GOD'S LITTLE DEVOTIONAL BOOK

FOR TEACHERS

RACINE, WI

God's Little Devotional Book for Teachers
ISBN: 979-8-88898-081-1 - *Paperback*
ISBN: 979-8-88898-082-8 - *Hardcover*
ISBN: 979-8-88898-083-5 - *Ebook*
Copyright © 2023 by Honor Books, Racine, WI

INTRODUCTION

Teaching is not just a job or a career; it is a "twenty-four, seven" identity—twenty-four hours a day, seven days a week. A teacher never stops being a teacher in the eyes of the students, no matter what day of the week, season of the year, or decade of life. Twenty years after having Miss Jones as a third-grade teacher, a student is still likely to greet and introduce her as "Miss Jones, my teacher."

What does this mean to teachers? It means they fill a role that requires a high sense of responsibility and nobility of character. It means teachers must face and overcome an ever-increasing volume and variety of problems with wisdom. And it means teachers face a great deal of stress—not only because ol the workload, but the inner stress of desiring to produce a lasting, good work in the lives of their students. No one needs inspiration and encouragement more than teachers!

What a teacher receives, a teacher gives. But the converse also is true. Unless a teacher receives, a teacher has little to give. Use this book to "fill up your cup" each day, and then let what you have received overflow to your students. Look for opportunities each day to share your faith in silent, yet powerful, ways.

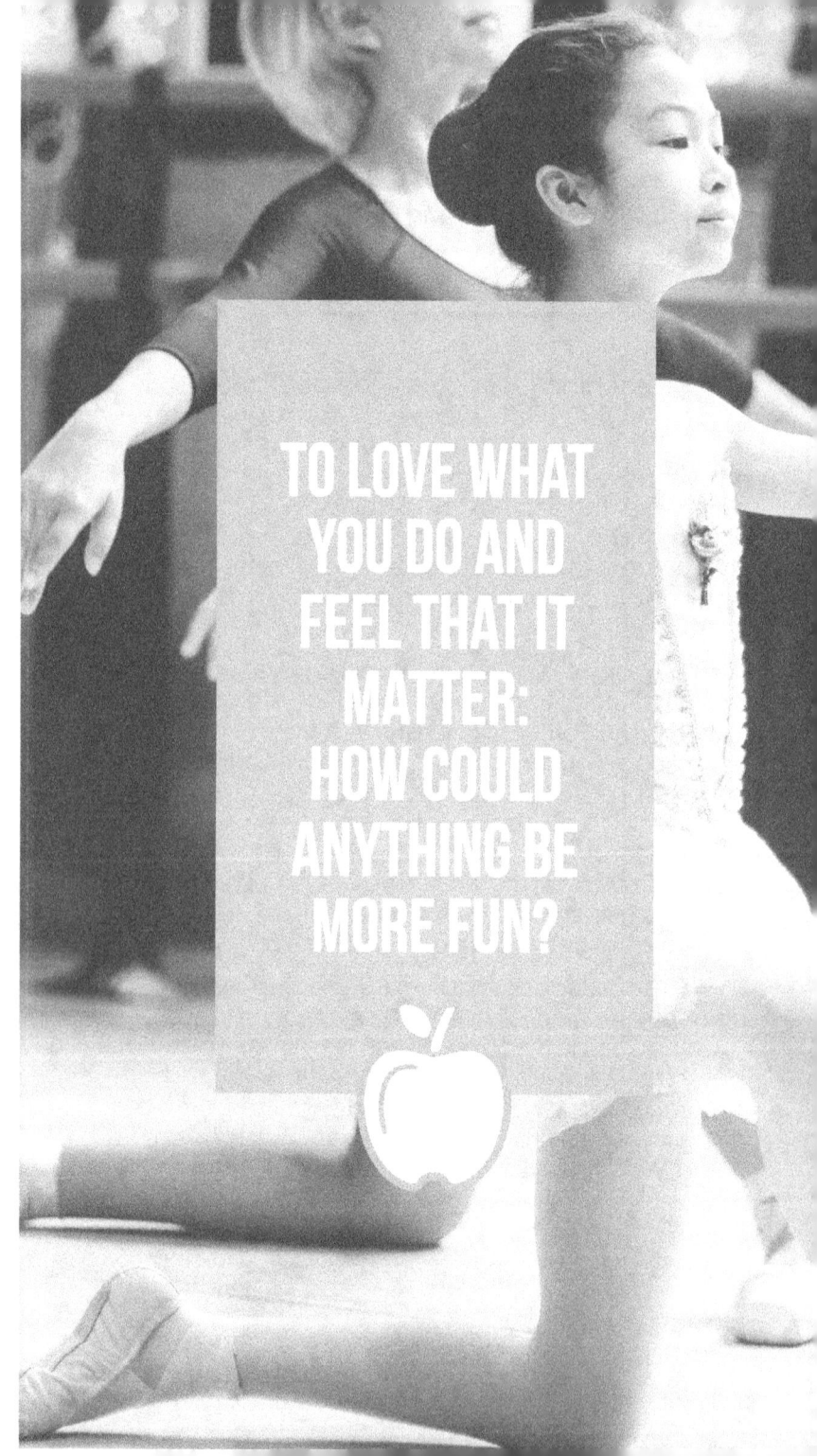

TO LOVE WHAT YOU DO AND FEEL THAT IT MATTER: HOW COULD ANYTHING BE MORE FUN?

Tom Chappell, founder of Tom's of Maine, was a man who seemed to have fulfilled "the great American dream." He had a wonderful family, a large New England home, and all the usual trappings of wealth. But he wasn't happy.

One day, Tom awoke and realized he had lost his enthusiasm. Not only that, he had started to question why he was in business. Tom embarked on a search for meaning for his life and work. He enrolled in divinity school, and one of the ideas he confronted was that making money did not have to be an empty, unfulfilling exercise. He developed a mission statement for his company that embraced social responsibility and care for the environment. In the process, Tom rediscovered his enthusiasm for his business and went on to introduce several new products that were well received. Work became more meaningful, and more fun.

If you have lost enthusiasm for teaching, ask yourself why. Consider writing a mission statement for yourself. Recapture the important meaning of why you became a teacher.[1]

For my heart rejoiced in all my labour.

ECCLESIASTES 2:10

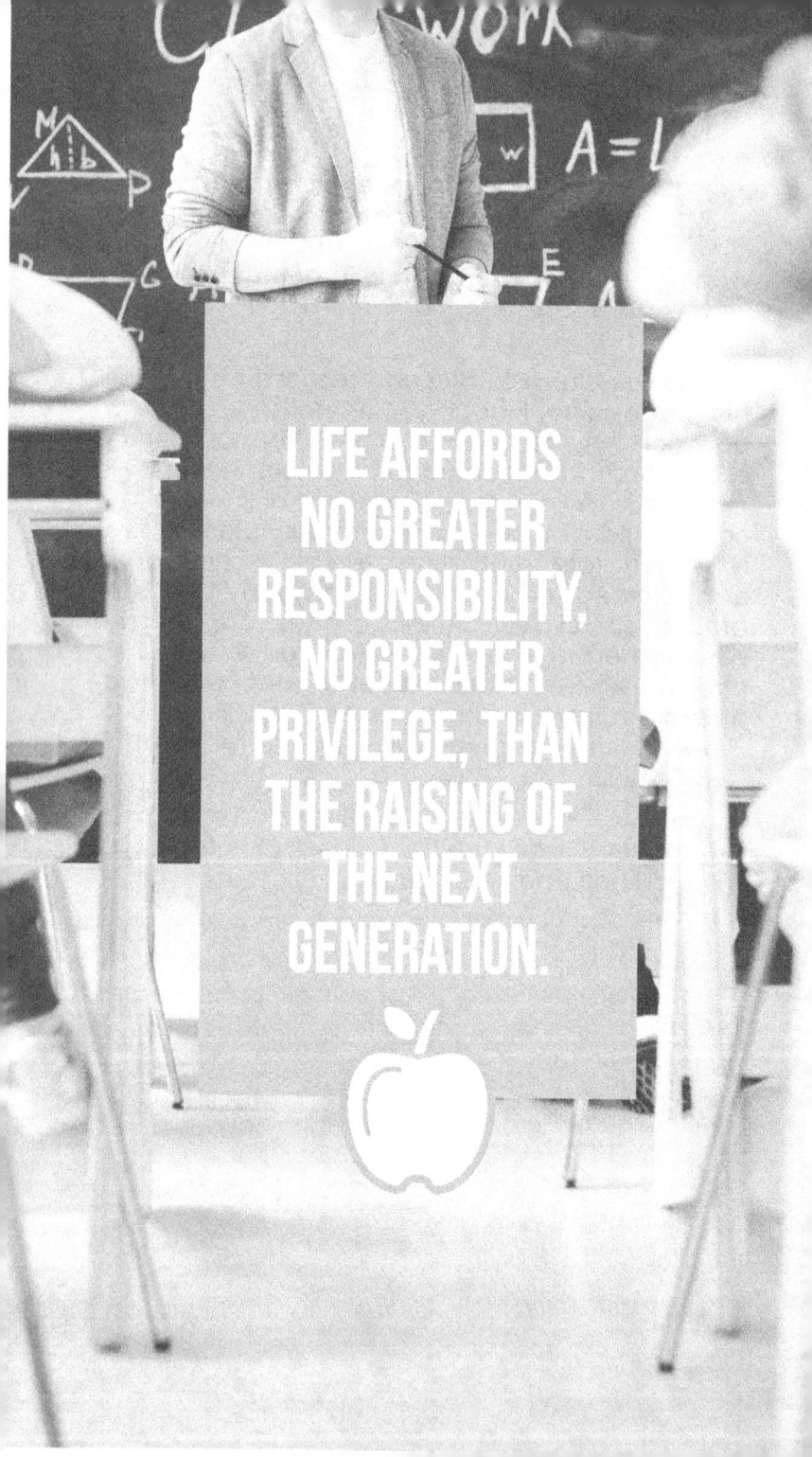

A small boy sat with his mother in church, listening to a sermon. The minister asked at several key places in his sermon, "What is a Christian?" each time pounding his fist on the pulpit for emphasis.

At one of these fist-pounding times, the boy whispered to his mother, "Mama, Do you know what a Christian is?"

His mother replied, "Yes, dear, now try to sit still and listen."

As the minister was wrapping up his sermon, he once again thundered, "What is a Christian?" and pounded especially hard on the pulpit.

At that the boy jumped up and cried, "Tell him, Mama, tell him!"

Rather than preach sermons, teachers speak volumes solely through their lives. They show children what a Christian is through their behavior, conversations, choices, and decisions. Children judge their elders not only by what they hear from them, but by their actions, as well.

A child will follow in the footsteps of those he or she admires most. Make sure your footsteps are worth following.

Teach them [God's commandments] to your children, talking about them when you sit at home and when you walk along the road, when you lie down and when you get up . . . so that your days and the days of your children may be many.

DEUTERONOMY 11:18,21 NIV

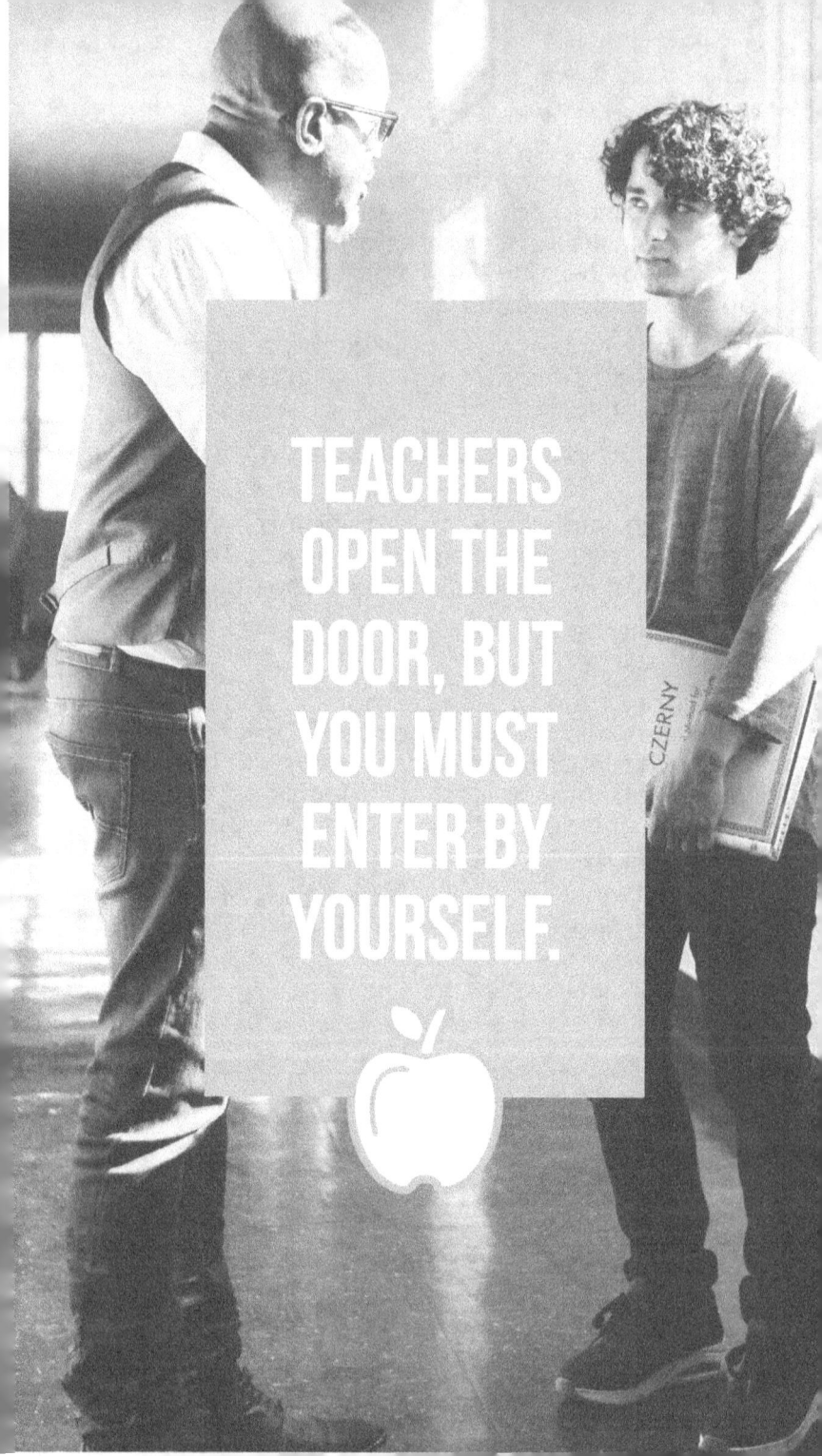

TEACHERS OPEN THE DOOR, BUT YOU MUST ENTER BY YOURSELF.

Della Reese, singer and star of the TV show, *Touched by an Angel*, considers Mahalia Jackson to have been her greatest teacher and mentor. As a teenager, she had the privilege of touring with Mahalia. On one occasion, Della recalls singing with all her might to wild applause. Then Mahalia rose and began to moan deep and low until she finally broke out singing, "Precious Lord, Take My Hand." She sang the entire song seated, speaking directly and only to God.

The audience responded with reverence and awe. Della thought, *What is it that she has that I don't have?*

After her third tour with Mahalia, she concluded that Mahalia was worshiping God, while she was just performing. Della's mother put it this way, "When Mahalia sings, you can feel God in her."

Mahalia had a different way of expressing it: "Deloreese," she said, "you are not in competition. You are in God's service." It was a lesson she never forgot, and a lesson she used throughout her life.

A teacher teaches character by example, not lecture. A student learns character by following and imitating, not memorizing.[3]

The hand of the diligent makes one rich.

PROVERBS 10:4 NKJV

Jake Steinfeld is best known as the founder of Body by Jake—the program that keeps many movie stars in shape. How did a proverbial weakling who stuttered as a child become a well-known fitness guru?

His book, *PowerLiving*, tells about the time his father stopped selling insurance and started his own business. It seemed like a crazy thing to do—after all, he had a wife and family to support. Even so, the elder Steinfeld had a dream of producing a magazine that real-estate agencies nationwide could hand out to people who were moving to a new town. He believed in his dream and was determined to succeed. His son admits that while watching his father in action, he was afraid of what might happen to him and his family. The magazine was a success. And that lesson gave Steinfeld the courage to launch his own business and pursue his own dreams.

It takes courage to take a chance, especially when those you care about are depending upon you to take care of them. What is true for students is also true for teachers. If you do your homework, truly believe in your dream, and work hard, you can accomplish great things![4]

And when Peter was come down out of the ship, he walked on the water, to go to Jesus.

MATTHEW 14:29

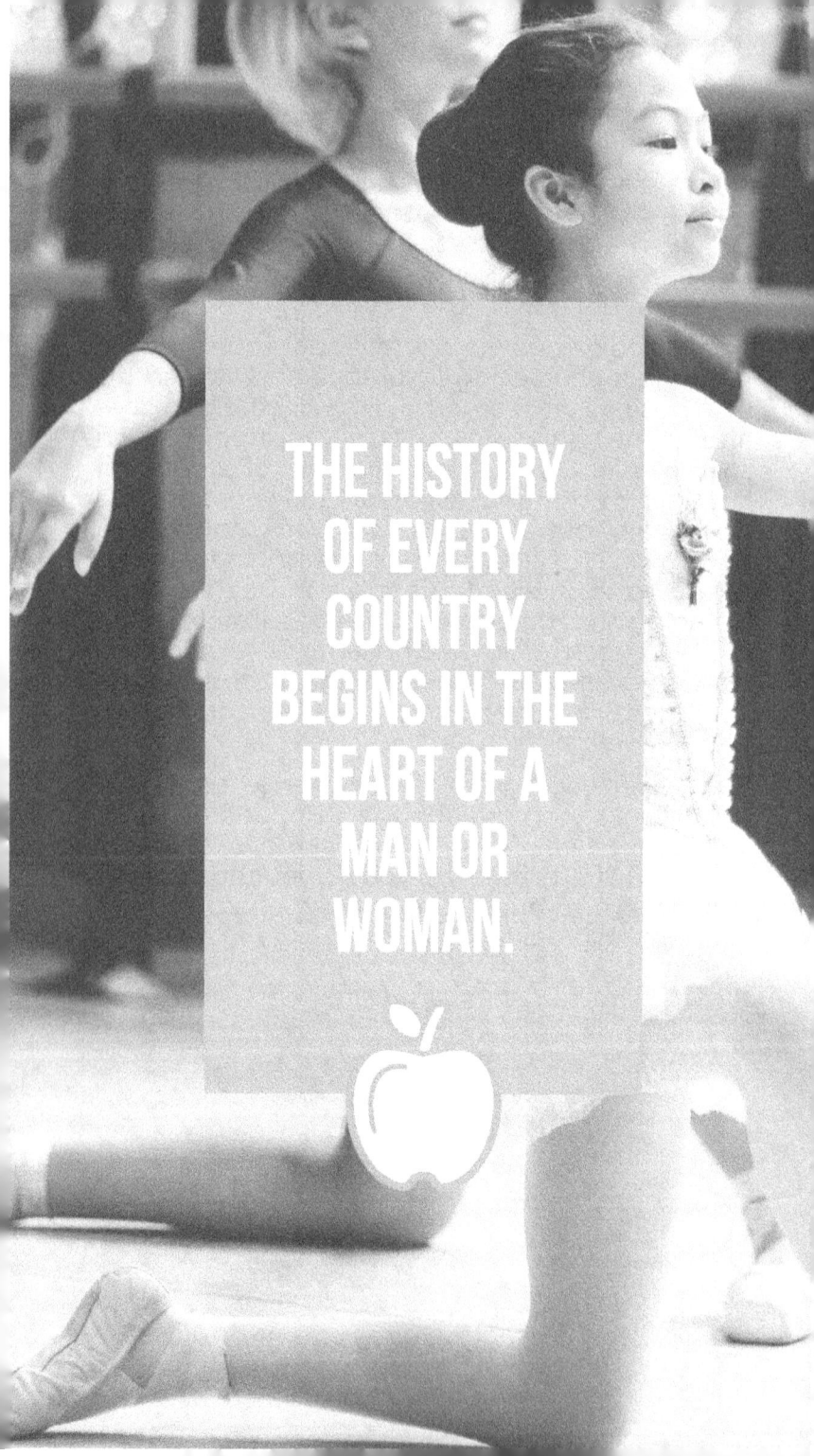

THE HISTORY
OF EVERY
COUNTRY
BEGINS IN THE
HEART OF A
MAN OR
WOMAN.

In 1957, Little Rock's school board unanimously voted to desegregate its schools, beginning with Central High. The city already had desegregated many public places, but the night before school started, Arkansas Governor Orval Faubus called in National Guard troops to prevent black students from entering the school. That decision sparked a battle in all branches of government that lasted several days. By Wednesday, September 25th, nine courageous black students were escorted into Central High under the protection of 1,000 members of the 101st Airborne Division of the U.S. Army, and history was made. Inside the school, the great majority of the 2,000 students, teachers, and administrators worked quietly and persistently for acceptance of the students and full implementation of the law. And the following year, Ernest Green, the school's first black graduate, was among 601 seniors who received their diplomas from Central High.

No matter how fierce a political or cultural storm may rage in your school, look for the quiet center in which to work effectively—that center may be your own heart!

Apply thine heart unto instruction, and thine ears to the words of knowledge.

PROVERBS 23:12

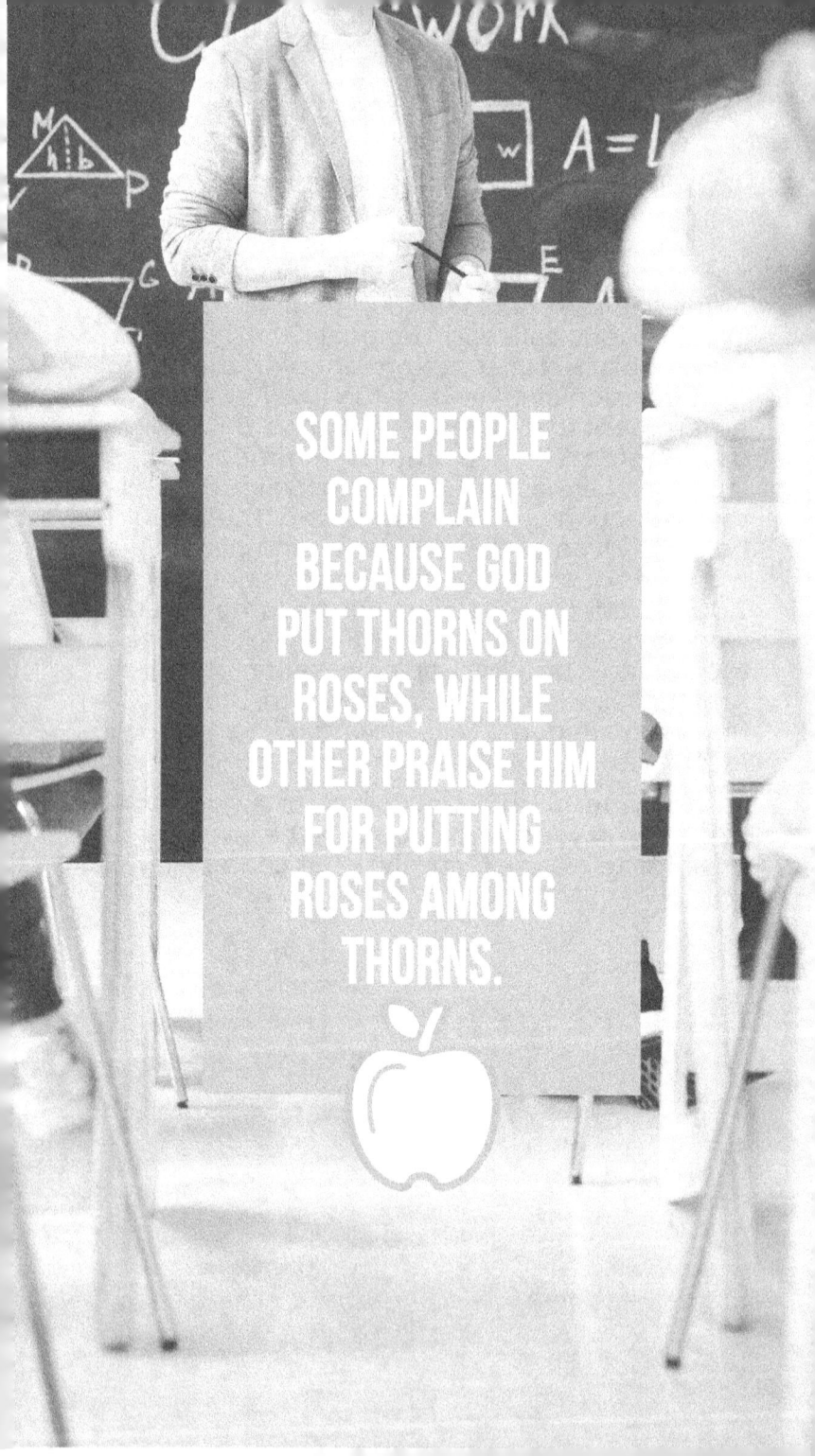

SOME PEOPLE COMPLAIN BECAUSE GOD PUT THORNS ON ROSES, WHILE OTHER PRAISE HIM FOR PUTTING ROSES AMONG THORNS.

S isters Pauline and Mary always were dose. They married and set up households within blocks of each other. Then in 1986, their lives changed. Pauline was told she had breast cancer. Although radiation and chemotherapy left her fatigued, Pauline had unflagging optimism. She decided, "If my life is going to be shorter, I want it to be better." She continued to live her life fully!

As Pauline approached her fifty-eighth birthday, Mary and a friend commissioned a piece of jewelry in her honor—a tulip-shaped sterling-silver bell with a tiny chime inside, symbolic of the church bell choir in which Pauline played. Through tears Mary told her sister that she was going to have more bells made to sell with the proceeds donated to cancer research.

Even after Pauline's death in June 1996, Mary continued to sell the bells. At last count, more than two thousand bells have been sold, raising more than $25,000 for cancer research. Mary has said, "Although cancer would ultimately take her body, Pauline refused to let it take her life!"

The seed of something good lies at the heart of every tragedy. Part of your challenge as a teacher is to find it and help it grow![6]

Finally, brethren, whatsoever things are true, whatsoever things are honest, whatsoever things are just, whatsoever things are pure, whatsoever things are lovely, whatsoever things are of good report; if there be any virtue, and if there be any praise, think on these things.

PHILIPPIANS 4:8

HE THAT THINKS HIMSELF THE WISEST IS GENERALLY THE LEAST SO.

Peter was one of those guys less talented people envy. He had an Ivy League education, the creativity of a true artist, and an overwhelming drive to succeed. What he didn't have was the ability to handle criticism or to consider other people's ideas.

During a meeting one day, one of Peter's colleagues came up with an idea that everyone liked . . . except Peter.

"That's interesting," Peter said. "I'll give it some consideration." The meeting adjourned, and Peter returned to his office where he immediately started working on one of his own ideas.

When his colleagues realized Peter was never going to give them a serious hearing, they began to avoid Peter and to leave him out of their "unofficial" meetings. Soon, their ideas were being championed and implemented, and high praise flowed from upper management. As Peter's ideas found less favor, his attitude became more irritating. He was the first to go when the company downsized its work force.

We each need others to succeed and to put legs on our good ideas. We must never assume that we know more than everyone else—even if we are the teacher![7]

When words are many, sin is not absent,
but he who holds his tongue is wise.

PROVERBS 10:19 NIV

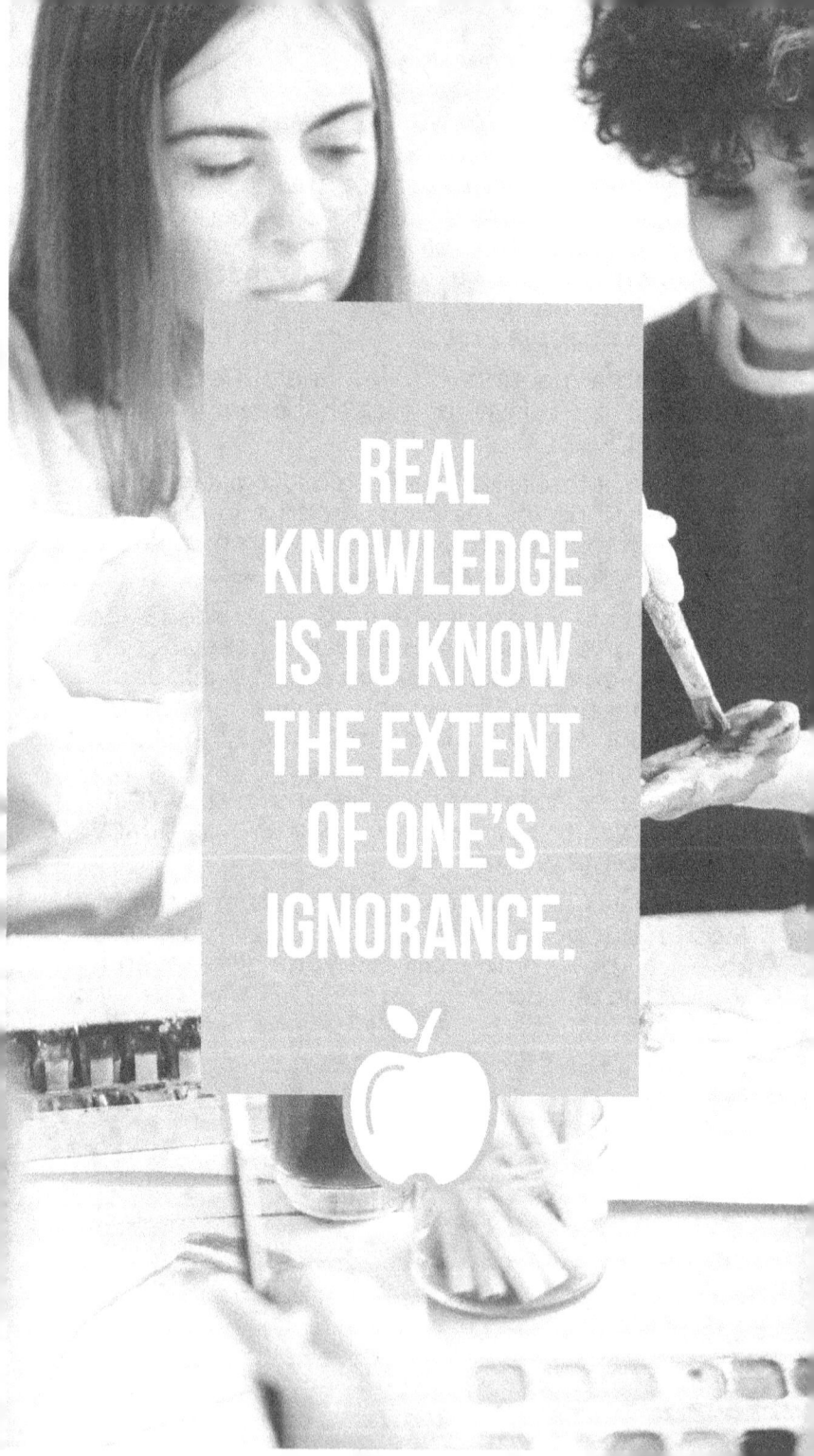

REAL
KNOWLEDGE
IS TO KNOW
THE EXTENT
OF ONE'S
IGNORANCE.

In an issue of *Guideposts*, Ronald Pinkerton describes a near accident he had while hang gliding. As he descended, a powerful blast of air hit his hang glider, plummeting him toward the ground.

He wrote, "I was falling at an alarming rate. Trapped in an airborne riptide, I was going to crash! Then I saw him—a red-tailed hawk. He was six feet off my right wingtip, fighting the same gust I was . . . suddenly he banked and flew straight downwind. If the right air is anywhere, it's upwind! The hawk was committing suicide . . . From nowhere the thought entered my mind: Follow the hawk. It went against everything I knew about flying. But now all my knowledge was useless. I followed the hawk . . . Suddenly the hawk gained altitude. Then a warm surge of air started pushing the glider upward. I was stunned. Nothing I knew as a pilot could explain this phenomenon. But it was true: I was rising."

From time to time, each of us is forced to admit we don't know what to do. Look around. God has placed somebody in your path to be your teacher in those moments. Choose to learn from them.[8]

But seek ye first the kingdom of God, and his righteousness; and all these things shall be added unto you.

MATTHEW 6:33

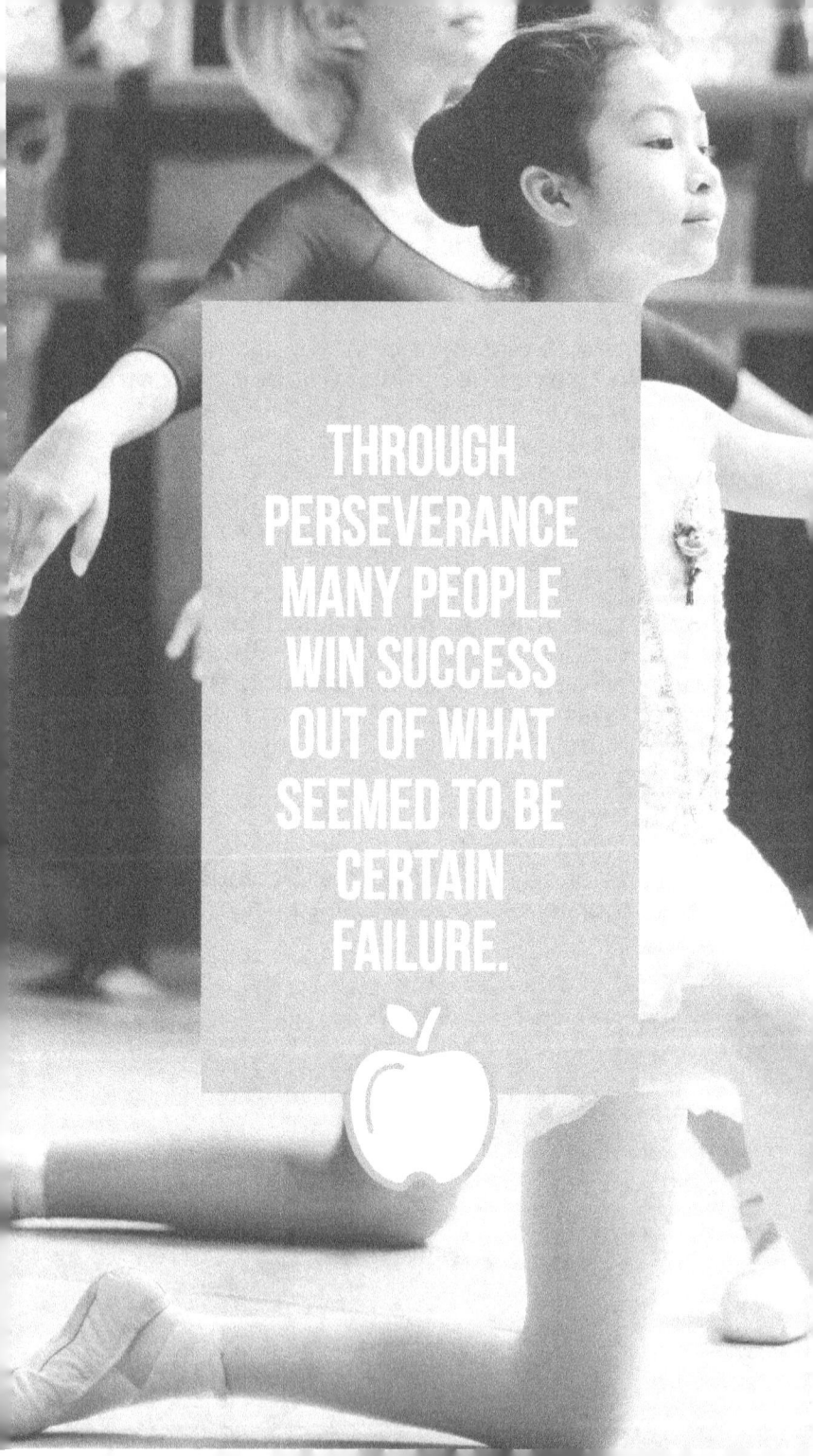

THROUGH
PERSEVERANCE
MANY PEOPLE
WIN SUCCESS
OUT OF WHAT
SEEMED TO BE
CERTAIN
FAILURE.

In 1931, Ted and Dorothy Hustead made a life-changing decision. They decided to move to a town with a good school, a good church, a good doctor, and an opportunity to make their business dream a reality. They chose Wall, South Dakota—a town in the "middle of nowhere" between the Badlands and the Black Hills. Since Ted was a pharmacist, they opened a drugstore.

The first year was tough—thick dust, intense heat, and swirling winds. However, tired, throat-parched travelers rarely stopped at the drugstore. After a period of soul-searching, Ted and Dorothy made signs and placed them along the highway; "*Free Ice Water at Wall Drugstore.*" For years, druggists had offered free ice water to thirsty customers. But no one had advertised the luxury like Ted and Dorothy did.

The result? Four to six-thousand people a day stop at Wall Drugstore. The sign itself also has become a novelty item—Wall Drugstore signs have been spotted all over Europe, Korea, India, Egypt, and even the North Pole!

When times get tough in your classroom, ask God for an idea. He has an unlimited supply of good ones. And once you have a good idea, stick with it.[9]

For with God nothing shall be impossible.

LUKE 1:37

W hich matters most a winning football record or building character in football players? A small private Midwestern university felt it had to answer that question when faced with the 48-wins-to-74-losses record of their football coach.

"Experts" predicted the coach would be fired and replaced with a coach who could rack up more wins. But the university decided to go a different way. In an unprecedented move, it gave the coach a huge vote of confidence and a four-year extension of his contract!

The athletic director said in announcing the university's decision: "I had to do what I really felt was best for this university and best for our student-athletes."

The university president said, "We want to win with class and dignity. We want to win well within the rules. No one questions the integrity of [our coach]."

Excellence is defined by more than external records and awards. It is a quality carried deep within the heart of a good teacher or a good student—a quality reflected by how well that teacher or student is able to communicate morality, character, and faith to others.[10]

Many daughters have done well, but you excel them all.

PROVERBS 31:29 NKJV

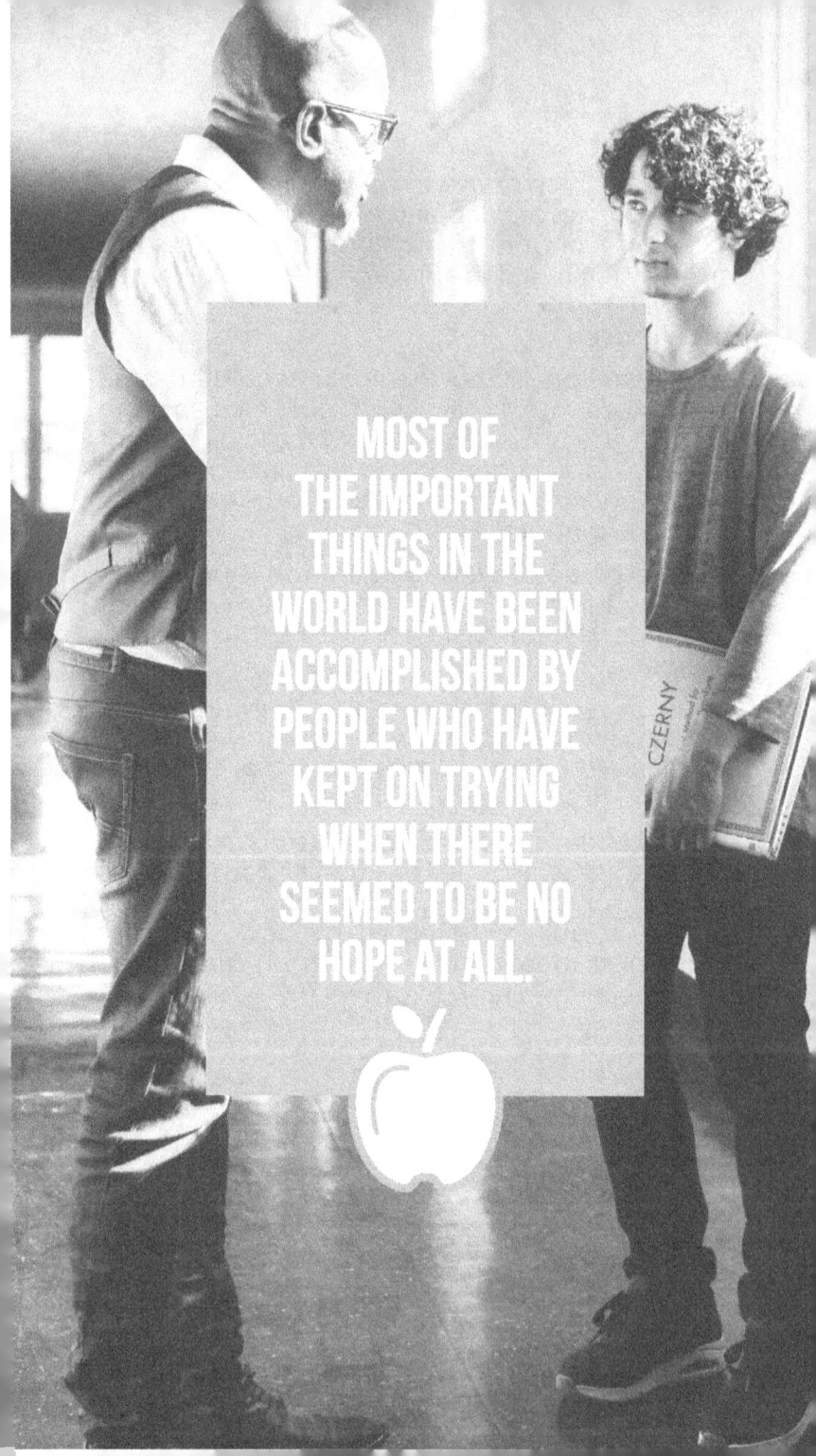

MOST OF THE IMPORTANT THINGS IN THE WORLD HAVE BEEN ACCOMPLISHED BY PEOPLE WHO HAVE KEPT ON TRYING WHEN THERE SEEMED TO BE NO HOPE AT ALL.

Victor Villasenor remained illiterate until adulthood because of dyslexia. Then a woman in his native country of Mexico taught him to read. Ironically, Victor decided he wanted to become a great writer and asked God to help him fulfill his dream.

For ten years, Victor worked hard at manual labor, digging ditches and cleaning houses. As he worked; he thought of interesting characters and plots. At night, he read voraciously, devouring more than five-thousand books, memorizing favorite opening lines, and analyzing literary styles. Then he started writing: nine novels, sixty-five short stories, and ten plays. He sent them all to publishers—and all were rejected. One publisher sent a two-word response: "You're kidding." Instead of being discouraged, Victor was happy that the publisher had read his work! In 1972 after 260 rejections, Victor sold his first novel, *Macho*. He then published a nonfiction book and an award-winning screenplay. He is best known for his saga about his own family, *Rain of Gold*, which took twelve years to write.

Encourage your students to dream big! Then motivate them to turn those dreams into reality![11]

I can do all things through Christ which strengtheneth me.

PHILIPPIANS 4:13

LIFE IS A PROGRESS, AND NOT A STATION.

A vibrant old woman astounded everyone with her consistent cheerfulness even though she seemed to have abundant troubles and few pleasures. When she was asked the secret of her upbeat personality, she said, "Well, the Bible says often, 'And it came to pass'—not 'and it came to stay!'"

One of life's greatest lessons is that we are all "works in progress." Your students won't be the same at the end of the year as they are on the first day of school. Neither will you be the same teacher!

A little girl was once asked by her Sunday school teacher, "Who made you?"

She quickly answered, "Well, God made a part of me."

The teacher asked, "What do you mean, God made a part of you?"

She replied, "Well, God made me real little, and I just growed the rest myself."

Certainly God makes Himself available to help us in our growth process, but He also expects us to grow through the decisions we make, the challenges we undertake, and the effort we put out Embrace the changes that come your way. They are part of God's ongoing process for you—both as a teacher and as a person.[12]

And shall be like a tree planted by the rivers of water, that bringeth forth his fruit in his season.

PSALM 1:3

DO NOT MISTAKE A CHILD FOR HIS SYMPTOM.

A junior class in a Chicago church was disrupted every Sunday by one boy. The teacher was in turmoil. She asked herself, *Is my responsibility to this boy or to the others in the class who are disturbed during the lesson?*

Finally, she went to the Sunday school superintendent who advised her the class came first and the problem-causing boy should be told to stay at home. The teacher, however, wasn't willing to settle for that solution. She felt concerned about the boy, whom she believed to be brilliant, and she could not bring herself to tell anyone if to stay away from church.

Then she had an idea. She asked the boy to come to her house the next Saturday to help prepare some of the materials for Sunday's lesson. He gladly came without embarrassment and provided real help to her. From that time on, he often came on Saturdays. He became an asset to the class and never again was a hindrance.

Not every behavior problem can be resolved so easily, but one thing is certain: God has a solution for every problem student. Ask the Lord to reveal the highly individualized solutions you need to reach each of your students effectively.[13]

And now a word to you parents. Don't keep on scolding and nagging your children, making them angry and resentful. Rather, bring them up with the loving discipline the Lord himself approves, with suggestions and godly advice.

EPHESIANS 6:4 TLB

One morning, a man stepped into a battered taxi in Brazil and gave the driver his destination. The driver responded, "That is the Bible House! Are you one of those kind of people?" The man replied that he had come to share what God had done for him. He then asked the taxi driver if he had ever experienced God's care in his life, and the driver gave a heartwarming testimony. The man then asked about his family.

The driver answered that he had never married. He had taken in one, then two, then three street orphans. He fed and clothed them and took them to school every morning. On Sundays, he took them to Sunday school and church. The children had become his life, leaving little time to search for a wife.

When the taxi arrived at the man's destination, he started to pay the fare, but the driver refused his money. He responded that it was his joy to drive him for free. He said that he had never had an opportunity to exercise hospitality to a foreign minister as the New Testament said believers should do, and he wanted to do this for the Lord.

Whose heart will you make happy within your school building today?[14]

Be not deceived; God is not mocked: for whatsoever a man soweth, that shall he also reap.

GALATIANS 6:7

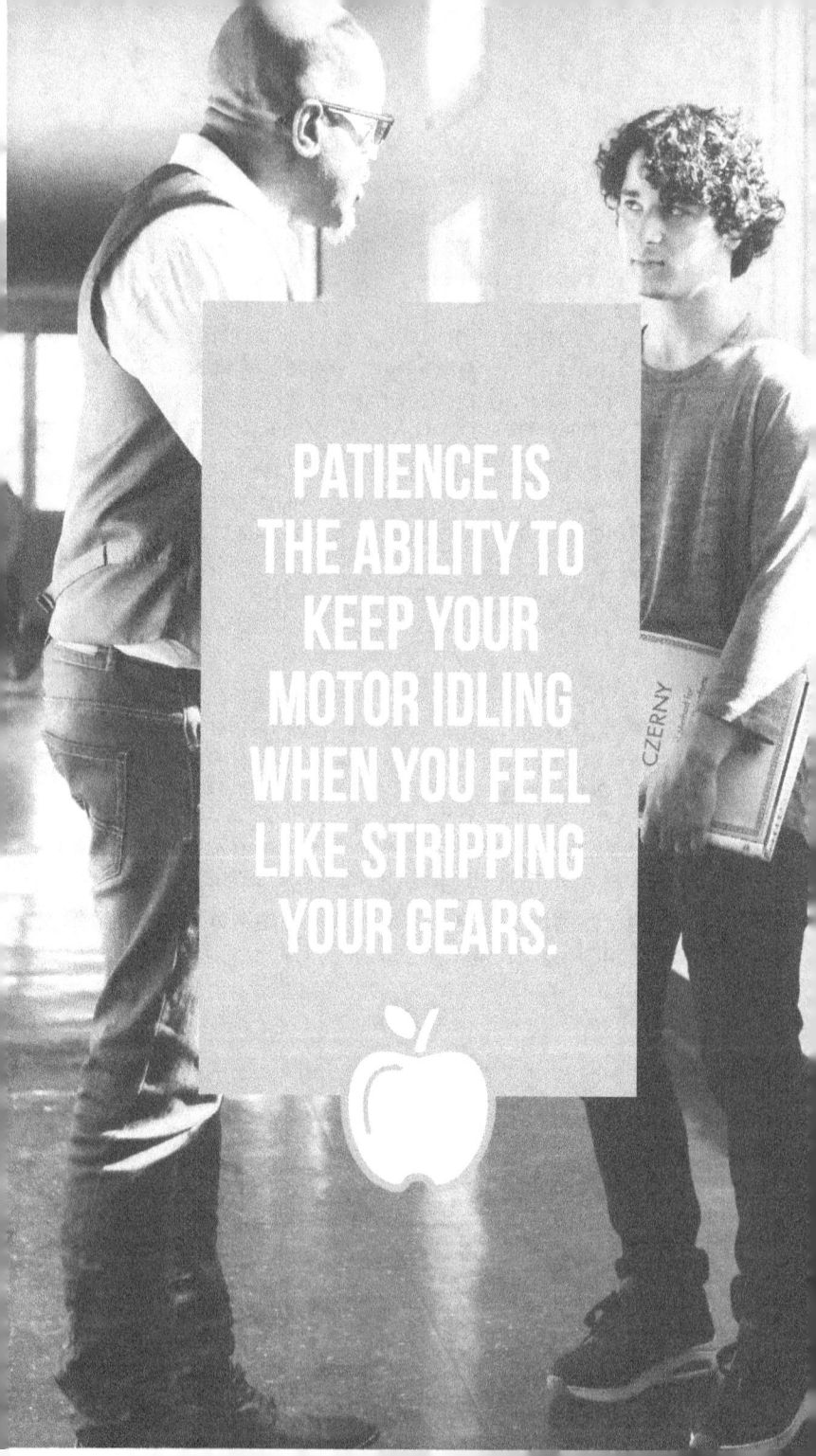

PATIENCE IS
THE ABILITY TO
KEEP YOUR
MOTOR IDLING
WHEN YOU FEEL
LIKE STRIPPING
YOUR GEARS.

The last place most people want to be is stuck on an ice-covered road in a traffic jam. Bill found himself in just this position at the base of an ice-covered hill one morning. He knew there was no hope except to turn around slowly. He maneuvered his vehicle off the pavement and onto the grassy shoulder where he thought he could gain more traction to turn his car around. *Patience, Bill*, he kept telling himself. It took him ten slow, frustrating minutes. But no sooner was he on the shoulder of the road than a car came up too quickly behind him, skid on the ice, and crashed at a ninety-degree angle into the truck immediately in front of him. He was trapped again—this time by an accident!

After checking to make certain both drivers were uninjured, Bill used his cell phone to call for a tow truck. *Why didn't I think of using my phone earlier?* he asked himself. For the next hour, Bill made phone calls—the same calls he would have made at his desk in the office. He accomplished an entire morning's work by the side of an icy road.

When delays come your way, trust God for two things a teacher needs every day: patience and options.

He that is slow to anger is better than the mighty; and he that ruleth his spirit than he that taketh a city.

PROVERBS 16:32

Danny's world was turned upside down when his father died—his home totally changed, and his mother became ill. Although his loved ones understood the reason for his insecurity, they didn't know how to deal with his tirades. A special teacher was consulted.

The teacher spent some time with Danny, and when he went into one of his "cyclone imitations," she quietly, but firmly, took hold of his arms and looked him steadily in the eyes. He looked back in fear, expecting her to punish him. Instead she said, "Danny, when little boys act that way I hold them like this until they get quiet inside."

He didn't struggle. After a moment he said, "You can let go now. I won't do it again."

The teacher said, "Fine," and let go.

The next day, Danny started on a rampage again, this time with one eye on his teacher. She walked slowly toward him as she had the day before, but before she reached him, he suddenly grabbed his own arms and said, "You don't have to hold me. I can hold myself." And he did.

Eventually, each young person must learn to discipline himself. It helps, however, to have a patient teacher who shows by example how to hold with arms of love.[15]

Teach a child to choose the right path, and when he is older he will remain upon it.

PROVERBS 22:6 TLB

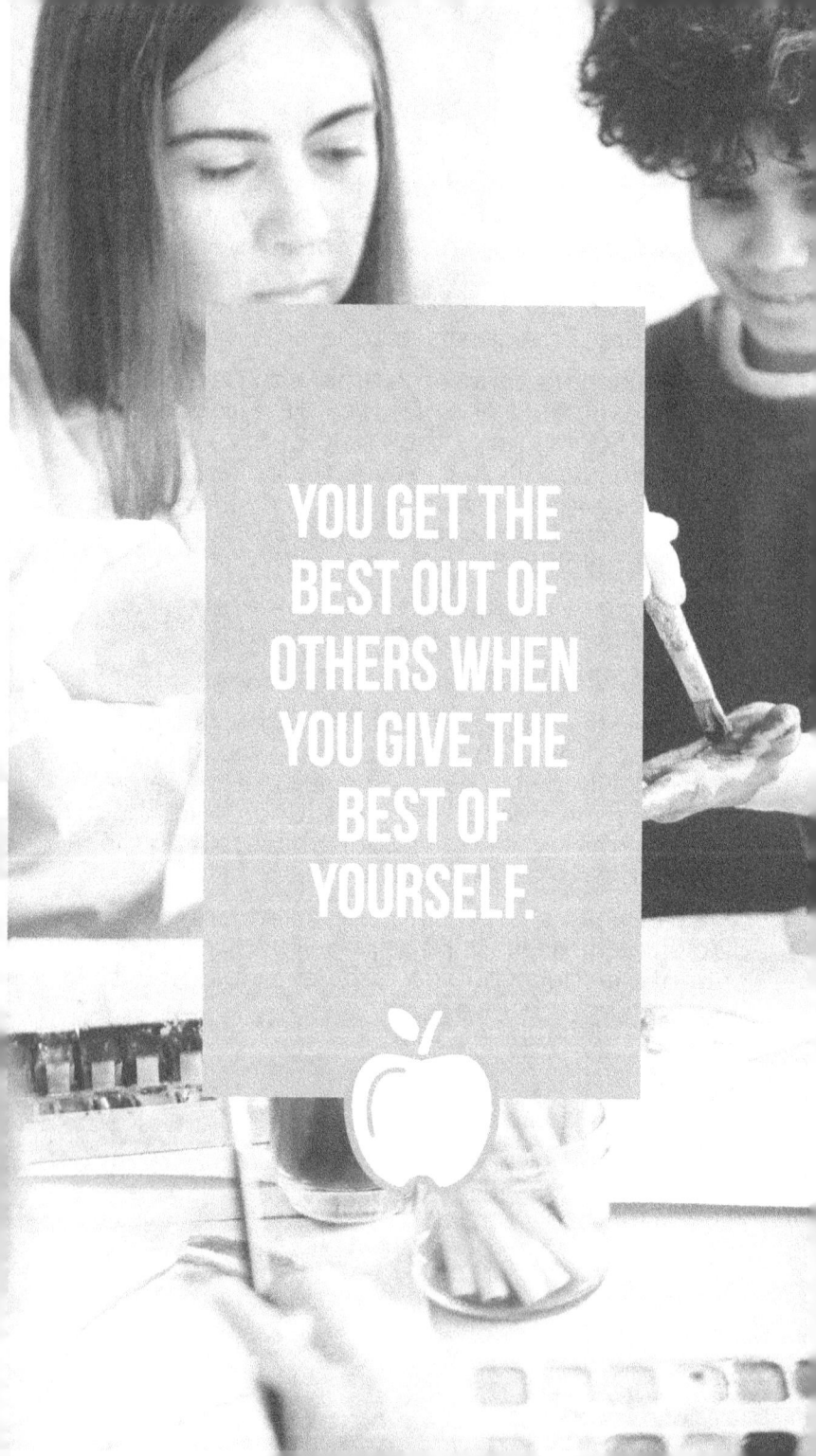

YOU GET THE
BEST OUT OF
OTHERS WHEN
YOU GIVE THE
BEST OF
YOURSELF.

One night while watching the news, Chuck Wall—a human relations instructor at Bakersfield College in California—heard a cliche that stuck in his mind: "Another random act of senseless violence . . ."

Wall got an idea. He assigned his students to perform an out-of-the-ordinary act of kindness and then write an essay about it. One student paid his mother's utility bills. Another bought thirty blankets from the Salvation Army and took them to homeless people who had gathered under a bridge.

For his part, Wall created a bumper sticker that read, "Today, I will commit one random act of senseless KINDNESS . . . Will you?" A bank and a union printed the bumper stickers, and some of the students sold them for a dollar each. The profits went to the county Braille center. The bumper stickers were pasted on all one-hundred and thirteen patrol cars in the county, and the message was repeated in pulpits, schools, and professional associations.

Wall commented later, "I had no idea our community was in such need of something positive."

Every community—and especially, every school—needs those who will give their best efforts, creative ideas, and kindness. As a teacher, will you lead the way?[16]

Let your light shine before men, that they may see your good deeds and praise your Father in heaven.

MATTHEW 5:16, NIV

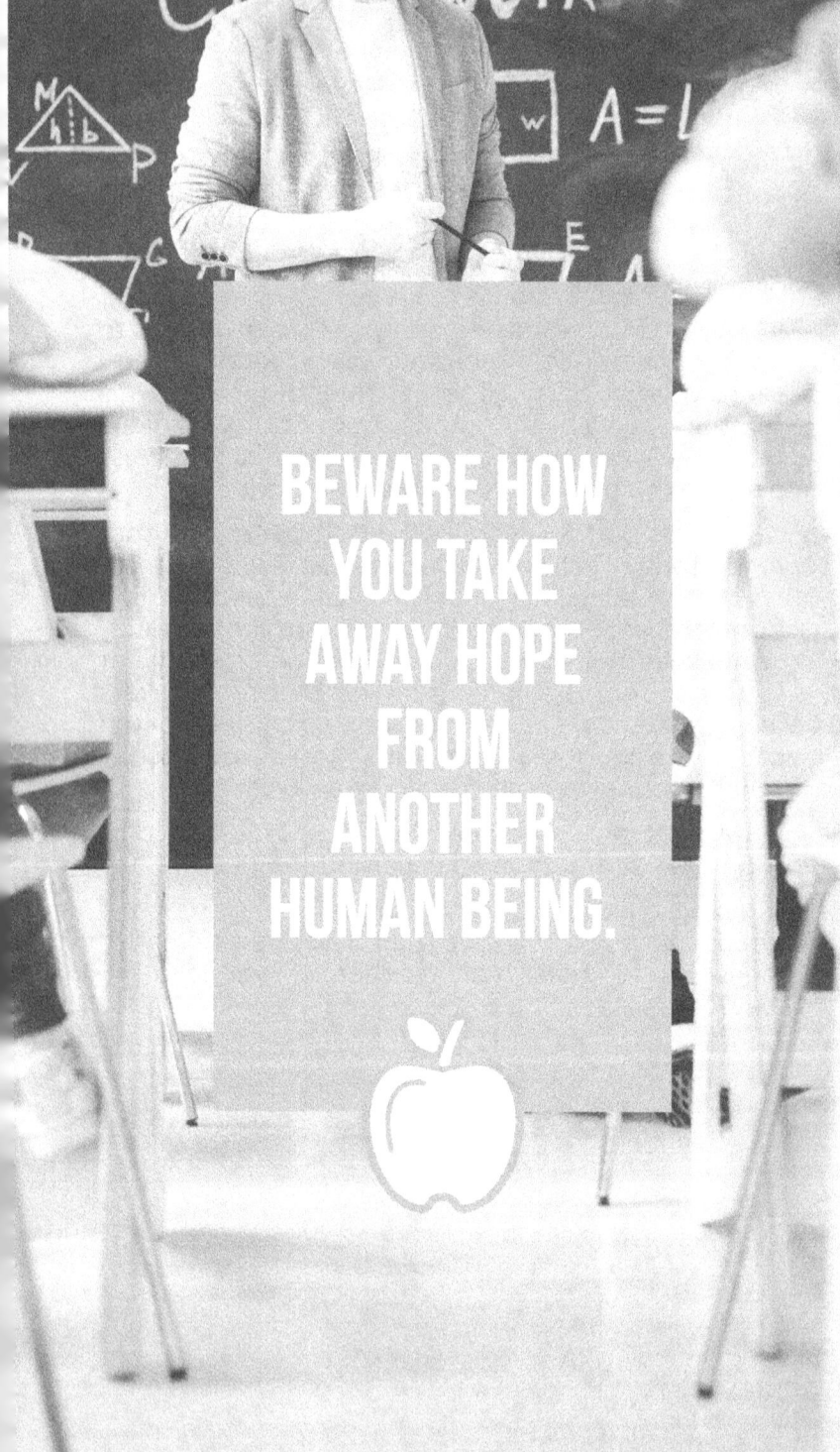

BEWARE HOW YOU TAKE AWAY HOPE FROM ANOTHER HUMAN BEING.

A couple was about to leave their home one evening to attend an elite society party when the phone rang.

"Hello, Mom," the caller said. "I'm back in the states with an early release from my army duties in Vietnam!"

"Wonderful!" the mother exclaimed. "When will you be home?"

"I'd like to bring a buddy home with me," the son replied. "Both of his legs have been amputated, one arm is gone, his face is disfigured, and one ear and one eye are missing. He's not much to look at, but he needs a home real bad."

"Sure, bring him home for a few days," she said.

"You don't understand," the young man said, "I want to bring him home to live there with you."

The mother stammered, "What would our friends think? It would be just too much for your father . . ." Before she could finish, she heard a dial tone.

Later that night when the couple returned home, they had a message to call the police department. The chief of police said, "Ma'am, we just found a young man with both legs and one arm missing. His face is badly mangled. He shot himself in the head. His identification indicates he is your son."

All of us need love and acceptance, especially those who face special challenges. Build up their hopes and support their dreams. Your own hopes as a teacher will be strengthened.[17]

A kind man benefits himself, but a cruel man brings trouble on himself.

PROVERBS 11:17 NIV

THERE IS A NAME FOR PEOPLE WHO ARE NOT EXCITED ABOUT THEIR WORK—UNEMPLOYED.

A man once walked into a store and took his place in line behind four other customers. Before long, he realized the line wasn't moving. A trio of clerks behind the counter were involved in a personal discussion, and it was only after they sensed the restlessness of those waiting that they turned to give them attention. Even then, they did not offer service cheerfully. They acted as if the customers were interfering with their social lives and continued their personal conversation.

After making his purchase, the man asked to see the manager Suddenly, the clerk's attitude changed. He became all smiles as he said, "I'm sorry if I kept you waiting."

The man smiled back and said, "Don't worry. It won't happen again. I can assure you it won't." If that sounded like a threat . . . it was. Little did the clerk know that he had neglected the owner of the store!

Most managers and teachers have tolerance for work that is not perfect, but few have tolerance for those who fail to show good effort or enthusiasm at their assigned tasks. A willing worker can be trained, even without the necessary experience. Encourage willingness in your students.[18]

Whatever you do, work at it with all your heart, as working for the Lord, not for men.

COLOSSIANS 3:23 NIV

THERE IS NO
MAN LIVING
THAT CAN NOT
DO MORE THAN
HE THINKS HE
CAN.

Researchers at Wright Patterson Air Force Base have been working on a project called "brain-actuated control." They are hoping to develop a means for pilots to fly airplanes with their minds.

In their experiments, the pilots wear scalp monitors that pick up electrical signals from various points in the brain. The scalp monitors are wired to a computer Using biofeedback techniques, the pilots are able to direct the electrical activity created by their own thought processes. The computer then translates the electrical signals into mechanical commands for the airplane.

Although controlling airplanes with the mind is yet to be perfected, the mind certainly has tremendous control over one thing—behavior. Eventually, thoughts erupt into actions. The height of our success only has one major ceiling: the height of our dreams.

One prisoner knew this. Suspended in a spread-eagled position, secured by manacles and chains above the damp floor of a dungeon, he looked up about forty feet to the only window in the cell. Immobile and pinned to the wall, he said to the other prisoner in his dungeon cell, "Here's my plan!"

God-given dreams are always big. Choose to dream them on behalf of yourself and your students.[19]

A man's heart deviseth his way: but the Lord directeth his steps.

PROVERBS 16:9

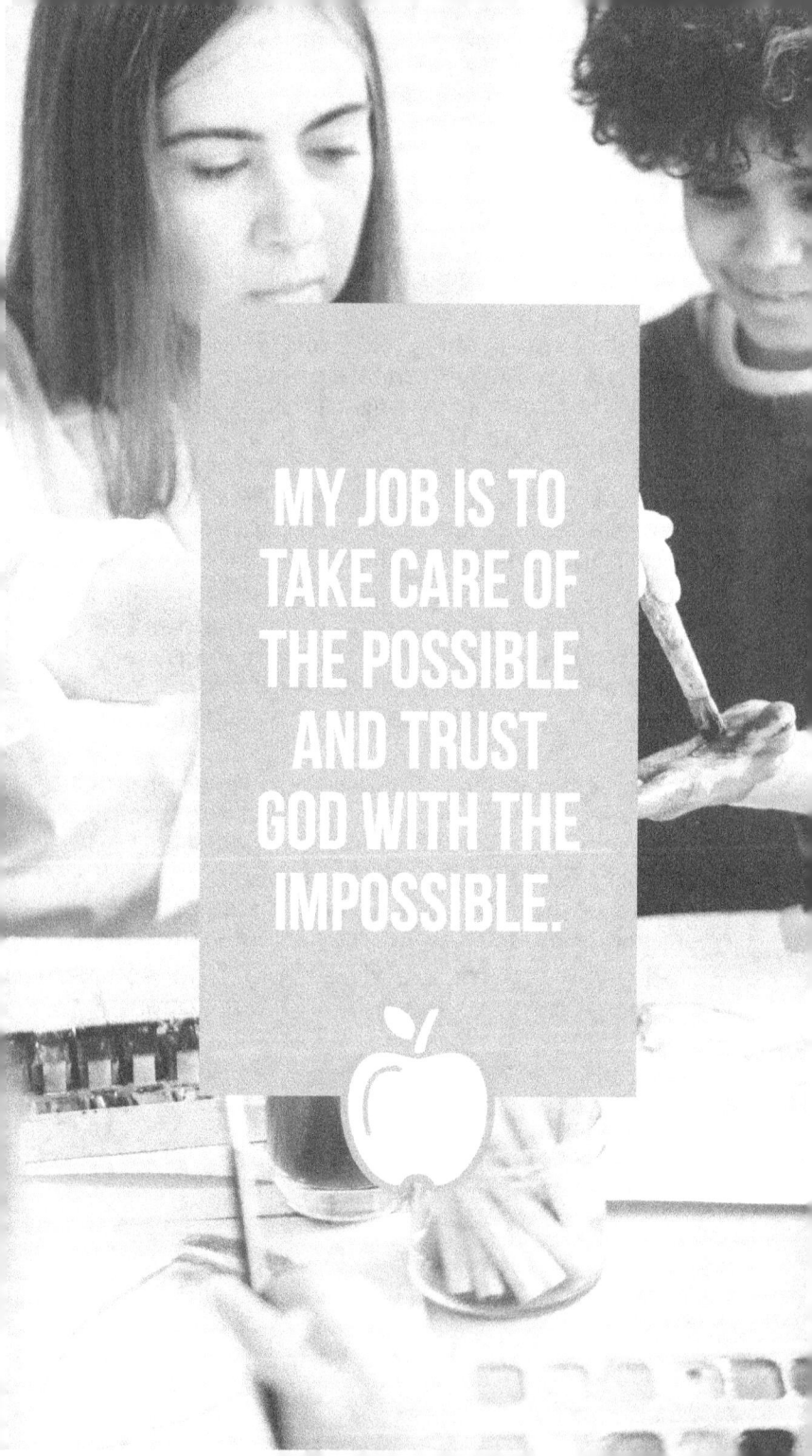

MY JOB IS TO TAKE CARE OF THE POSSIBLE AND TRUST GOD WITH THE IMPOSSIBLE.

I n *God: A Biography*, Steven Mosley tells a story about Robert Foss and his Aunt Lana, who experienced a vision that intruded her prayers. Upon reflection and research, they concluded this "picture from God" was of a quiet cove near the Quinault Indian reservation.

Since the family had clothes to deliver to the reservation, Robert and his aunt decided to deliver them immediately. On the way, they found the exact spot Aunt Lana had seen in her vision. However, nothing unusual happened when they stopped at the beach she had seen.

Upon arrival at the reservation, an old Indian grandmother said happily, "You've come! I've been expecting you." As they unloaded the clothes, she told about the trouble in her family and the lack of warm clothing for her grandchildren. One day, she had gone to a quiet place on the beach to ask for God's help. As they compared notes, they discovered her prayer had been at the exact day and hour the "picture" first came to Aunt Lana's mind!

Every teacher has finite vision, unable to see all that is going on backstage in God's unfolding plan. We need to keep our attention on the current assignment, and then trust God daily that He is arranging all things for eternal benefit—both in our lives and in the lives of our students.[20]

And they that know thy name will put their trust in thee, for thou, Lord, has not forsaken them that seek thee.

PSALM 9:10

LOOK AT EVERYTHING AS THOUGHT YOU WERE SEEING IT FOR THE FIRST TIME FOR THE LAST TIME. THEN YOUR TIME ON EARTH WILL BE FILLED WITH GLORY.

W hile preparing to speak at a convention, a woman wanted her husband to go out for sandwiches while she got ready for the event. She requested a chicken sandwich with no mayonnaise. She made sure he understood the order, even to the point of his replying, "Yep, I got it. N-o-o-o-o mayo."

When the sandwich arrived, however, she found it smothered with mayonnaise. Her husband seemed totally to have forgotten her request. She launched into a tirade of "you never listen—you only care about yourself" statements. Tension filled the air in their hotel room for a full hour before she finally asked her husband to forgive her.

Later that evening after she had spoken, a woman came to her and said, "It's lovely to see how much you and your husband love each other. Treasure one another!" She walked away with tears in her eyes.

A woman standing nearby said, "She lost her husband last month. He died of a heart attack. They had been married only two years."

The speaker thought, *How would I feel if the last thing I got to say to my husband was that he blew my sandwich order?*

What was the last thing you said to your students as they walked out of the classroom? Express gratitude if for their lives rather than irritation at their faults.[21]

Know ye that the Lord he is God: it is he that hath made us, and not we ourselves; we are his people, and the sheep of his pasture.

PSALM 100:3

ANGER IS NEVER WITHOUT A REASON BUT SELDOM A GOOD ONE.

A man and woman were driving a van in the far left lane of Chicago's Northwest Tollway. Their two children were buckled in the back. Unexpectedly, a white Cadillac pulled up behind them, tailgating mere inches from their bumper. The van driver slowed down, and the Cadillac driver whipped into the right lane, passed quickly, then swerved back in front of the van. The van driver dodged violently to avoid a collision, and the Cadillac sped away.

The van driver chased the Cadillac, and when he eventually pulled alongside the white car, the two men began yelling at each other and gesturing angrily. The driver of the Cadillac then pulled a handgun and fired at the van. The bullet hit the van driver's baby girl in the head. She lived, but is blind in one eye, half-blind in the other, partially deaf, and suffers severe mental and physical disabilities. The man who fired the shot was an ex-convict, who was sent back to prison. The little girl's parents live in deep regret.

The results of angry expressions are more often tragic than triumphant. As teachers, we are wise to turn down the temperature of our anger before expressing our opinions. Anger may be justified, but lashing out in anger at a student is never justifiable.[22]

An angry man stirreth up strife, and a furious man aboundeth in transgression.

PROVERBS 20:22

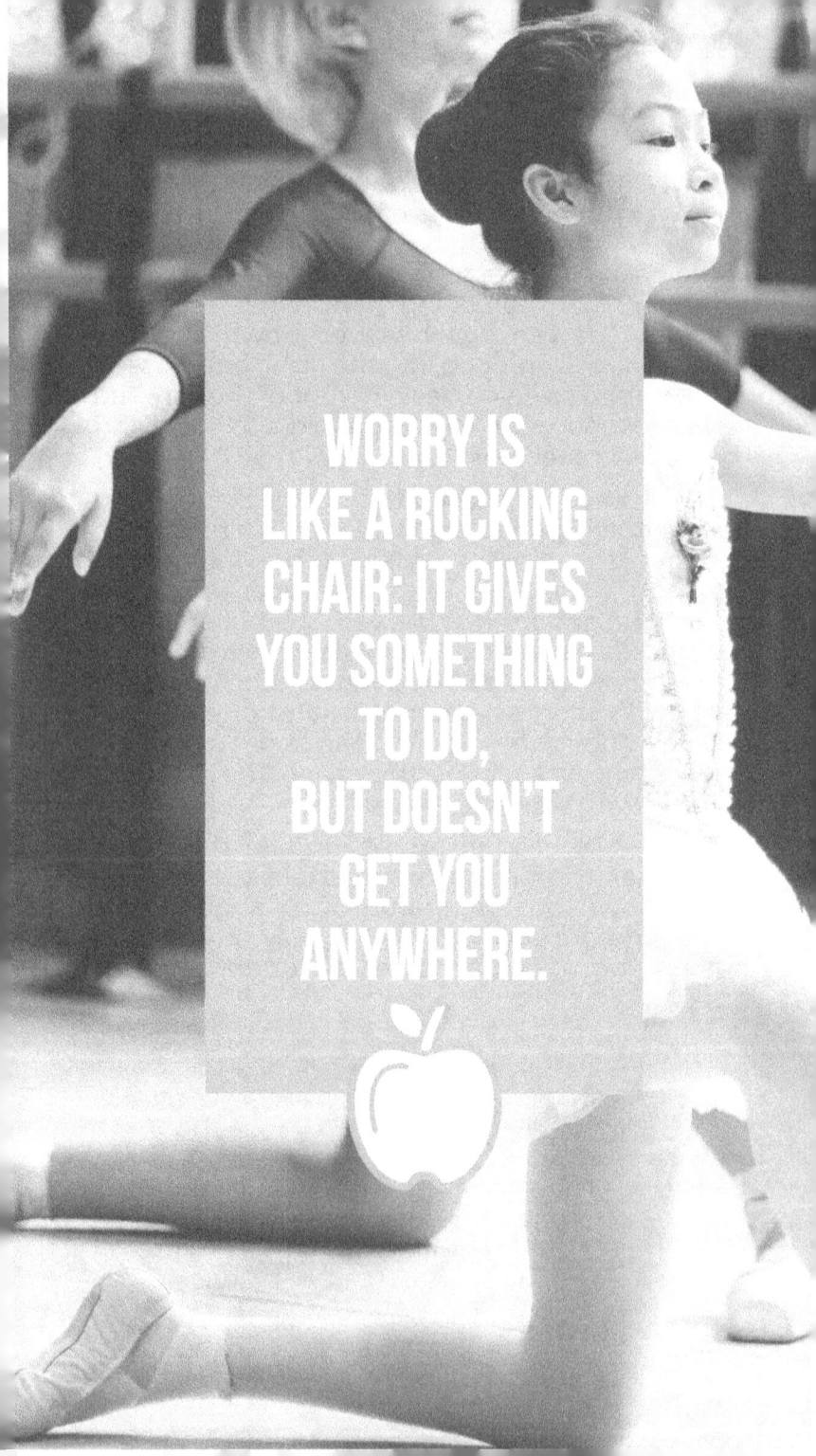

WORRY IS
LIKE A ROCKING
CHAIR: IT GIVES
YOU SOMETHING
TO DO,
BUT DOESN'T
GET YOU
ANYWHERE.

A woman once recalled a number of admonitions she had heard down through the years from her father:

"Don't walk with a spoon in your mouth. You'll trip and that spoon will go right down your throat."

"Don't race around that coffee table. You'll split your head on the corners. They should pad corners!"

"Don't eat raw cookie dough. You might get salmonella poisoning."

"Did you wash your hands?"

"Watch out for waiters. You don't want to get hot coffee poured on your head."

"Be sure to check the lead content of those mini-blinds you are buying."

"Watch how you use that cleaning fluid. It's poisonous."

"Watch your step when you board the train. You don't want to fall onto the tracks."

She now realized that when her elderly father comes to visit and she takes him to the station to return home, she finds herself saying as she waves good-bye, "Be careful, Dad."

Concern for students and fellow teachers is a sign of love, but worry is a sign of doubt and fear. We each must learn the difference.[23]

Casting the whole of your care [all your anxieties, all your worries, all your concerns, once and for all] on Him, for He cares for you affectionately and cares about you watchfully.

1 PETER 5:7 AMP

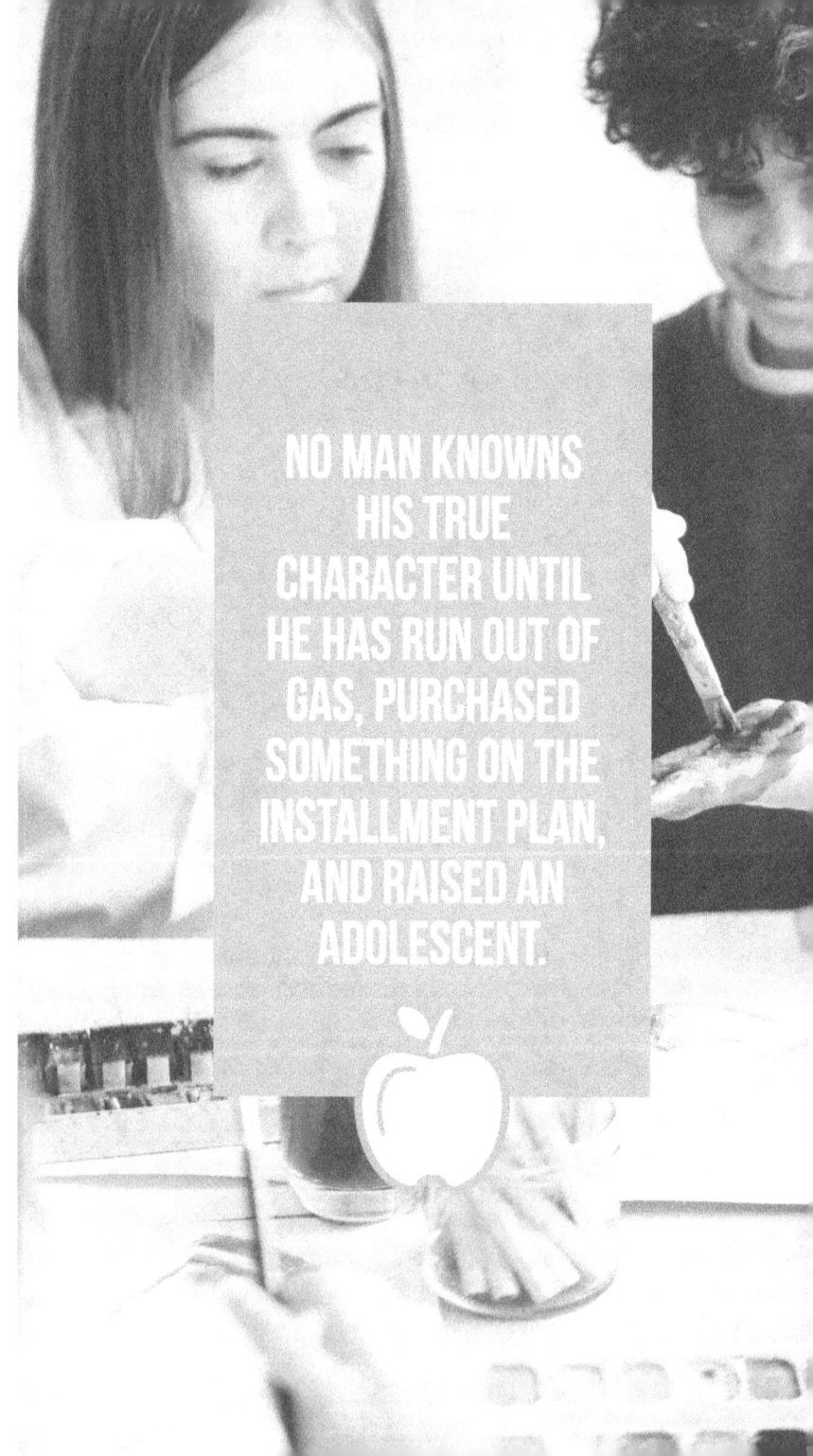

NO MAN KNOWNS
HIS TRUE
CHARACTER UNTIL
HE HAS RUN OUT OF
GAS, PURCHASED
SOMETHING ON THE
INSTALLMENT PLAN,
AND RAISED AN
ADOLESCENT.

Chuck Givens was on his way to conduct a workshop some two hundred miles from his home. He left in plenty of time and looked forward to the drive. He enjoyed taking the tight mountain curves in his sports car. On that particular day however, his fan belt broke, and the car immediately overheated. Nevertheless, he decided to press on in hopes of finding a gas station with a fan belt.

A few minutes later, the engine froze. He faced another choice. He could call and cancel his workshop, or he could try to get to his destination some other way. He decided to hitchhike. Although there wasn't much traffic, within ten minutes a car stopped. Not only did the driver deliver him to his exact destination, but the driver decided to enroll in the workshop!

At the end of the program, he asked those in attendance, "Is anybody heading my way?" Ten hands shot up. He got a ride home. At the day's close, he felt calm and successful, rather than angry and frustrated.

This instructor's conclusion? Events control our lives only if we give them that power. It's often better to take the challenge of pressing on, rather than becoming buried in the problem of the moment.[24]

Consider it all joy, my brethren, when you encounter various trials, knowing that the testing of your faith produces endurance.

JAMES 1:2-3 NASB

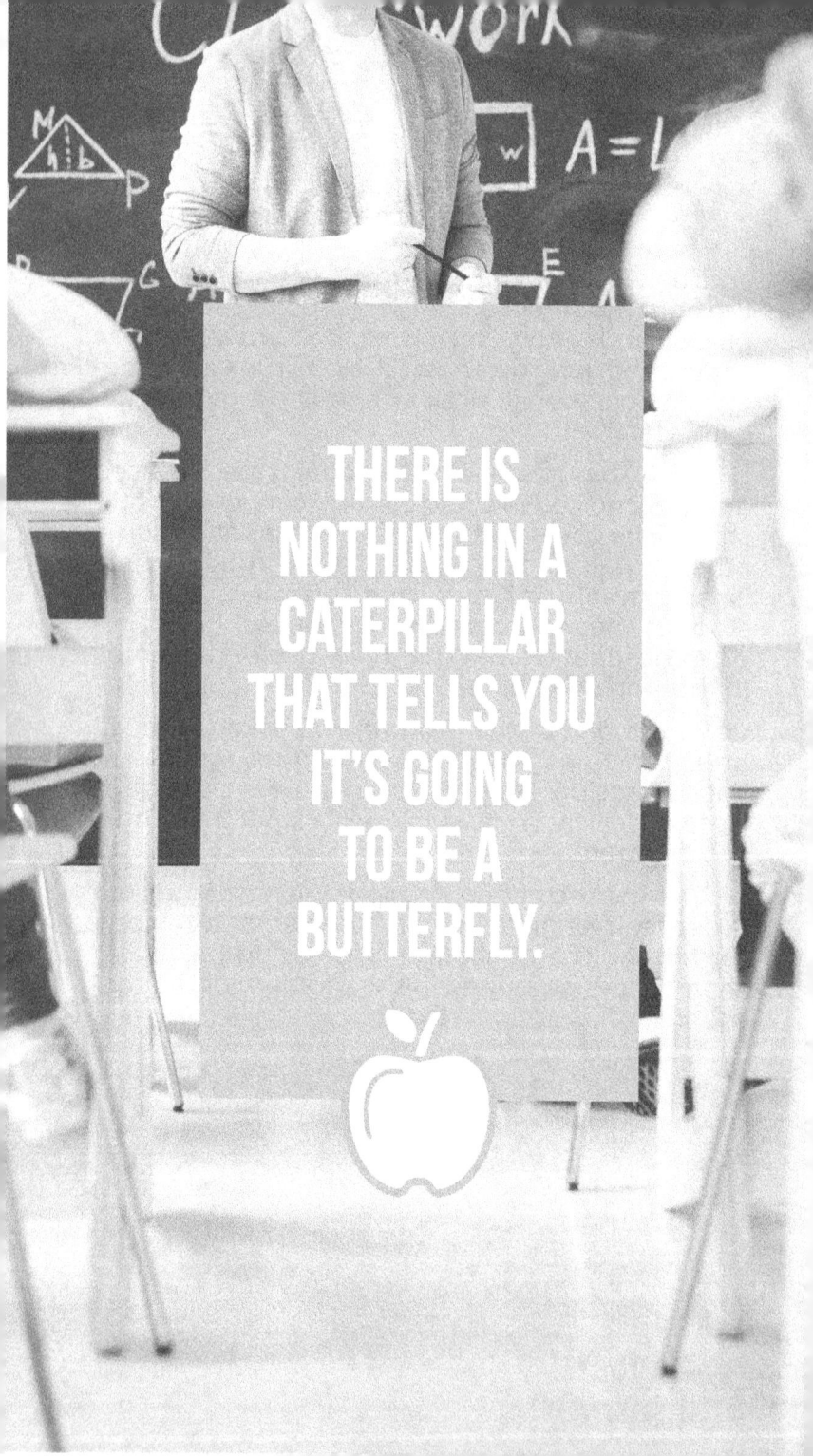

Nikola Tesla is the scientist who invented the method of generating electricity that is called "alternating current." Many scientists regard him as an even greater genius than the more widely recognized Alexander Graham Bell.

Tesla had an unusual habit During thunderstorms, he would sit on a black mohair couch by the window and applaud each lightning strike. It was as though one genius was recognizing and appreciating the work of another! Tesla knew better than anyone the wonder of lightning, because he had spent years researching electricity.

For thousands of years, lightning was feared and avoided. There was nothing in lightning strikes that would lead man to conclude he might generate and harness a similar power and that such a power might be used for good purposes.

Rather than applauding the workmanship of God in others, we too often are critical, unloving, and even fearful. What a difference it makes when we see others—students, fellow teachers, and administrators—as bearers of God's grace, love, and goodness.[25]

Beloved, let us love one another: for love is of God; and every one that loveth is born of God, and knoweth God.

1 JOHN 4:7

n Lewis Carroll's famous book, *Through the Looking Glass*, he presents a conversation between Alice and the queen:

"I can't believe that!" said Alice.

"Can't you?" the queen said in a pitying tone. "Try again, draw a long breath, and shut your eyes."

Alice laughed. "There's no use trying," she said. "One can't believe impossible things."

"I daresay you haven't had much practice," said the queen. "When I was your age, I always did it for half an hour a day. Why, sometimes I've believed as many as six impossible things before breakfast."

One of the things we must recognize is that most of the inventions and major achievements of the past century have been rooted in what was once considered to be impossible.

Can a man fly? Can a machine process information faster than a man can write? Can a person walk on the moon? Can a person's voice and picture be sent around the world without the person moving an inch? Can you become the teacher you truly would LIKE to be? It's not impossible![26]

Aim for perfection.

2 CORINTHIANS 13:11 NIV

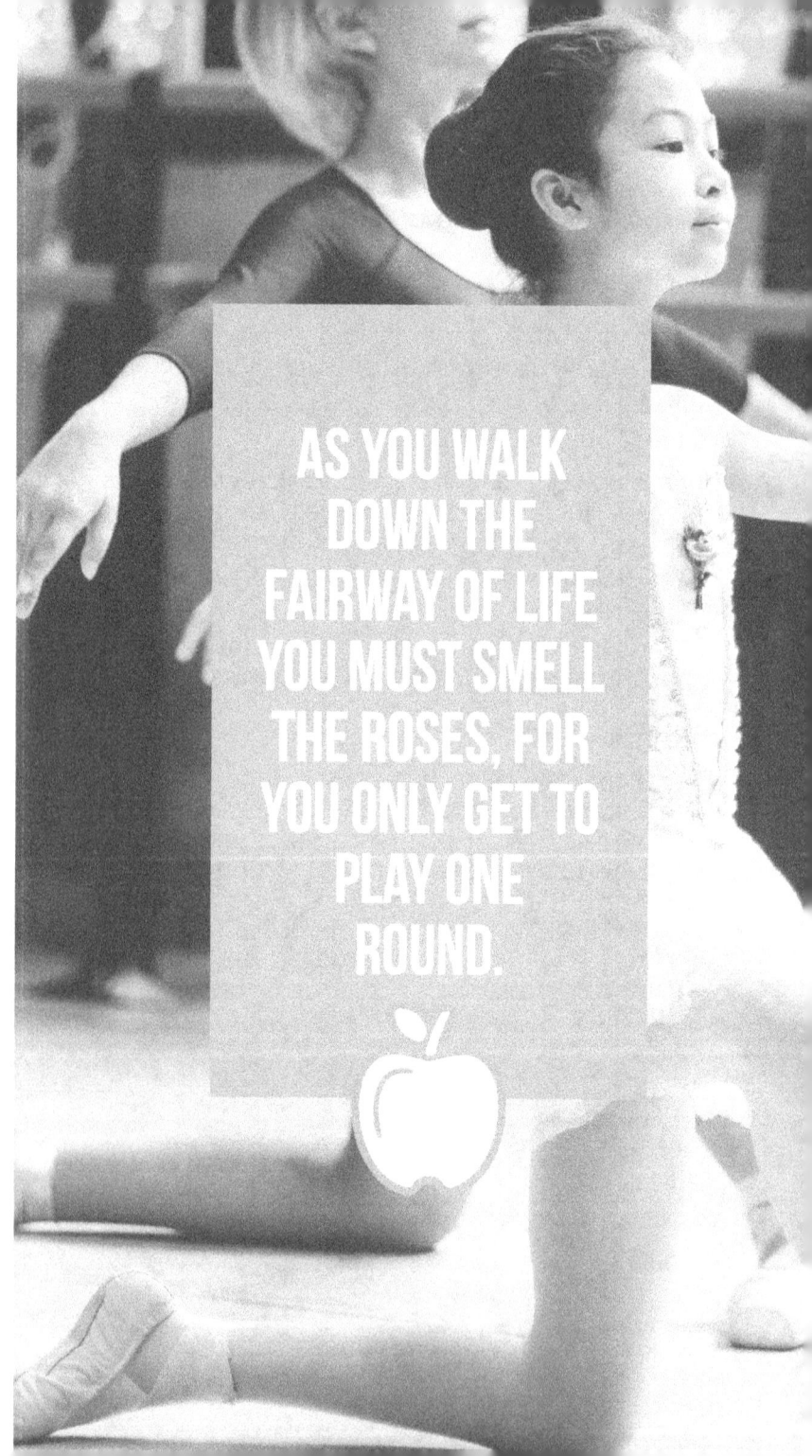

AS YOU WALK DOWN THE FAIRWAY OF LIFE YOU MUST SMELL THE ROSES, FOR YOU ONLY GET TO PLAY ONE ROUND.

Most of us try to prove ourselves by working extra hard to get ahead. Yet despite our best efforts, the volume of work seems to increase geometrically. Not only do we find we're not moving ahead, but we're not even keeping pace! Rather than stop and regroup, we push ahead and eventually develop burnout.

That's what happened to Denise. Her job ate up her life to the point where every surface in her home was cluttered with unfinished work. Each time a friend called, Denise had to cut the call short, claiming she had "too much work to do."

Finally, Denise's friends decided enough was enough. They showed up at her door one Saturday morning and announced, "We're the cleaning crew you've been meaning to call. We're going to help you get your life back." True to their word, they brought order back into Denise's life, and even concluded the day with dinner at a fine restaurant. Their fee? A promise from Denise that she would stop neglecting her friends and make time for a real life.

Today, step back, regroup, clean off your teacher's desk, and reprioritize your life.[27]

Lord, make me to know mine end, and the measure of my days, what it is: that I may know how frail I am.

PSALM 39:4

NO PLAN IS
WORTH THE
PAPER IT IS
PRINTED ON
UNLESS IT
STARTS YOU
DOING
SOMETHING.

A young farmer was learning to plow. Seated on the tractor, he pulled the lever that dropped the plow to the ground and started across the field. After he had gone a few yards, he turned around to look at the furrow he was making. He was entranced by the rushing flow of rich black topsoil along the blade.

Too late, he caught himself and quickly turned back to look where he was going. He realized that in turning around to look at his work, he had strayed from his initial straight line. He pulled the tractor back into line, and then after a few more yards, he looked back at his furrow again. He repeated this process several times. By the time he reached the end of the field and turned the tractor around, he found he had created a wavering line that was of little use in plowing the rest of the field. The young farmer soon learned that the only way to plow a straight furrow was to place his sights on a permanent marker across the field and keep the nose of his tractor squarely aimed at that point. No turning around to check his work!

We are wise when we set our sights on what God tells us to do, and then do it with all of our might, leaving all the consequences of our teaching to Him.[28]

But be ye doers of the word, and not hearers only, deceiving your own selves.

JAMES 1:22

Betty felt affirmed greatly by a statement that her son Rick made to her while he was a college student Betty and Rick were discussing the fact that a neighbor boy, Steve, who always seemed to be in trouble, was now driving his third car, having wrecked the first two cars his parents had given him. Betty expressed her gratitude to Rick for being a son who had never given her or his father a problem in all his twenty-one years. She then voiced her regret that they had not been able to afford to give Rick even one car.

Rick responded, "You and Dad gave me something more important, Mom. It was something Steve never had. You were parents who were always there."

Children not only need parents who are "there" for them in times of major crisis, but parents who are there to hear their successes, moments of indecision, feelings, reactions, opinions, and responses. Children need the same in their teacher— a teacher who is not only consulted to answer questions and resolve problems, but a teacher who makes himself or herself available to discuss life.

God is always available and accessible to us as teachers, so let's reflect those traits to our students.[29]

As a father has compassion on his children, so the Lord has compassion on those who fear him.

PSALM 103:13 NIV

THE BEST BRIDGE BETWEEN HOPE AND DESPAIR IS OFTEN A GOOD NIGHT'S SLEEP.

John H. Timmerman once wrote, "In the back corner of my yard, partitioned by a rose bed and a 40-year-old lilac bush, rests a pile, 8 feet long, 4 feet wide, and 4 feet high—my compost pile. Old-fashioned chicken wire stapled to well-anchored stakes holds it in place. Into it toss every bit of yard scrap and a heavy dose of kitchen scrap . . . a bit of lime now and then . . . and an occasional handful of fertilizer. The compost pile burns hot, never smells, and each October yields about 70 bushels of fine black dirt, dark as midnight, moist and flaky, that I spread in the garden . . . It nurtures 80 roses and a half-dozen beds of perennials and annuals."

Each night when we go to bed, we are wise to turn the day's "garbage" over to the Lord in prayer and to trust God to transform our mistakes and errors into something if useful. As we rest our bodies, we must also rest our hearts, believing that God can turn all things to good. And indeed He does. The garbage of our lives often becomes the compost for spiritual fruit.

The key is not in "sleeping on a problem," but rather in choosing to sleep in *spite* of a problem. We must trust God as the only One who truly can turn a day of classroom disaster into a dawning of hope.[30]

It is vain for you to rise up early, to sit up late, to eat the bread of sorrows: for so he giveth his beloved sleep.

PSALM 127:2

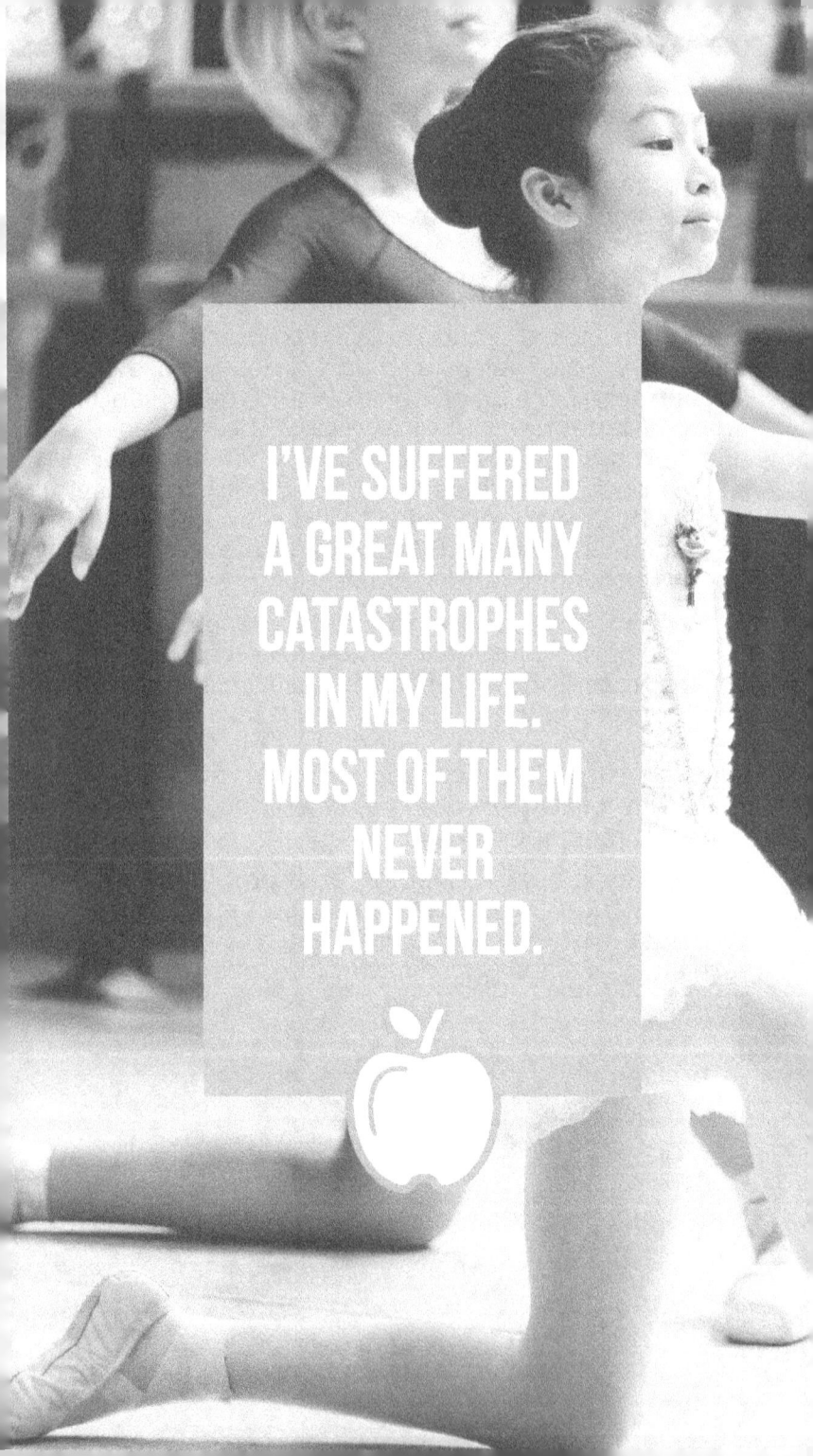

I'VE SUFFERED A GREAT MANY CATASTROPHES IN MY LIFE. MOST OF THEM NEVER HAPPENED.

Worry is often linked to the fact that we don't know how to respond to potential, past, or current events in our lives —or what to do about potential consequences. We don't know whether the long-term effect of a situation will be good or bad.

A man in China raised horses for a living, and one day one of his prized stallions ran away. His friends gathered at his home to help him mourn his loss. But the next week, the horse returned, bringing with it seven strays. The same friends gathered again, this time to celebrate his good fortune. That afternoon, the horse kicked the owner's son and broke his back. The friends came again to express their sorrow and concern. But a month later, war broke out and the man's son was exempt from military service. Again, the friends came together to rejoice.

Often at the time we are going through an experience, we truly can't tell a catastrophe from a cause for celebration. God asks us to trust Him with each circumstance as it arises, and to walk out each day with faith. We are to expect the best, believing that God can and will work all things for both His and our eternal benefit and the eternal benefit of our students.[31]

For God hath not given us the spirit of fear; but of power, and of love, and of a sound mind.

2 TIMOTHY 1:7

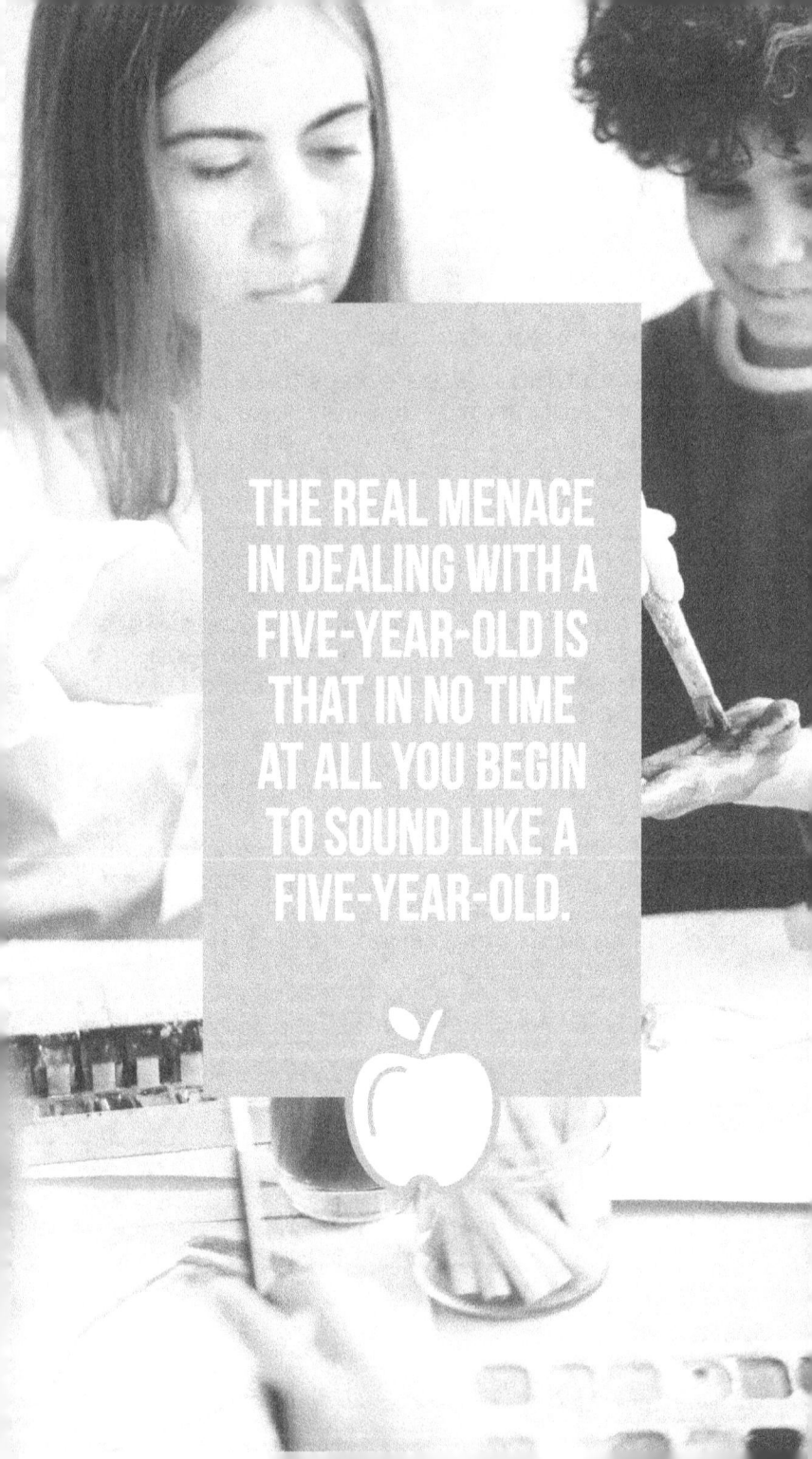

THE REAL MENACE
IN DEALING WITH A
FIVE-YEAR-OLD IS
THAT IN NO TIME
AT ALL YOU BEGIN
TO SOUND LIKE A
FIVE-YEAR-OLD.

An extreme example of an adult acting like a child is portrayed in the movie "Mommie Dearest" based upon a book by Christina Crawford. In one scene, the mother insists that her daughter finish eating a piece of steak on her plate. The daughter refuses, insisting that the meat is raw.

Long after the rest of the family has left the table, the daughter is forced by her mother to remain at the table. The mother is determined to win this battle of wills. The daughter falls asleep at the table, only to find the piece of steak on her breakfast plate the next morning. The battle continues for several meals, the piece of meat appearing on each plate put before the child until finally the mother gives in and disposes of the offensive, rotting meat.

What lesson does the daughter learn in this? Sadly, the only lesson to her seems to be that adults can be as stubborn as children.

Are you in a contest of wills with a student today? Is eternity at stake? Is evil truly afoot? Or are you simply engaged in a battle to save face or a contest to determine who is more powerful? Those who seek peace—and use peaceful means to reach it—are generally the winners in the long run.

Peacemakers who sow in peace raise a harvest of righteousness.

JAMES 3:18 NIV

THE BEST INHERITANCE A PARENT CAN GIVE TO HIS CHILDREN IS A FEW MINUTES OF HIS TIME EACH DAY.

A s Lisa's two daughters entered their teen years and began to walk straight to their rooms after arriving home from school each day, she became concerned about her ability to communicate with them. Her solution? She implemented "tea time."

Each day, she prepared a pot of hot tea—or a big pitcher of ice tea—and put out small sandwiches, fruit, and sweets on a tray which she decorated with fresh flowers and pretty dishes and napkins. Lisa would sit down with her own cup of tea so that when her daughters arrived home, both tea and Mom might be available. At first, her daughters ignored the tray of goodies. Then gradually, they began to stop by to say "hi" and pick up a sandwich or cookie. Soon, however, they began to stop and have tea and conversation with Mom. For her part, Lisa chose primarily to listen and pour tea. The more willing she was to listen, the more her daughters shared their feelings and experiences about their day. Lisa concluded, "I want my daughters to know there is a time each day when they know where to find me and when they know I'll listen."

Do your students know when you have time for them? What about your own children?

Be very careful then, how you live—not as unwise but as wise, making the most of every opportunity.

EPHESIANS 5:15-16 NIV

Each day, a man routinely walked to and from his office along Lake Michigan—a beautiful way to combine his commute to work with exercise. He enjoyed the walk on most days, but was frustrated by the automated sprinkler systems along the walkway. Specifically, he found it annoying that the sprinklers sprayed water beyond the lawns onto the sidewalks.

One day as he swerved to avoid the sweep of a sprinkler, he noticed a woman jogging past him. She headed straight for the sprinkler, and when she reached it, she simply stopped in her tracks, her Walkman still clamped to her ears, and let it soak her completely. The executive found himself chuckling inside at the obvious joy she took in being sprayed by the sprinkler. He noticed that several others also were smiling, obviously enjoying the freedom she seemed to experience Reflecting on this as he continued his walk, the executive concluded the jogger was someone who was more glad about life than she was mad, sad, or afraid. He found himself interested in wanting to know why.

Today, respond to everything you experience with joy and delight. A joyful response to life is one of the greatest witnesses a teacher can have![32]

Live such good lives among the pagans that though they accuse you of doing wrong, they may see your good deeds and glorify God on the day he visits us.

1 PETER 2:12 NIV

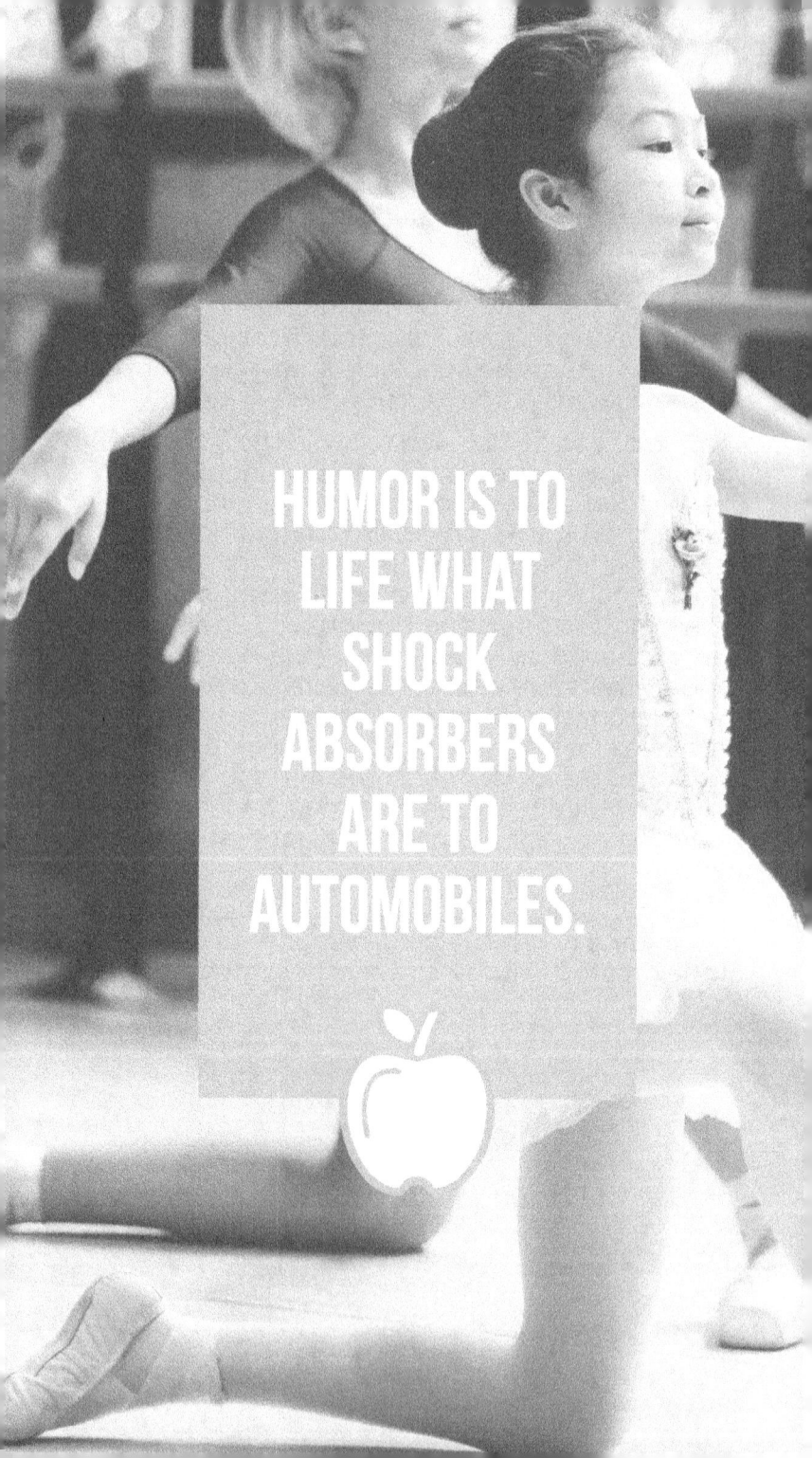

HUMOR IS TO LIFE WHAT SHOCK ABSORBERS ARE TO AUTOMOBILES.

D r. Fry has called laughter a stationary jogger. He has said, "There is hardly a system in the body a hearty laugh doesn't stimulate."

Norman Cousins, former editor of *Saturday Review*, believed that his recovery from a deadly form of spinal arthritis was due to massive doses of vitamin C and a tremendous amount of laughter every day. More than seventy years ago, Bernard MacFadden wrote that laughter is a form of exercise. He and his followers derived so much benefit from laughter exercise that he called it his Laugh Cure.

Laughter has long been regarded as a sign of mental health. In the recent movie "Patch Adams," Dr. Hunter Adams, while still a medical student, gives a long list of laughter's benefits to a supervising physician, including a greater release of endorphins and other hormones to the brain, relaxed muscle systems, increased circulation, and lower blood pressure.

Choosing to have fun and laugh heartily at life's foibles may be one of the best choices a teacher can make for health and genuine quality of life. It certainly is worth a try since laughter has no known negative side effects![33]

A merry heart doeth good like a medicine:
but a broken spirit drieth the bones.

PROVERBS 17:22

SOME PEOPLE SUCCEED BECAUSE THEY ARE DESTINED TO, BUT MOST PEOPLE SUCCEED BECAUSE THEY ARE DETERMINED TO.

The movie, "Rudy," is based upon the life of Daniel E. Ruettiger. Rudy grew up listening to legends about Notre Dame football. He dreamed of playing there one day but friends advised him that he was neither a good enough student to be admitted to the university, nor a good enough athlete to make the team. Rudy forfeited his dream and went to work in a power plant.

Then a friend of his was killed in an accident at work. Shaken, Rudy realized in a flash that life is too short not to pursue one's dreams. At the age of twenty-three, he enrolled at Holy Cross Junior College. He made good enough grades to transfer to Notre Dame, and he worked until he made the football squad as part of the scout team—players who help the varsity prepare for games, but who never suit up for the games.

Because Rudy requested it, the coach allowed Rudy to suit up for the final game of his senior year. In the final minutes of the game, a student in the stands began yelling, "We want Rudy!" Others joined in. With only twenty-seven seconds left on the game clock, Rudy took the field—and made the final tackle. He had persisted until he reached his goal.

Never give up on a student. A goal is worth pursuing until it is reached.[34]

Having done all . . . Stand therefore.

EPHESIANS 6:13-14

WISDOM IS
THE WEALTH
OF THE WISE.

In *The Hiding Place*, Corrie ten Boom tells about a lesson she learned from her father one day while they were riding a train. She asked her father, "What is sex sin?"

Her father looked at her for a moment, then stood up, lifted his traveling case from the rack over their heads, and set it on the floor of the train car. "Will you carry it off the train, Corrie?" he asked.

Corrie stood up and began to tug at the case, which was filled with watches and spare parts he had purchased that morning. "It's too heavy," she said.

"Yes," he said, "and it would be a pretty poor father who would ask his little girl to carry such a load. It's the same way, Corrie, with knowledge. Some knowledge is too heavy for children. When you are older and stronger, you can bear it. For now you must trust me to carry it for you."

There are many issues and questions which children are too young to carry. Wisdom is knowing what knowledge is necessary, and when and how it should be learned and applied. A good teacher is wise not to teach everything he or she knows and not to bother learning what is unimportant to teach.[35]

For the value of wisdom is far above rubies; nothing can be compared with it.

PROVERBS 8:11 TLB

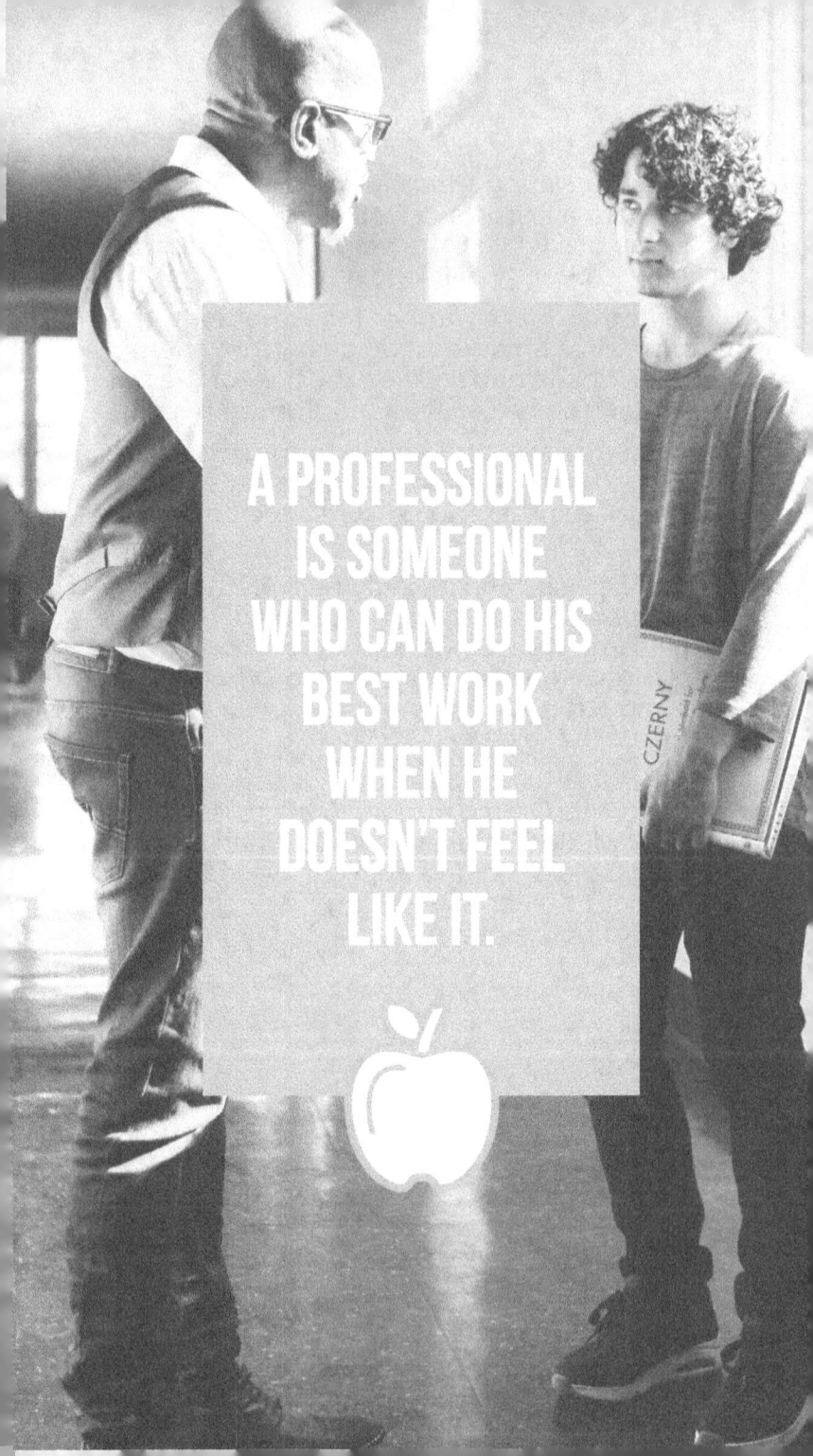

A PROFESSIONAL
IS SOMEONE
WHO CAN DO HIS
BEST WORK
WHEN HE
DOESN'T FEEL
LIKE IT.

Several years ago, well-known author and pastor Bill Hybels played on a park district football team. He was assigned to play defensive middle linebacker, which was fine with him since his favorite professional athlete was Mike Singletary, All-Pro middle linebacker for the Chicago Bears.

Hybels writes in *Honest to God*: "I crouched low and stared intently at the quarterback, readying myself to explode into the middle of the action in typical Singletary style The battle raged . . . and reality struck with a vengeance. Using a simple head fake, the quarterback sent me in the opposite direction of the play, and the offense gained fifteen yards. So went the rest of the game. By the fourth quarter, I came to a brilliant conclusion: If I wanted to play football like Mike Singletary, I would have to do more than try to mimic his on-the-field actions. I would have to get behind the scenes, and practice like he practiced. I would have to lift weights and run laps like he did. I would have to memorize plays and study films as he did. If I wanted his success on the field, I would have to pursue his disciplines off the field."

No teacher can be a classroom "star" without back-stage homework. The same is true in the Christian life.[36]

To win the contest, you must deny yourselves many things that would keep you from doing your best.

1 CORINTHIANS 9:25 TLB

HAPPINESS
IS THE
HARVEST OF
A QUIET EYE.

There is an old legend that once upon a time, God decided to become visible to a king and a peasant. He sent an angel to tell His plans.

"O king," the angel said, "God has deigned to be revealed to you in whatever manner you wish. In what form do you want God to appear to you?"

The king royally proclaimed, "How else would I wish to see God, except in majesty and power? Show God to us in His full glory of power." God granted his wish. A bolt of lightning struck and instantly vaporized the king and his court.

The angel then said to the peasant, "God has deigned to reveal Himself to you in whatever manner you wish. In what form do you want to see God?"

The peasant thought for a while and then said, "I am a poor man and am not worthy to see God face to face. If it is God's will to reveal Himself to me, let it be in those things I know—the earth I plow, the water I drink, and the food I eat. Let me see His presence in the faces of my family, neighbors, and—if God deems it good—even in my own reflection." God granted his wish, and he lived a long and happy life.

How are you expecting to see God? Expect to see Him in your students and your classroom today.[37]

My heart is steadfast, O God; I will sing and make music with all my soul.

PSALM 108:1 NIV

HONESTY IS
THE FIRST
CHAPTER OF
THE BOOK OF
WISDOM.

A high school student announced to his mother one day, "I won't be going to school this morning."

"Are you sick?" the mother asked.

"No, but it's senior skip day, and everybody will be at home."

She replied, "Everybody may skip, but you'd better be there." She knew that the assistant principal made it a priority to call about each child that didn't show up at school.

Sure enough, the assistant principal called her that I evening, asking, "Is John sick?"

"No," the mother said, "I told him to be in school and he disobeyed me."

The next day her son walked out of the house angry and mumbling at his long "grounding" sentence.She expected him to return home in that same mood. To her surprise, he entered the house and said, "Thank you."

"For what?" she asked.

He said, "The principal said he called parents for fourteen hours and you were the only one who told him the truth. I think it's cool to have the only mom brave enough to tell the truth."

It takes courage to tell the truth. Kids need to learn that lesson as much as teachers need to remember it.[38]

Provide things honest in the sight of all men.

ROMANS 12:17

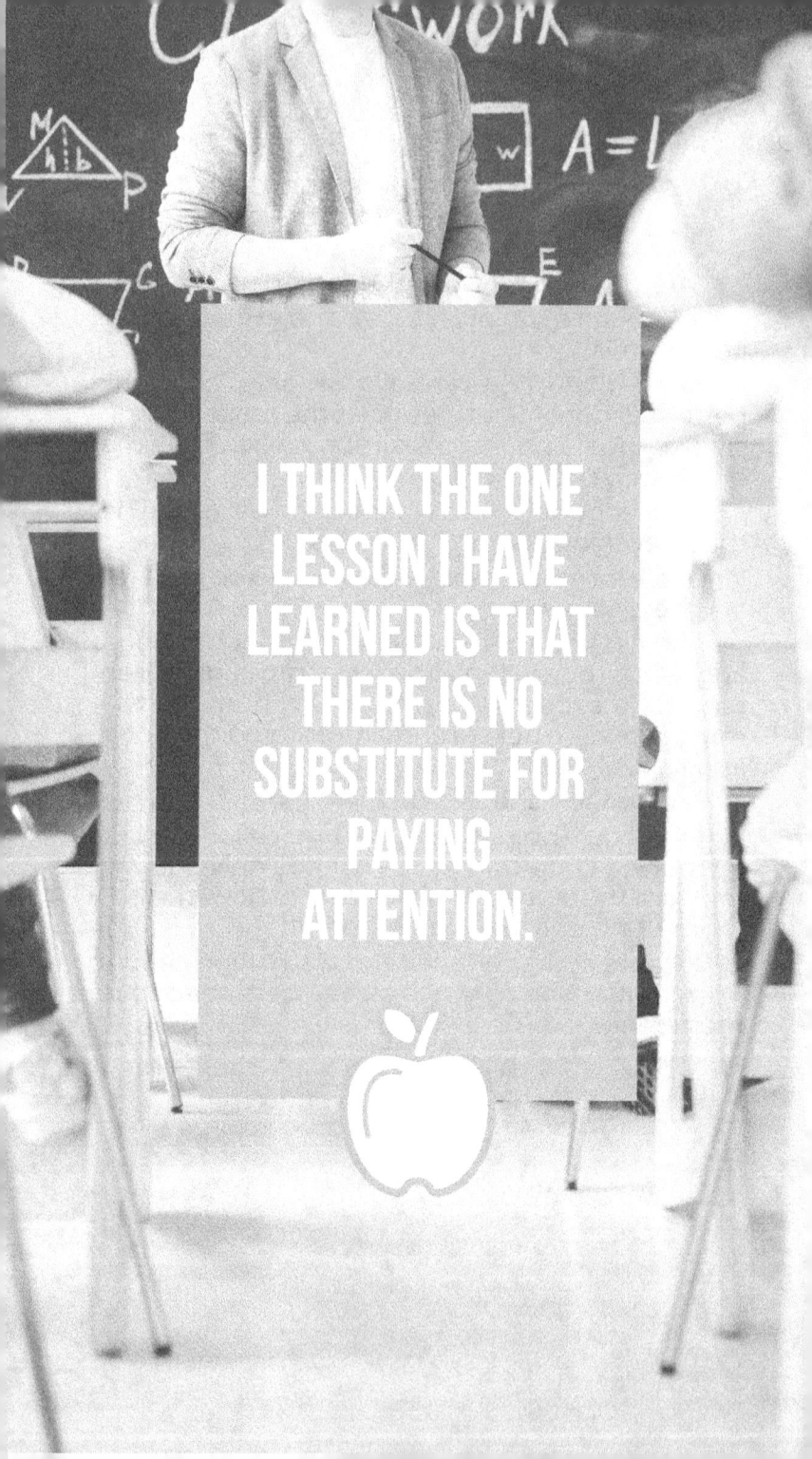

I THINK THE ONE LESSON I HAVE LEARNED IS THAT THERE IS NO SUBSTITUTE FOR PAYING ATTENTION.

One day, a rather reckless steel worker in Indiana gathered a group of men and bet each one of them five dollars that he could take his naked finger and whip it rapidly through the inch-thick stream of fiery iron without harm to his finger. They all covered his bet. The man stooped to the floor, took up a handful of the powdery dust all around the furnace, and used it to dry all the body oil from his finger. Coating his finger with this hot, dry dust, he thrust it at the liquid iron and caused sparks to fly in many directions. His finger survived the molten iron, and he won his bet.

Another worker watched this incident, then went to another place in the mill where a similar stream of iron was being poured. He made a similar bet with the men in that area and they, too, covered his bet This man, however, did not know the secret of wiping the body oil from his finger with the parched dust When he made his attempt, he burned his finger badly and was rushed to a first-aid station. A surgeon later had to remove his entire finger. For want of a little dust, this man lost a finger.

Teach your students by your own example to pay attention to detail. It could change the circumstances of their lives.[39]

Therefore we ought to give the more earnest heed to the things which we have heard, lest at any time we should let them slip.

HEBREWS 2:1

CARVE YOUR NAME ON HEARTS AND NOT ON MARBLE.

A strange group of gravestones stands in Mt. Hope Cemetery in Hiawatha, Kansas. A man named Davis had them made. When his wife died, Davis erected an elaborate statue in her memory. It showed both her and him at opposite ends of a love seat. He was so pleased with the result, he commissioned another statue, this time of himself placing a wreath as he kneeled at her grave. He was so impressed by this one that he had a third monument made, one of his wife—now with angel wings on her back—placing a wreath at his future grave. One idea led to another, and in the end he spent more than a quarter million dollars on monuments to himself and his wife.

Meanwhile, when anyone in the town tried to get him interested in helping with a community project— such as a hospital or park—the old miser frowned, set his jaw, and shouted back, "What's this town ever done for me? I don't owe this town nuthin'!"

John Davis died at 92, a lonely and bitter resident of the poorhouse. Few attended his funeral And the monuments? Each is sinking into the Kansas soil, owing to time, vandalism, and neglect.

Teachers are challenged daily to carve their legacy on young hearts.[40]

The only letter I need is you yourselves!
They can see that you are a letter from
Christ written by us . . . not one carved on
stone, but in human hearts.

2 CORINTHIANS 3:2-3 TLB

A prisoner with a long criminal record was on trial for his latest crime spree. The judge found him guilty on twenty-six counts and sentenced him to one hundred thirty years. Already middle-aged, the prisoner burst into tears. He knew there was no hope of parole with a sentence that long and that the rest of his life would be spent behind bars.

The judge noted this show of remorse and said, "I know I've imposed an unusually severe sentence. You don't have to serve the whole time." Then with a benign smile, he leaned toward the prisoner, whose tears had suddenly dried, and said, "Just do as much as you can."

It's unlikely any of us will ever accomplish as much as we would like to accomplish in a lifetime—to learn as much as we would like to learn, to experience as much as we would like to experience. What we must ask God to provide for us is the wisdom to know where and how to apply ourselves. Each day we are wise to ask, "What do You want me to learn today? What do You want me to experience?" When we ask God to set the curriculum of our lives, we can trust Him to teach us the most important lessons first and to reinforce them with patience and love.[41]

So teach us to number our days, that we may apply our hearts unto wisdom.

PSALM 90:12

EVEN A MOSQUITO DOESN'T GET A SLAP ON THE BACK UNTIL IT STARTS TO WORK.

I n a "Peanuts" comic strip by Charles Shultz, Charlie Brown tells Lucy about his birdhouse project, saying, "Well, I'm a lousy carpenter. I can't nail straight. I can't saw straight, and I always split the wood. I'm nervous, I lack confidence, I'm stupid, I have poor taste, and absolutely no sense of design."

Then in the last frame of the strip he concludes, "So, all things considered, it's coming along okay."

Many people approach their work as only a step toward being able to afford and to do what they really want to do. They endure the Monday-to-Friday grind solely so they can "live" on Saturdays and Sundays. In their work, they are choosing to make a living rather than make a life. The result is often a less-than-best effort at work and a superlative effort at hobbies and recreational pursuits. Choose work that is truly satisfying. If teaching isn't something you really enjoy and find fulfilling, choose a career that is rewarding to you, not only financially, but mentally, emotionally, and spiritually. Life is too short to waste effort on the *majority* of your days solely to enjoy a *few* of your days. Live each day with maximum effort, diligence, and performance.[42]

Work hard so God can say to you, "Well done." Be a good workman, one who does not need to be ashamed when God examines your work.

2 TIMOTHY 2:15 TLB

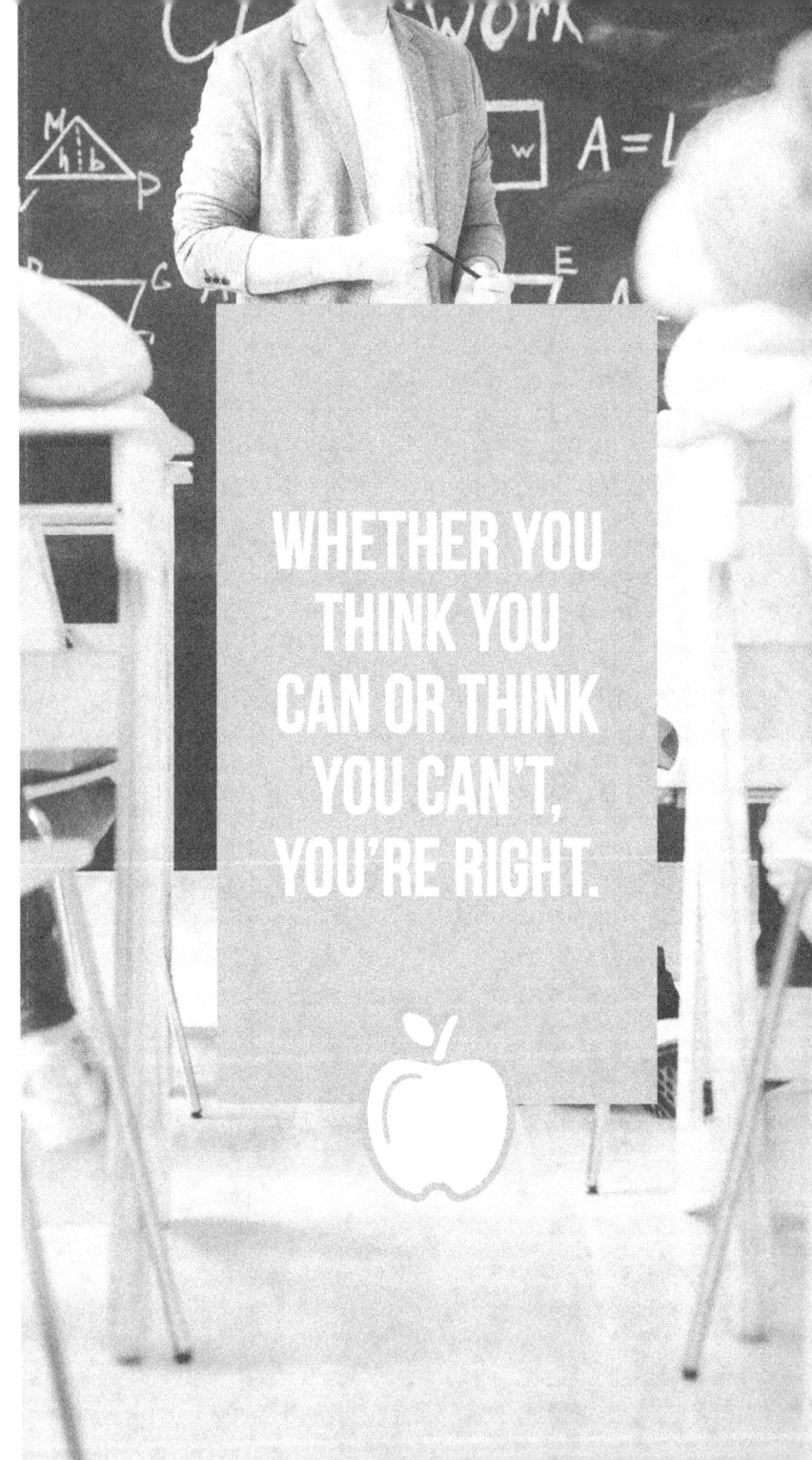

Lou Holtz, famous head football coach at Notre Dame, is a man known for winning—winning seasons, a lifetime winning record, a winning attitude. Holtz admits, however, that he didn't always have a winning attitude. Holtz's first job as a head coach was at the College of William and Mary. Upon reviewing the schedule his team faced, Holtz concluded that he didn't think his team could even be competitive. He was right. Week after week, his team lost.

By the second year, Holtz felt he could field a competitive team, but he didn't believe the team could beat its powerhouse opponents. Again, the team did as expected—it never lost a game by more than six points, but it consistently lost to the "big" schools when winning mattered most to fans and recruits.

Finally, Holtz realized what was happening. He concluded that confidence was the one factor that was making the difference. When the team played expecting to lose, it did. He made a life-changing decision; Expect the best from yourself and others, and then you won't be surprised when you get it.

Are you expecting your students to pass or fail today? What are you expecting from yourself?[43]

As he thinketh in his heart, so is he.

PROVERBS 23:7

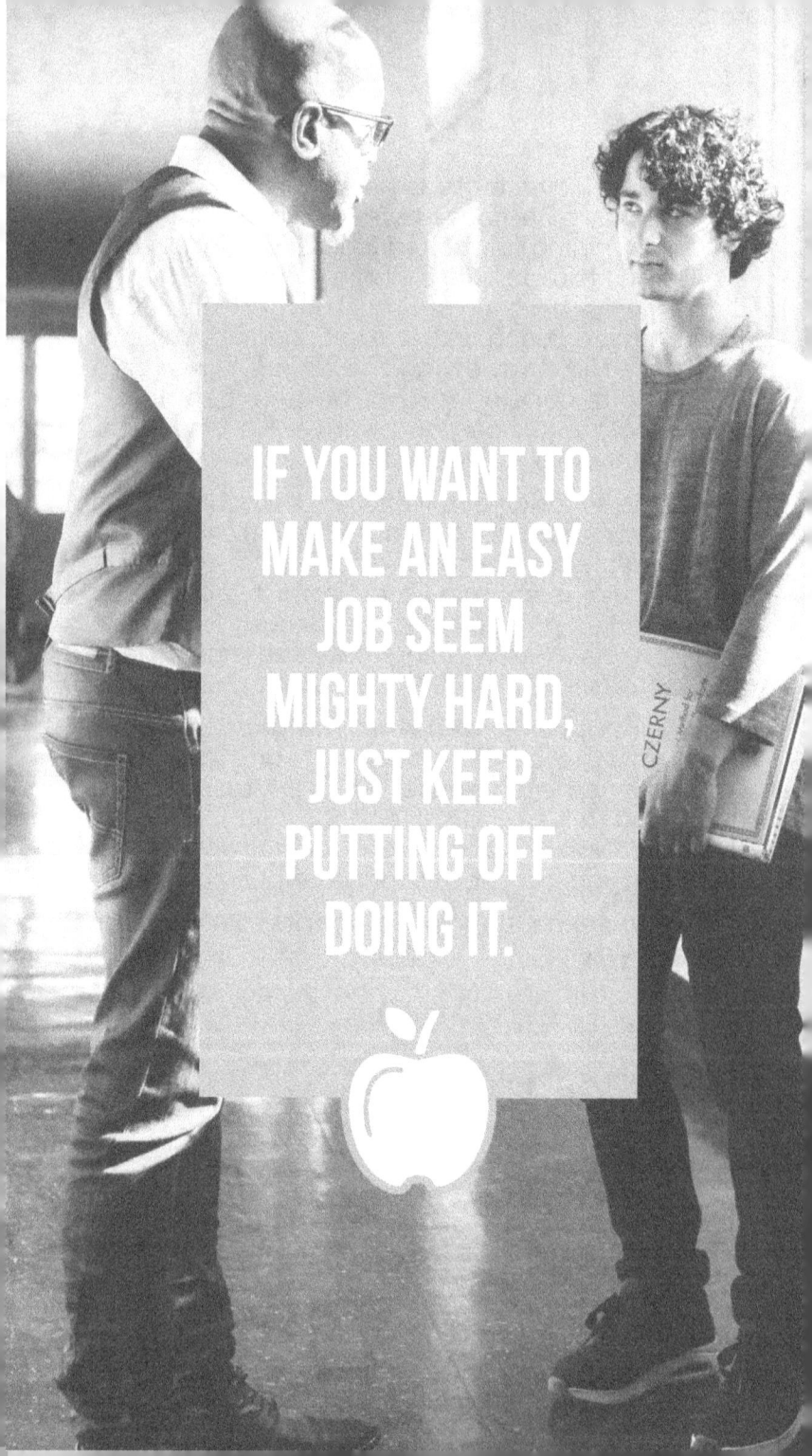

IF YOU WANT TO MAKE AN EASY JOB SEEM MIGHTY HARD, JUST KEEP PUTTING OFF DOING IT.

Once a year, an aerospace company held a savings bond drive. The job of getting employees to sign up for bonds was routinely assigned to the most junior engineer in a department. Most did only the minimum work possible . . . except for one man. He jumped right in and took charge!

He convinced every engineer and every manager in his department to buy and he even called all over the nation to convince those on temporary assignments elsewhere. He said to each one, "At the end of this bond drive, they post results. We can be number one!" Amused old-timers bought bonds and even found themselves getting excited about the drive. They especially were excited when their department came out ahead by a mile.

The effort did not go unnoticed by the company's president, who also noted an increase in morale and productivity in this "fired-up" department. He believed that if this engineer could accomplish so much with a bond drive, he could accomplish even more as a manager. He soon was promoted over twenty other engineers with more seniority. And not long after, he was promoted again to be a vice-president.

Don't wait. Jump into the challenge of the new course or the new school year with enthusiasm![44]

How long are ye slack to go to possess the land, which the Lord God of your fathers hath given you?

JOSHUA 18:3

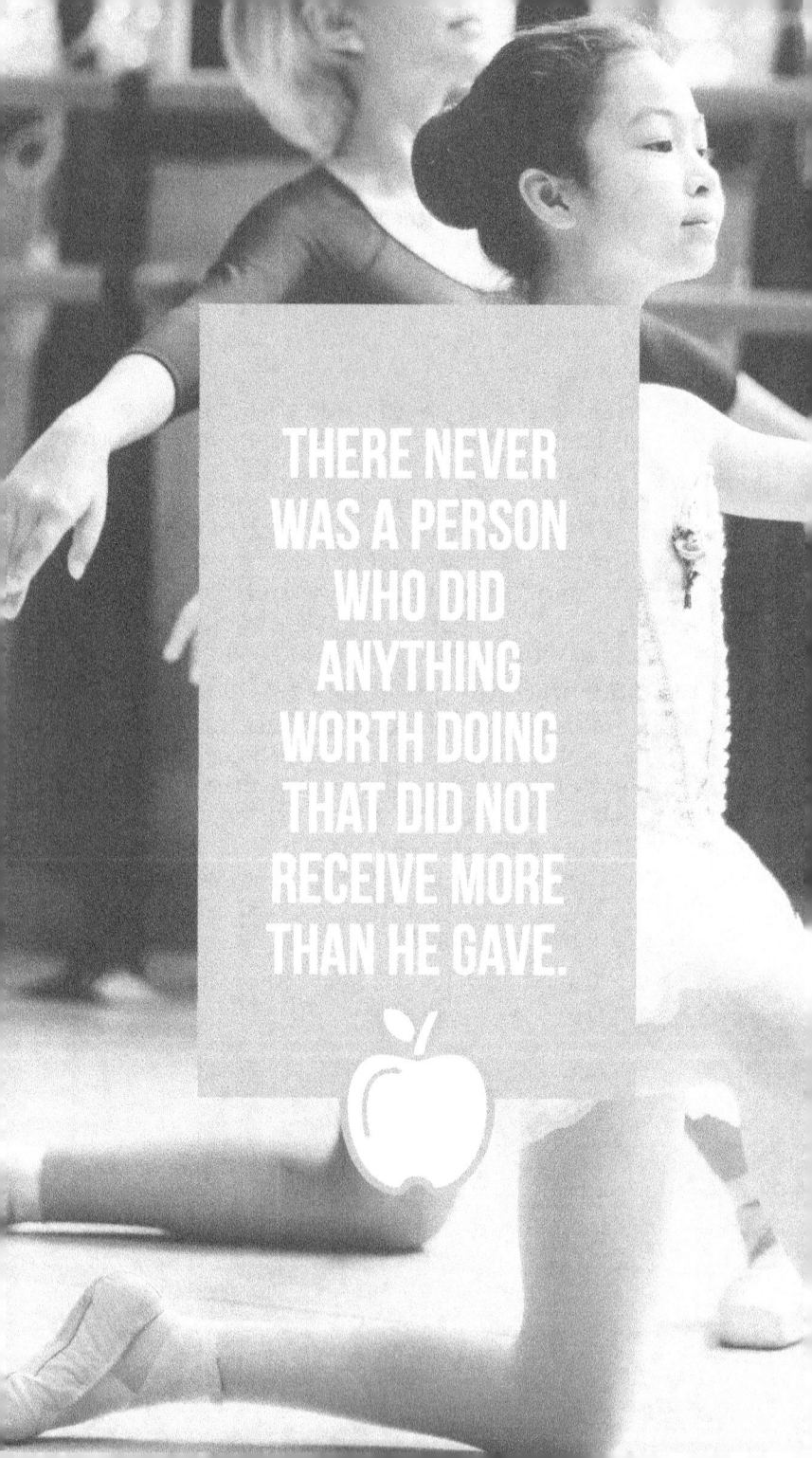

THERE NEVER
WAS A PERSON
WHO DID
ANYTHING
WORTH DOING
THAT DID NOT
RECEIVE MORE
THAN HE GAVE.

Millard Fuller was a successful law school graduate of the University of Alabama. He possessed an entrepreneurial spirit, and even as a student he made lots of money selling cookbooks, delivering flowers, and providing birthday cakes to students. A few years after graduation, Fuller had made more than a million dollars. However, it didn't make his wife happy.

"If all you want to do is make money," she said, "I'm leaving."

"I'll give away all my money if you won't leave me," Fuller responded. And he did. He gave away every cent he had earned, moved to a rural area in Georgia, and began to build homes for poor people in need. After spending three years in Zaire, he moved back to the United States and organized Habitat for Humanity, a program that provides housing for families in need of a home.

Today Habitat has chapters in forty nations. There is no "charity" involved. Families spend at least five hundred hours working on their own houses—one fourth of the total construction time. They pay full price, but receive interest-free loans. In its first sixteen years, Habitat has built more than twenty-thousand homes, all because one man—a lawyer, and not a very good carpenter—chose to care for others more than he chose to earn money.

Whatever a teacher gives to his or her students always comes back in the form of a rich reward.[45]

For God so loved the world that he gave his one and only Son, that whoever believes in him shall not perish but have eternal life.

JOHN 3:16 NIV

I DON'T KNOW THE SECRET TO SUCCESS, BUT THE KEY TO FAILURE IS TO TRY TO PLEASE EVERYONE.

At age sixty, Mary's mother developed severe pelvic pain. Exploratory surgery revealed osteoporosis, and Mary was told her mother would spend the rest of her life in a wheelchair.

Mary began to take over the chores of cleaning and cooking for her parents. One day her mother said to her, "Mary, unless you are just coming for a cup of tea and a chat, stop coming over here. I want you to stop cleaning my house, bringing me flowers, and cooking."

Mary asked, "Why don't you want me to help you? It's one way I can give back to you."

Her mother replied, "I want to let go of everything that looks like a reward for being sick. I want to heal. I'm going to put all of my energy into getting well and strong." Within six months, the doctors were amazed that her mother's pelvic bone was regenerating itself. A few months later, she was walking again. At age seventy-five, Mary's mother went sky-diving!

Mary discovered that doing all she could to please her mother was not actually what was best for her mother. Before giving a student all the answers, we should ask God what He desires for that student and then line up our teaching efforts accordingly. Sometimes less immediate help yields long-term results.[46]

Am I now trying to win the approval of men, or of God?

GALATIANS 1:10 NIV

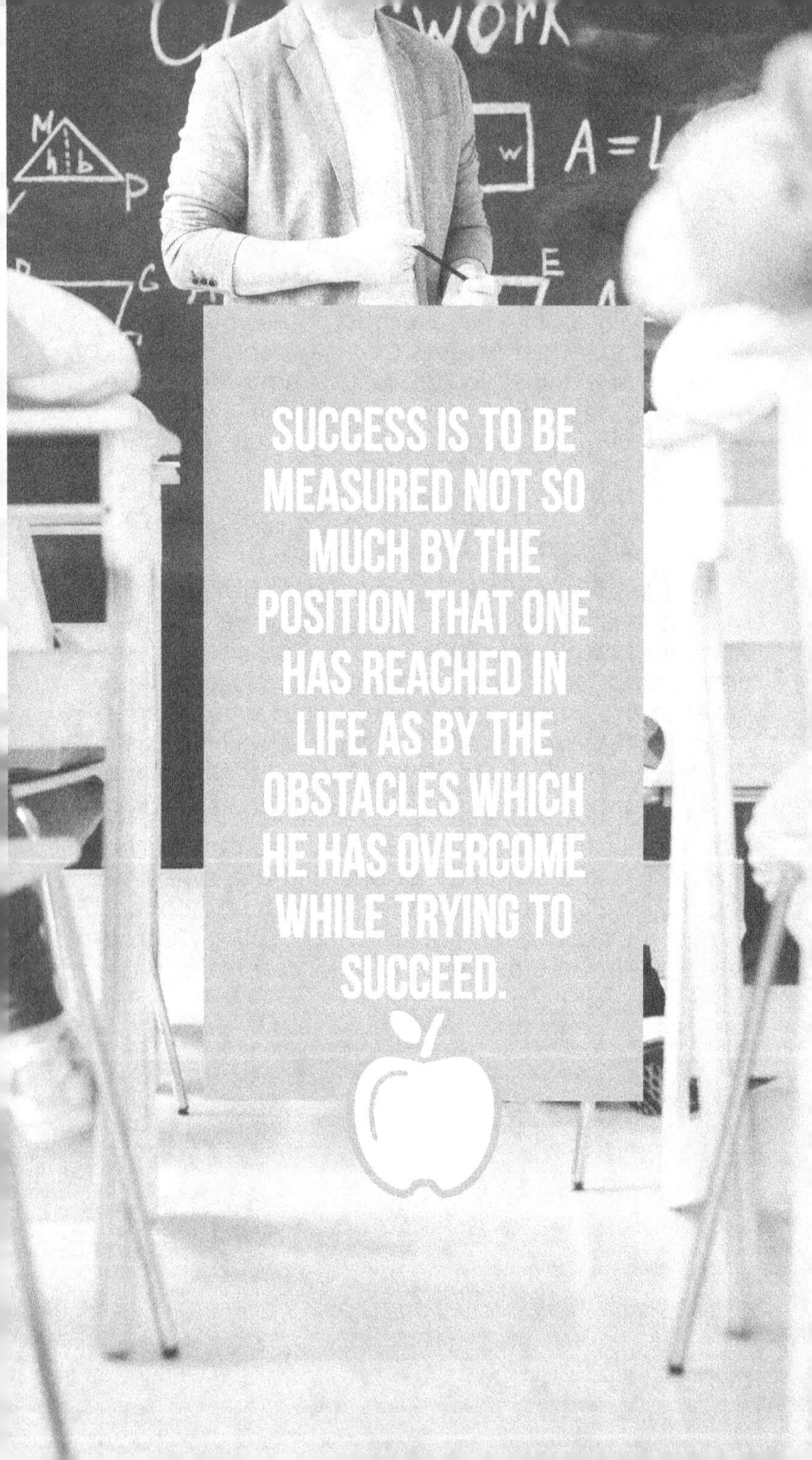

"Life is a test," Marnita Lloyd told her fellow classmates and teachers during graduation exercises at Detroit's Denby Technical and Preparatory High School. "You either pass or fail—it's up to you."

Marnita went on to a full scholarship at Wayne State University, but the road to academic achievement for this valedictorian was marked by plenty of setbacks and obstacles. When she was eleven, her brother was killed in a drug dispute. When she was sixteen, her mother died of heart disease. During her senior year, a sixteen-year-old friend was fatally stabbed at his locker and an eighteen-year-old friend was gunned down at a church carnival.

Marnita went to class rather than get involved in the commotion of the school slaying. She chose to stay home and study rather than participate in a neighborhood anti violence parade after the carnival murder. "Those [parades] are good," she said, "but it won't help me study for my government test." Marnita kept her eyes on her personal goal: a medical career as an obstetrician-gynecologist. She chose to place her emphasis on new life, not death.

If chaos is swirling in your classroom, set your students' sights on a higher goal.[47]

Blessed is the man who perseveres under trial, because when he has stood the test, he will receive the crown of life that God has promised to those who love him.

JAMES 1:12 NIV

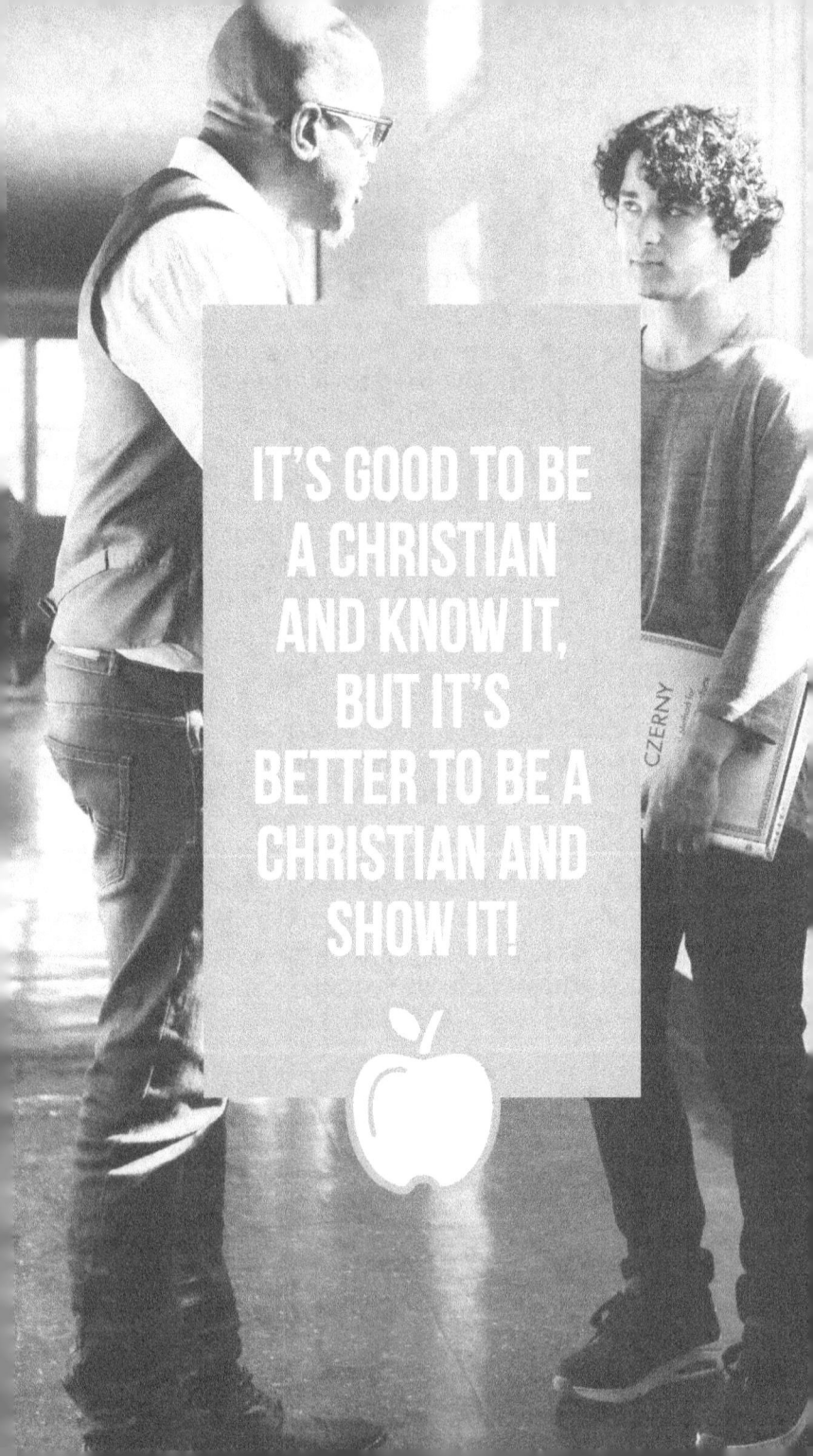

Paul Azinger tells about receiving a phone call from a golf pro with whom he hadn't talked in a while. Paul was expecting the usual questions about his cancer treatments, but this golf pro immediately launched into a long tale of woe, most of which stemmed from the fact that he had lost his job.

All the while he was talking, Paul was thinking about what a selfish, insensitive jerk the guy was in not asking about Paul's health. The golf pro then asked Paul to write a letter of recommendation. It was only after Paul had agreed to do the favor that the pro finally asked Paul how he was feeling.

"I feel great!" Paul replied. Suddenly, he felt a new positive attitude about the phone call. He realized he had been wrapped up in his own world and just as self-centered as this golf pro. He also realized this was the opportunity he had been praying for—a chance to be an inspiration to others by telling how he had drawn peace and strength from the Lord during his cancer treatments. "In a very real way," Paul said, "that phone call helped me to get well . . . truly well."

Seek today to have a positive influence in the life of a student who has a negative attitude. Consider that student to be your own personal "mission field!"[48]

Your strong love for each other will prove to the world that you are my disciples.

JOHN 13:35

WHEN THE
BLIND MAN
CARRIES THE
LAME MAN,
BOTH GO
FORWARD.

CBS newsman Charles Osgood once told a story of two women who lived in the same convalescent center. Each had suffered a debilitating stroke. Ruth's stroke damage was all on her right side; Margaret's stroke had left her left-side restricted.

Both Ruth and Margaret had once been accomplished pianists, but their strokes had forced them to face the fact that they might never play again. Then the convalescent center director asked the two women to try playing the center's piano together, Ruth taking the left-hand part and Margaret the right. They did . . . and the music they made together was beautiful. A friendship developed, and both women felt a renewal of meaning and joy in their lives.

As Christians, we are called to work together with other believers—each person sharing his or her skills with others, and in turn receiving the gifts of others in his or her own area of lack. In this way, the entire Body of Christ is made strong and effective as a whole, and the specific needs of each individual are met. What one teacher cannot do alone in your school, perhaps two or more can do together.[49]

And the prayer offered in faith will make the sick person well; the Lord will raise him up. If he has sinned, he will be forgiven.

JAMES 5:15 NIV

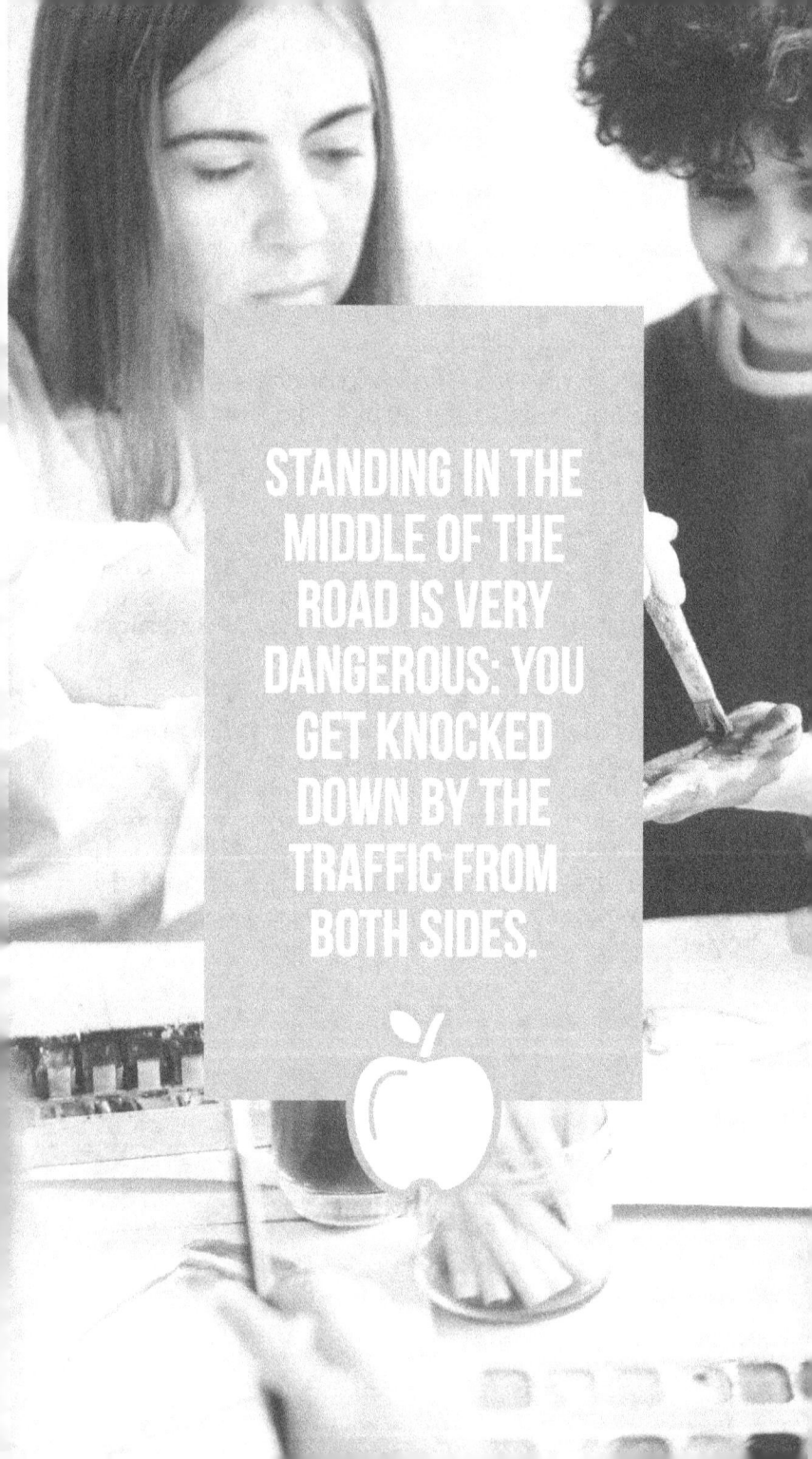

STANDING IN THE MIDDLE OF THE ROAD IS VERY DANGEROUS: YOU GET KNOCKED DOWN BY THE TRAFFIC FROM BOTH SIDES.

While walking down a road one day, a turtle fell into a pothole in the center of a country road. He spun his little legs but couldn't free himself. A rabbit friend came hopping along and offered assistance, but no matter what they tried, the turtle remained stuck in the muddy hole.

"It's no use," the turtle finally said. "There's no help for me." Various other animal friends passed his way, but the turtle refused their help, believing his destiny was sealed in the muck of the hole in which he had fallen. He sighed, "It's hopeless," and pulled his head inside his shell.

Then he heard a rumble. And peeking from his shell, he spotted a tractor heading straight for the pothole in which he sat. Without another thought, he scrambled out of the hole and across the road to safety.

Later that day, some of his animal friends saw him and asked, "How did you get free? We thought you couldn't get out of that pothole."

The turtle replied, "Oh, I couldn't . . . but then I had to!"

Don't wait for a crisis to develop in your class-room before you decide to take action on your problem or make a difficult decision. Act now. You'll save yourself stress and panic later.[50]

I know your deeds, that you are neither cold nor hot. I wish you were either one or the other!

REVELATION 3:15

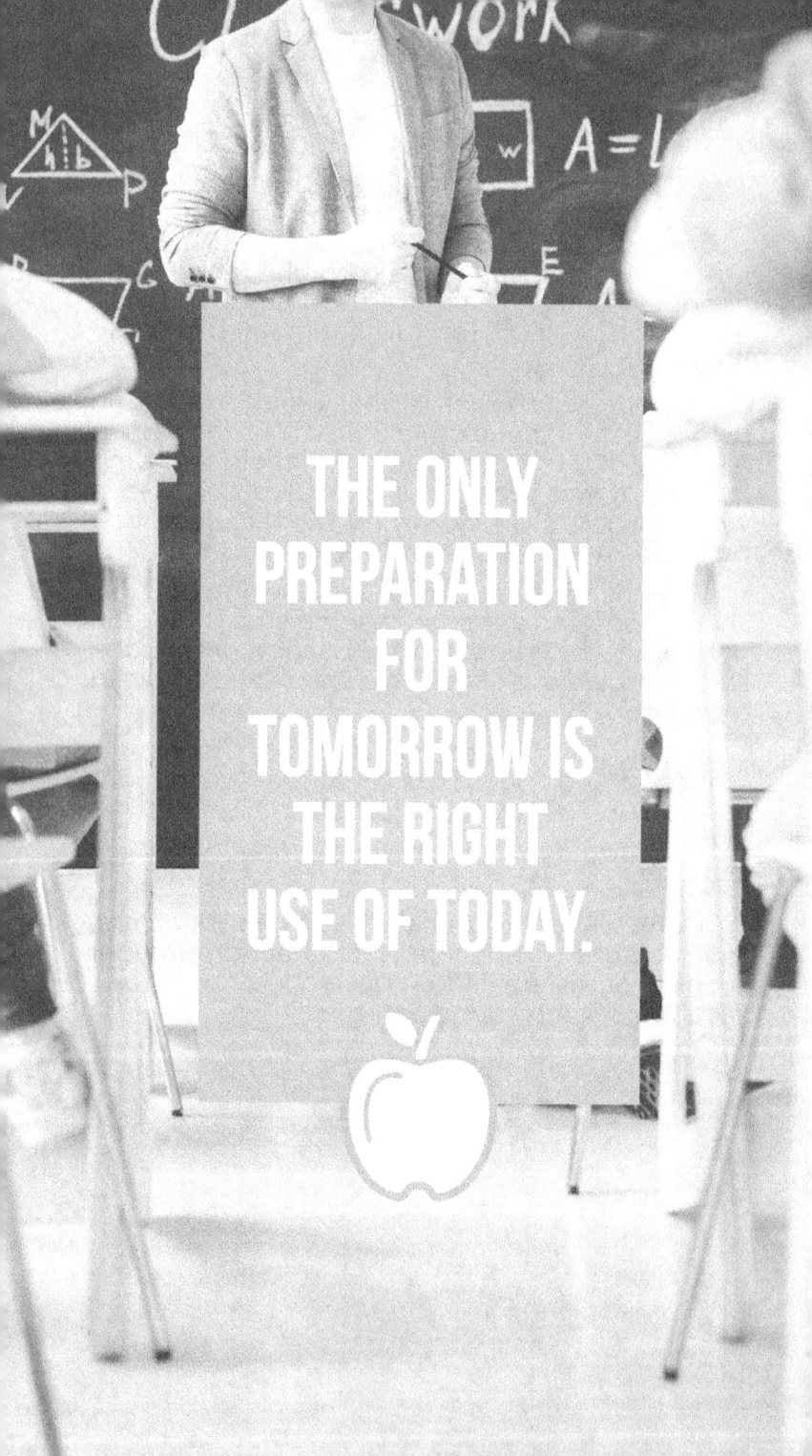

THE ONLY PREPARATION FOR TOMORROW IS THE RIGHT USE OF TODAY.

Could you give up a salary of $50,000 a week? Jonathan Taylor Thomas, one of the young stars of the *Home Improvement* television series, did just that, and for a good reason; he decided to pursue a college education.

When it came to life, Thomas didn't want to develop a case of tunnel vision. He wanted to see what else the world had to offer and to meet people whose opinions could help him form his own. He wanted to know more than how to hit his mark or memorize lines that someone else had written. He has stated often that he regards Hollywood as an industry, not a lifestyle. Family, friends, and church are all important to him.

The world's definition of success is often a shallow one. Real success is doing what we were created to do—developing and using all of the talents and abilities we have been given, not only for our own benefit but for the benefit of others. Real success is the product of good decisions made each day—decisions to be God's person, decisions to pursue one's own potential and to live in moral excellence, and decisions to love others and do good to them.

What you decide today will become who you are as a teacher tomorrow.[51]

Take therefore no thought for the morrow: for the morrow shall take thought for the things of itself. Sufficient unto the day is the evil thereof.

MATTHEW 6:34

A man once found the cocoon of an emperor moth and took it home to watch the moth emerge. One day a small opening appeared, and for several hours the moth struggled but couldn't seem to force its body past a certain point. Deciding that something was wrong, the man cut the remaining bit of cocoon with scissors. The moth then emerged easily—its body large and swollen, its wings small and shriveled.

The man continued to watch, expecting that in a few hours the wings would spread out into their large natural beauty. That didn't happen. The moth spent its entire life dragging around a swollen body and shriveled wings—it never did fly.

The man consulted a biologist to discover what had happened to the moth. He learned that the constricting cocoon and struggle are both normal and necessary. The struggle actually causes fluid from the moth's body to move into its wings, reducing the size of the body and making the wings strong and larger.

The struggle and pressure you are under today is not without value in your life. Trust God to use it as a means of developing your endurance, building your patience, and perhaps even forcing you to reevaluate your priorities. Stress can be a teacher's teacher.[52]

Knowing this, that the trying of your faith worketh patience. But let patience have her perfect work, that ye may be perfect and entire, wanting nothing.

JAMES 1:3-4

When he was in eighth grade, all Chuck Swindoll wanted for Christmas was a new basketball. His father, who worked in a machine shop, had made him an iron hoop for a basket. Chuck practiced until he could sink nine out of ten free throws, and he worked hard on a two-hand set throw.

Then one November evening, his old tattered basketball burst. With six weeks to go before Christmas, he dropped numerous hints and did his chores with renewed energy, even volunteering to wax the kitchen floor! Sure enough, a brightly wrapped box appeared under the Christmas tree—the right shape, the right sound when shaken, and with Chuck's name written on it. He could hardly wait. On Christmas Day, he tore at the wrapping only to discover a world globe inside. It had no bounce to it.

Disappointed at the time, Chuck has reflected back on this experience: "My mother's vision eclipsed my fantasy and became my reality. I still enjoy watching basketball, but what really excites me is the idea of sharing our Savior with people in places like Singapore and Moscow, Delhi and Montreal."

What are your dreams? What dreams are you instilling in those you teach? Are they God's dreams?
53

After this manner therefore pray ye . . . Thy kingdom come. Thy will be done in earth, as it is in heaven.

MATTHEW 6:9-10

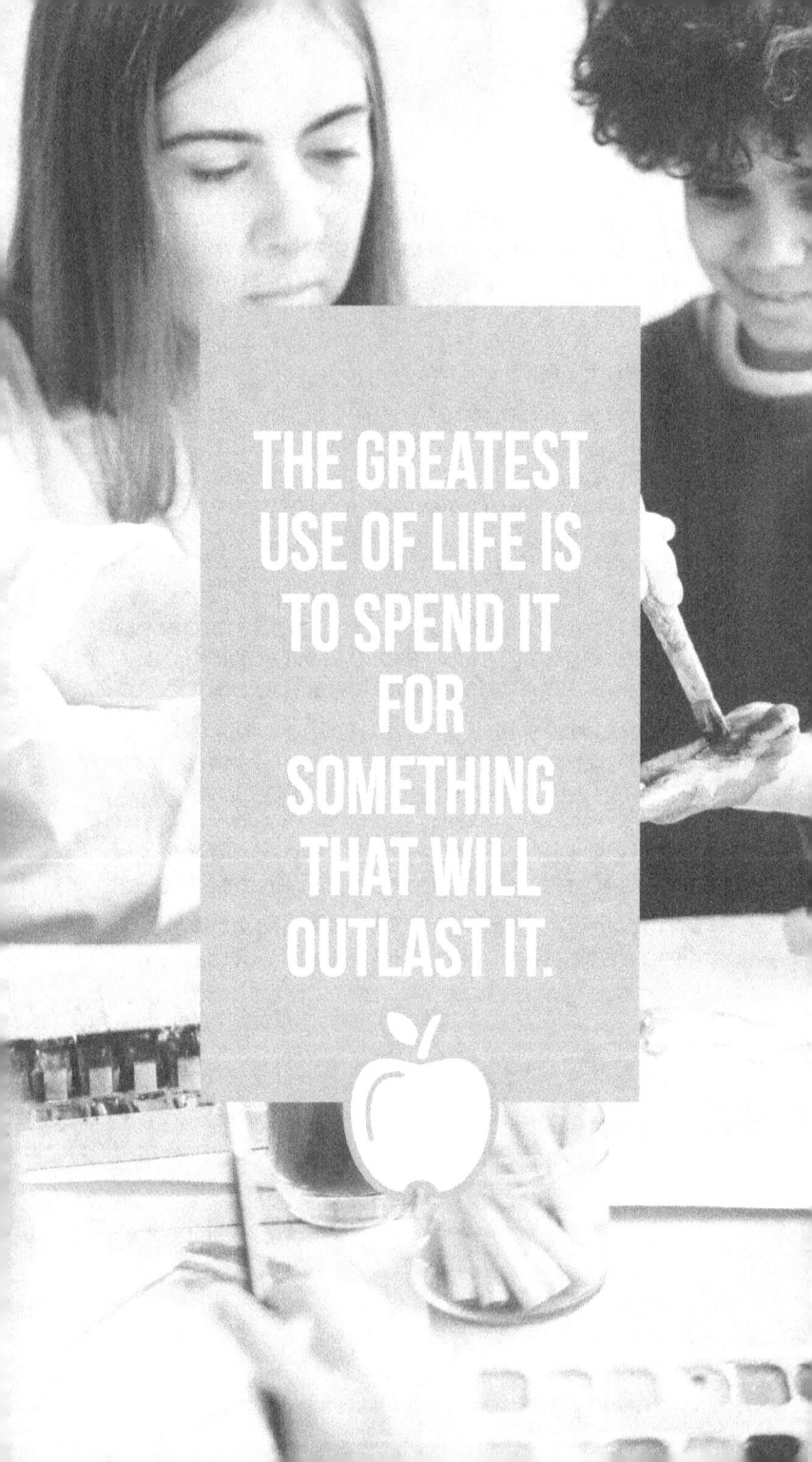

THE GREATEST
USE OF LIFE IS
TO SPEND IT
FOR
SOMETHING
THAT WILL
OUTLAST IT.

Those who visit Mount Rushmore in South Dakota generally come away with a much greater appreciation for all that was involved in the tremendous undertaking to sculpt the faces of America's most beloved presidents—Washington, Lincoln, Jefferson, and Theodore Roosevelt—into the side of a cliff.

For fourteen years, the sculptor Gutzon Borglum worked on the mountain. His other well-known works—the head of Lincoln for the Capitol Rotunda in Washington, D.C., and the twelve apostles for the Cathedral of St. John the Divine in New York City—are grand, but certainly not on the scale of Mount Rushmore. Of one thing Borglum could be certain as he hung on scaffolding month after month, year after year: Mount Rushmore wasn't going anywhere. His work there would remain long after his lifetime.

Teaching is much like sculpting. The end product may take years to produce, and the "work in progress" may seem unimpressive at times. When a child becomes an adult, however, and begins to put the lessons of his childhood to good use, he becomes a blessing to everyone around him.

Rather than think about teaching knowledge today, focus on the fact that you are sculpting lives!

54

But store up for yourselves treasures in heaven, where moth and rust do not destroy, and where thieves do not break in and steal.

MATTHEW 6:20 NIV

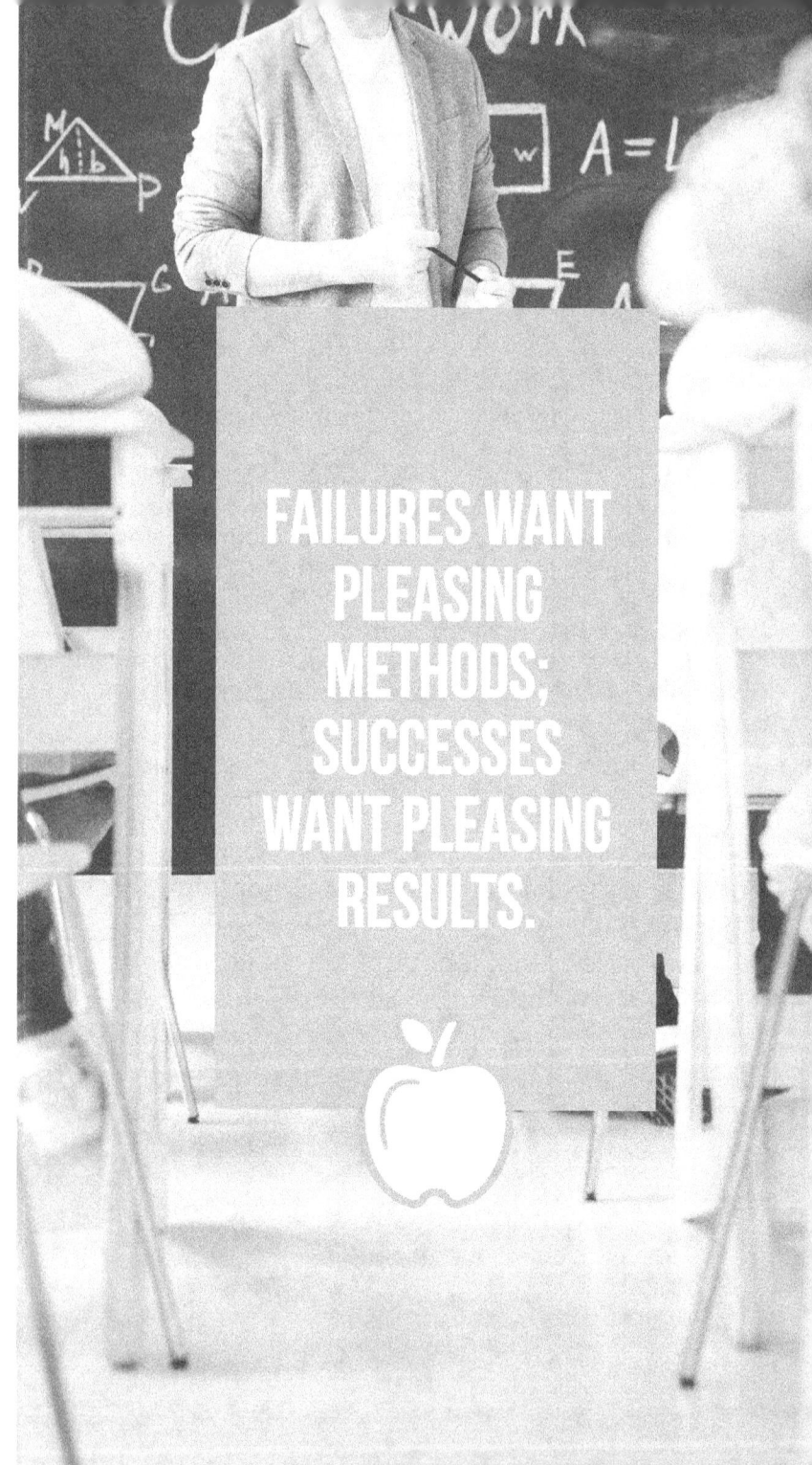

FAILURES WANT PLEASING METHODS; SUCCESSES WANT PLEASING RESULTS.

A young college student asked to teach a Sunday school class at a church near the campus. He was assigned a small area, a class book, and one eleven-year- old boy to teach. He taught this boy—who later brought a friend to class—for several weeks.

Discouraged at the small turnout, the teacher went to the superintendent to resign. The superintendent said, "I didn't want to give you this class in the first place, because I didn't think you were dedicated. I was right" This response made the young man so angry that he refused to quit. Instead, he went back to his dorm room and prayed.

Each afternoon for a week, he prayed for several hours. As he prayed, he realized that if he wasn't faithful in little things, God would never bless him with big things. He especially prayed for the boy and his friend, and he asked God for help and direction.

The next Sunday, new boys came to the class— he included them and their friends and families in his prayers. By the year's end the class had grown to fifty-six boys. All had accepted Christ, and many of their families also had come into the church.

Work faithfully with the students God has given to you. Pray for them and believe for their best![55]

No discipline seems pleasant at the time, but painful. Later on, however, it produces a harvest of righteousness and peace for those who have been trained by it.

HEBREWS 12:11 NIV

SCHOOL SEEKS TO GET YOU READY FOR EXAMINATION; LIFE GIVES THE FINALS.

When you get what you want in your struggle for self,
  And the world makes you king for a day,
  Just go to a mirror and look at yourself,
  And see what that man has to say.

  For it isn't your father or mother or wife,
  Whose judgment upon you must pass;
  The fellow whose verdict counts most in your life,
  Is the one staring back from the glass.

  Some people may think you're a straight-shooting chum,
  And call you a wonderful guy,
  But the man in the glass says you're only a bum,
  If you can't look him straight in the eye.

  He's the fellow to please, never mind all the rest,
  For he's with you clear up to the end,
  And you've passed your most dangerous, difficult test,
  If the man in the glass is your friend.

  You may fool the whole world down your pathway of years,
  And get pats on the back as you pass,
  But your final reward will be heartache and tears,
  If you've cheated the man in the glass.

ANONYMOUS[56]

Examine yourselves to see whether you
are in the faith; test yourselves.

2 CORINTHIANS 13:5 NIV

Robert D. Ballard is a man accustomed to looking for things other people have "lost." To date he has led or participated in nearly one-hundred deep-sea expeditions. Among the "lost" things he has found are the R.M.S. Titanic, the German battleship Bismarck, and eleven warships that were part of a fleet lost at Guadalcanal.

Did Ballard find these ships on his first try? No. As he once said in a commencement address, "My first voyage to find the Titanic ended in failure. My first expedition to find the Bismarck failed as welL The test you must pass is not whether you fall down or not, but whether you can get back up after being knocked down."

Ballard also noted, "Every major adventure I have been on over the years has tested me severely with violent storms and lost equipment . . . The hardest tests of all . . . look to see how determined you are to live your dream, how strong is your heart."

If you truly believe your teaching career is pleasing to God and a fulfillment of your life's purpose, never allow your journey to end. Always walk toward the next horizon. Consider failure only as an opportunity to regroup and strengthen yourself.[57]

For a just man falleth seven times, and riseth up again.

PROVERBS 24:16

FRIENDSHIP IMPROVES HAPPINESS AND ABATES MISERY BY DOUBLING OUR JOY AND DIVIDING OUR GRIEF.

A man named Paul once received a new car as a gift from his wealthy brother. One evening as Paul was leaving work, he noticed a poor child eyeing his shiny new car. "Is this your car?" the boy asked.

Paul nodded and said, "My brother gave it to me for Christmas."

The boy said, "It didn't cost you nothing? Boy, I wish . . ." Paul expected the boy to wish that he had a generous brother, but what the boy said astonished Paul. He said, "I wish I could be a brother like that."

He asked the boy if he'd like a ride home. The little boy hopped in quickly. Paul smiled, figuring that the boy was eager to show off to his neighbors and family. Again, he was wrong. When the two pulled up in front of the boy's house, the boy asked Paul to wait a minute. He then ran up the steps and soon returned carrying his crippled brother. Paul was moved deeply when he heard him say, "There it is, Buddy, just like I told you upstairs. His brother gave it to him. Someday I'm gonna give you one just like it."

Generosity is a vital aspect of friendship and community—in a school as well as a church. Be a giver. Joy will be the result, not only to those to whom you give, but also in your own heart.[58]

A friend loves at all times, and a brother is born for adversity.

PROVERBS 17:17 NIV

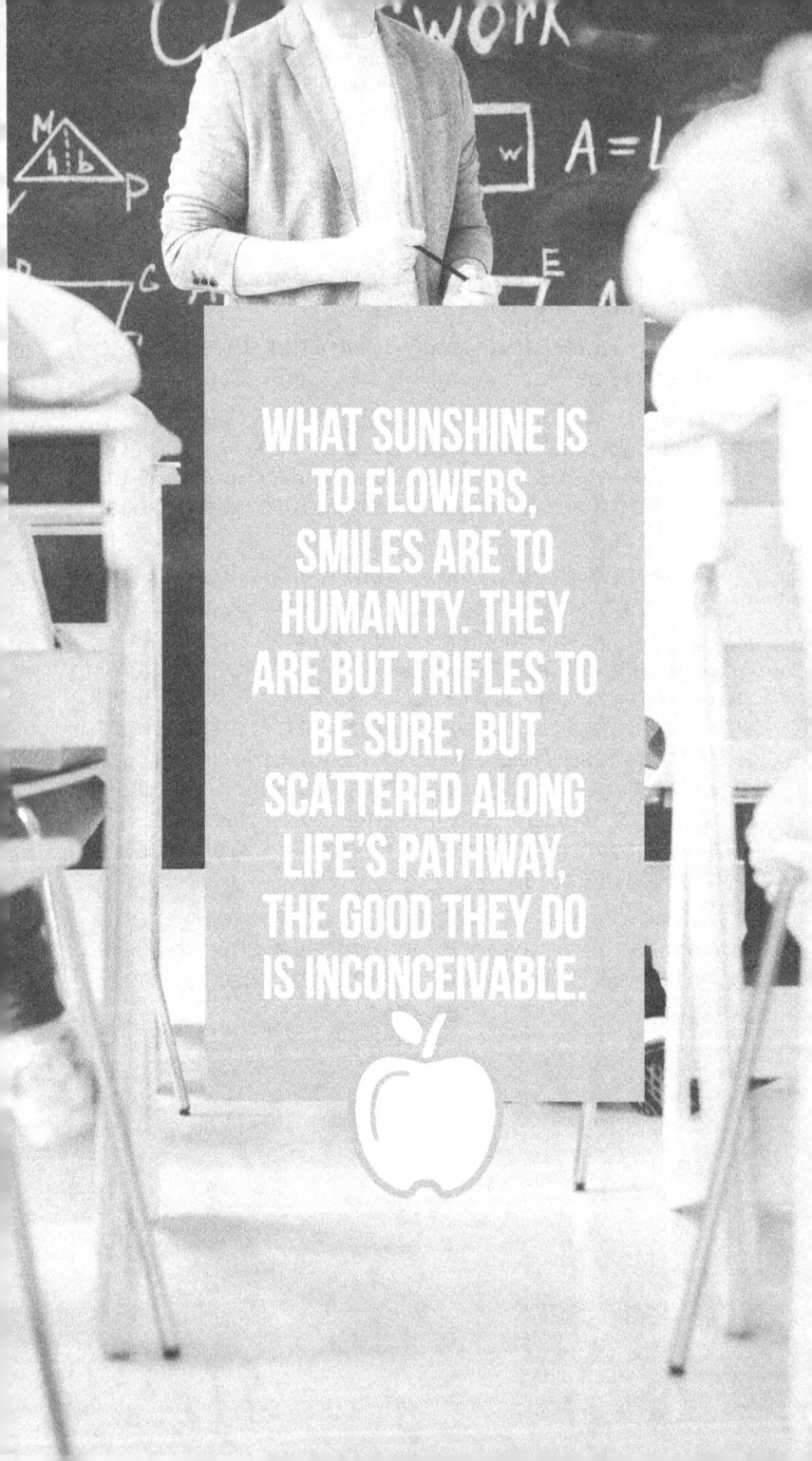

WHAT SUNSHINE IS TO FLOWERS, SMILES ARE TO HUMANITY. THEY ARE BUT TRIFLES TO BE SURE, BUT SCATTERED ALONG LIFE'S PATHWAY, THE GOOD THEY DO IS INCONCEIVABLE.

Barbara Johnson was having a rotten day. She had overslept and was late for work. Everything at the office had been done in a frenzy. By the time she reached the bus stop for her trip home, her stomach was in a knot. As usual, the bus was late and over-filled—she had to stand in the aisle.

A few moments after the bus pulled away, she heard a deep voice from the front of the bus say, "Beautiful day, isn't it?" She couldn't see the man, but she could hear him as he commented on the spring scenery. He called attention to each passing landmark the church, the park the cemetery, the firehouse. All the passengers began gazing out the windows, taking in the sight of spring foliage and late-after noon sunshine. His enthusiasm was so contagious that even Barbara found herself smiling.

When the bus reached her stop, she maneuvered toward the door, glad to finally get a look at the "guide" who had brought a smile to her face. What she saw was a plump man with a black beard, wearing dark glasses, and carrying a thin, white cane.

What we "see" as teachers has more to do with i inner vision than physical eyesight. Choose to see those things that bring happiness to your heart.[59]

A happy heart makes the face cheerful.

PROVERBS 15:13 NIV

During World War II, General MacArthur called in one of his Army engineers and pointed to a map. "How long will it take to throw a bridge across this river?" he asked.

The man immediately responded, "Three days."

MacArthur snapped back, "Good. Have your draftsmen make drawings right away."

Three days later, MacArthur sent for the engineer and asked how the bridge was coming along. The engineer reported, "The bridge is ready! You can send your troops across it right now—if you don't have to wait for the plans. They aren't done yet."

There are many times when effort is far more valuable than planning. When confronting injustice, time is critical. As teachers, we are not only stewards of financial resources and supplies, but we are also accountable for our time. When we only dream about what we will accomplish one day but never act on our dreams, we rob ourselves and the lives of others.

Ask God, and He will help you to invest your time wisely.[60]

Redeeming the time, because the days are evil.

EPHESIANS 5:16 NKJV

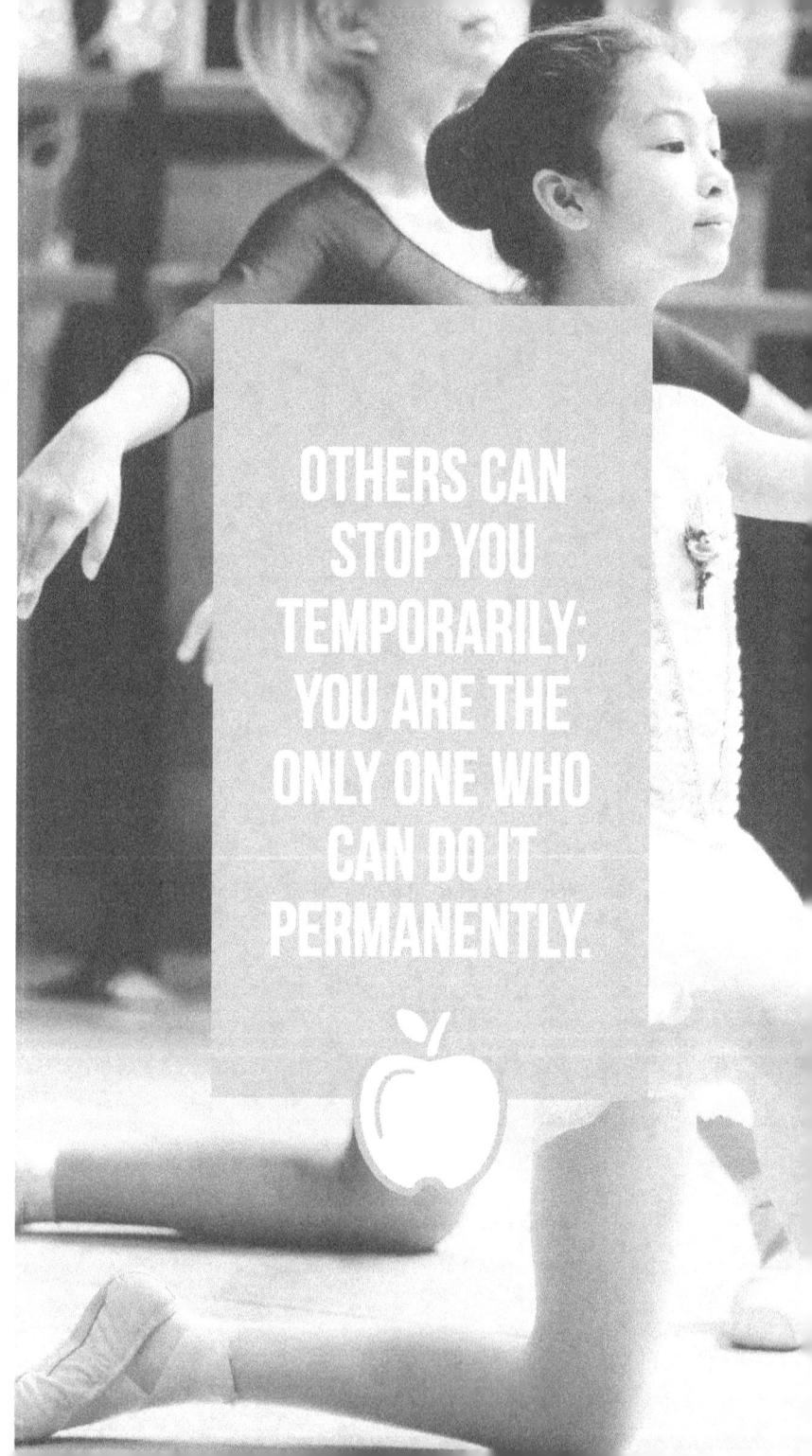

OTHERS CAN STOP YOU TEMPORARILY; YOU ARE THE ONLY ONE WHO CAN DO IT PERMANENTLY.

I n the novel, *Gone with the Wind*, the prospective brother-in-law of Scarlett O'Hara gives this eulogy about her father:

"There warn't nothin' that come to him from the outside that could lick him. He warn't scared of the English government when they wanted to hang him. He just lit out and left home. And when he come to this country and was pore, that didn't scare him a mite neither. He went to work, and he made his money. And he warn't scared to tackle this section when it was part wild and the Injuns had just been run out of it . . . And when the war come on and his money begun to go, he warn't scared to be pore again. And when the Yankees came through Tara and might of burnt him out or killed him, he warn't fazed a bit and he warn't licked neither."

And then facing the reality that O'Hara had died as a consequence of riding his horse while drunk, the eulogy ended, "But he had . . . failin's, too, 'cause he could be licked from the inside. I mean to say that what the whole world couldn't do, his own heart could . . . That weakness that's in our hearts can lick us in the time it takes to bat your eye."

Only God can transform inner weakness into strength. Ask Him to make you a better teacher today.[61]

> Do you not know that in a race all the runners run, but only one gets the prize? Run in such a way as to get the prize.
>
> 1 CORINTHIANS 9:24 NIV

YOU CAN BUILD
A THRONE WITH
BAYONETS, BUT
YOU CAN'T SIT
ON IT FOR LONG.

Mahatma Gandhi is a man who had a clearly defined value system, one rooted in peace.

Gandhi founded his campaign of nonviolent civil disobedience on the term *satyagraha*, which means "a force born of truth and love." Even when his followers were fired upon by the British, Gandhi condemned any form of violence in retaliation. He was arrested and imprisoned repeatedly, but always released. He gained control of his nation without firing a shot.

Gandhi accomplished his goals not only by means of moral pressure, but through a thorough knowledge of British law and culture. In essence, Gandhi said to the English, "I believe in your legal system, and I believe it is rooted in values that are higher than your methods."

For many teachers, the classroom is a battle-ground. But rather than fight fire with fire, perhaps there is a way that is "higher"—the pursuit of even greater goals by peaceful means. Perhaps it is time to say to angry students, "I believe in your potential. Let's pursue what you can be. Let's work together to overcome what is and create what will be!"

Too idealistic? No student of India's history thinks so.[62]

So are the ways of everyone who gains by violence; it takes away the life of its possessors.

PROVERBS 1:19 NASB

GOD NEVER
ASKS ABOUT
OUR ABILITY
OR OUR
INABILITY—
JUST OUR
AVAILABILITY.

Jockeys who consistently ride into the winner's circle are in complete control of their horses during a race. The winning horse is referred to as the "meekest on the track." Why? Because a winning horse responds quickly to the jockey's commands and is totally submitted to its rider. Self-willed and factious horses frequently are left at the gate. And even though they may run faster than the others, they make mistakes and rarely finish with the leaders.

This understanding of meekness on the horse track is related to an ancient definition of meekness: "yielding the will to the bit and the bridle."

If we willingly yield our lives to God—to the "bit and the bridle" of His will—then we are in the best position to win life's race. Jesus said, "Blessed are the meek: for they shall inherit the earth" (Matthew 5:5). Teachers who make themselves *available* to God are those who are used by God.[63]

Then I heard the voice of the Lord, saying, "Whom shall I send? And who will go for us?" And I said, "Here am I. Send me!"

ISAIAH 6:8 NIV

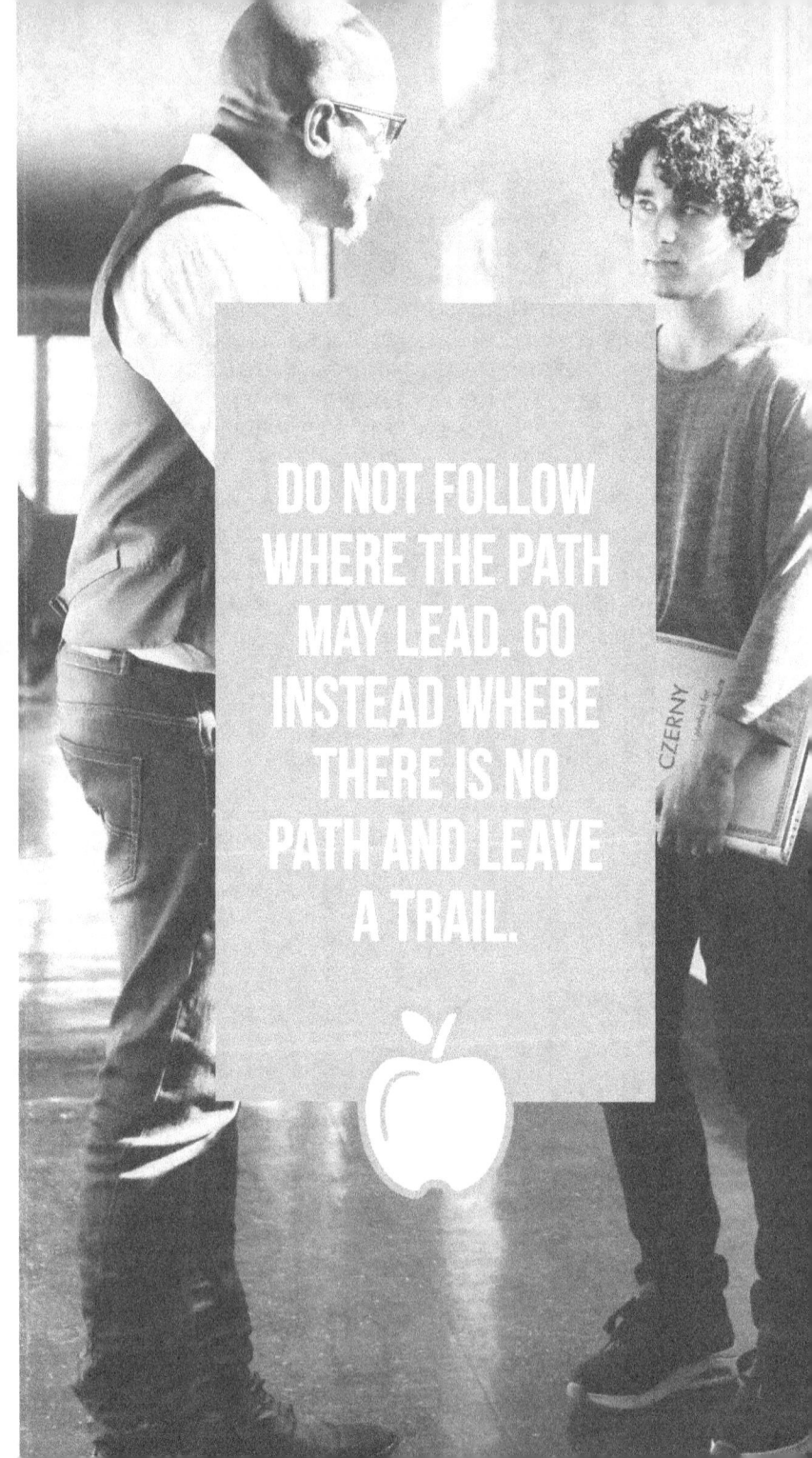

DO NOT FOLLOW WHERE THE PATH MAY LEAD. GO INSTEAD WHERE THERE IS NO PATH AND LEAVE A TRAIL.

During the summers of his childhood, Cleve Francis walked with his mother to her work as a maid at the "big house" in town. The seven-mile round trip was a long, hot journey, but Cleve enjoyed those times because it gave him a chance to talk with his mother.

One day when he was twelve, he asked her, "Mama, why am I black?"

His mother responded without hesitation, "God is a good God. He made the heavens and the earth. He made the great mountains, rivers, and oceans. He made all living creatures, and He made you. He gave you a beautiful black color. God makes no mistakes, Cleve. You were put here on this earth for a purpose, and you must find it."

Joy filled the young boy's heart at the knowledge that he was just who God wanted! He was proud to be one of God's chosen creatures, and he eagerly sought out God's plan for his life. Cleve found his purpose as a physician and an entertainer, and he won respect in both fields. Helping a child appreciate his unique gifts and talents and then helping a child discover his purpose in using those talents is the challenge of every teacher. Today, ask God to help you trail blaze His path in the lives of those you serve.[64]

Your ears shall hear a word behind you, saying, "This is the way, walk in it."

ISAIAH 30:21 NKJV

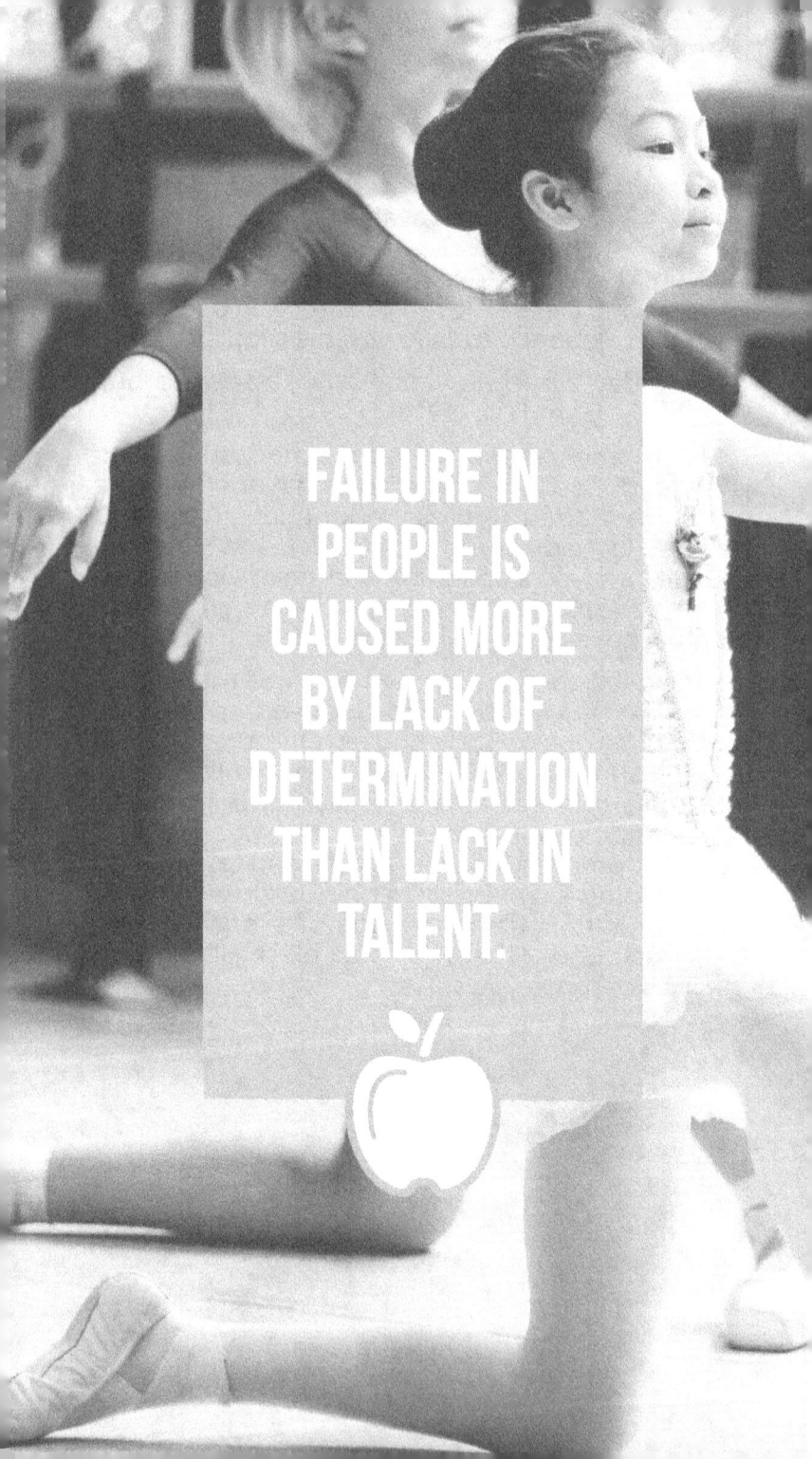

FAILURE IN PEOPLE IS CAUSED MORE BY LACK OF DETERMINATION THAN LACK IN TALENT.

The literary world did not offer immediate stardom to Agatha Christie, one of the foremost mystery writers of all time. Her first novel, in which she introduced master sleuth Hercule Poirot, was a failure. So were her next four books. It was only with her sixth book that she gained widespread recognition.

What many people don't know about Agatha Christie is that she was determined to be more than a mystery writer. In addition to her detective novels, she wrote numerous short stories, plus six novels, under the pseudonym Mary Westmacott. Her play, "The Mousetrap" debuted in London in 1952 and set a record for its continuous run of more than three decades. She set herself the personal goal of "producing a book every year, and possibly a few short stories." She more than met her goals. Friends and publishers remember her as a woman who approached her work in a "straightforward fashion, with no illusions." In good times and bad and regardless of personal tragedies, she kept writing—sixty-six mysteries in all.

A person rarely is born a genius. Genius usually is cultivated by students who refuse to take their hands off the plow of their own talent and by teachers who inspire them to plow their own unique field.[65]

And let us not be weary in well doing: for in due season we shall reap, if we faint not.

GALATIANS 6:9

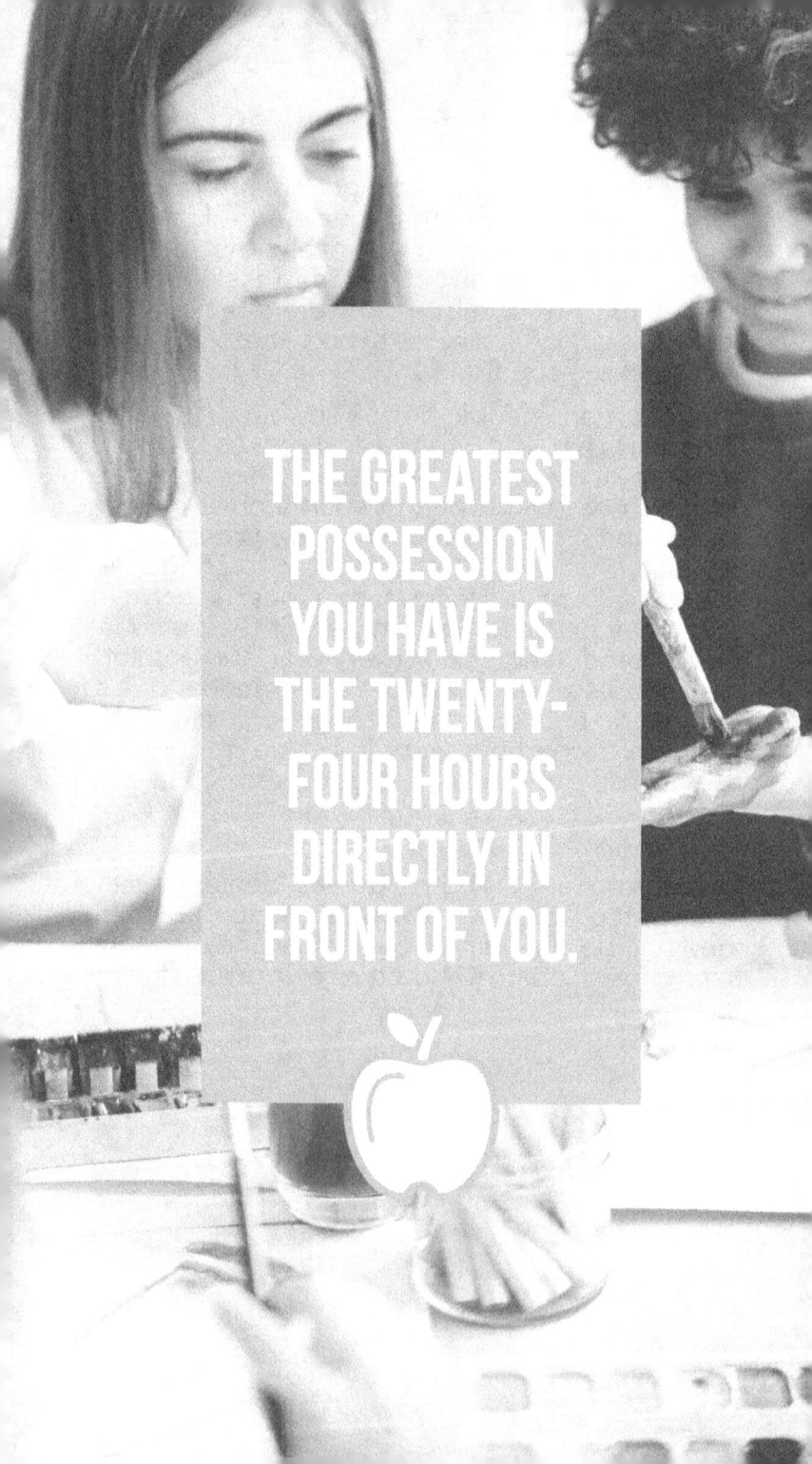

THE GREATEST POSSESSION YOU HAVE IS THE TWENTY-FOUR HOURS DIRECTLY IN FRONT OF YOU.

A time-management expert set a one-gallon mason jar on a table in front of the class he was teaching. He carefully placed a dozen fist-sized rocks into the jar. "Is the jar full?" he asked.

The class responded with one voice, "Yes."

Then he said, "Really?" He reached under the table and pulled out a bucket of gravel. He dumped some of it into the jar, and the pieces worked their way into the spaces between the large rocks. "Is the jar full?" he asked.

Some responded, "Probably not."

The teacher then brought out a bucket of sand. He dumped sand into the jar, allowing it to settle in the spaces between rocks and gravel. "Now is the jar full?"

The class responded, "No!"

"Good!" said the teacher as he poured water into the jar, filling it to the brim. "Now" he said, "what is the point of this illustration?"

One student quickly responded, "No matter how full your schedule, you can always fit in something else."

"No," the teacher replied. "The truth of the illustration is this: If you don't put the big rocks in first, j you'll never get them in at all."

When you make God your most important priority, everything else falls into place.[66]

For there is a time for every purpose and for every work.

ECCLESIASTES 3:17

HE THAT HAS LEARNED TO OBEY WILL KNOW HOW TO COMMAND.

General George S. Patton Jr. had an unusual method for filling leadership positions. He would line up the candidates and say, "Men, I want a trench dug behind warehouse ten. Make this trench eight feet long, three feet wide, and six inches deep."

"While the candidates are checking their tools out at the warehouse," General Patton explained, "I watch them from a distance. They puzzle over why I want such a shallow trench. They argue over whether six inches is deep enough for a gun emplacement. Some complain that such a trench should be dug with power equipment. Others gripe that it is too hot or too cold to dig. If the men are above the rank of lieutenant, there will be complaints that they should not be doing such lowly labor. Finally, one man will order, 'What difference does it make what [he] wants to do with this trench! Let's get it dug and get out of here.' That man will get the promotion.'"

General Patton chose leaders who could get the job done. And God needs the leadership skills of classroom teachers to raise up the leaders of tomorrow Little is accomplished by procrastination or complaining in the teachers' lounge. Purpose that your efforts will make a lasting contribution to the world of tomorrow.[67]

The wise in heart accept commands, but a chattering fool comes to ruin.

PROVERBS 10:8 NIV

THE FUTURE
BELONGS TO
THOSE WHO
BELIEVE IN
THE BEAUTY
OF THEIR
DREAMS.

A little boy named Johnny used to hang out at the local corner market. The other boys teased him constantly, saying that Johnny was two bricks shy of a load or two pickles short of a barrel. Puzzled about their behavior, the store owner eavesdropped on their conversation one day.

Johnny stood silently as the boys offered him a choice between a nickel or a dime. Johnny took the nickel. The boys immediately laughed, saying he was too dumb to know that the bigger coin was worth less.

The store owner took him aside and said, "Johnny, those boys are making fun of you. They think you don't know a dime is worth more than a nickel. Are you really grabbing the nickel because it's bigger?"

Johnny turned to the store owner and with a big grin on his face, he said, "Well, if I took the dime, they'd stop playing the game. And so far, I've saved twenty dollars!" The other boys in the neighborhood may not have had any faith in Johnny, but Johnny certainly had faith in his own abilities!

Even if no one else in your school trusts God as you do, don't stop trusting Him. In the end, your wisdom will prevail.[68]

Anything is possible if you have faith.

MARK 9:23 TLB

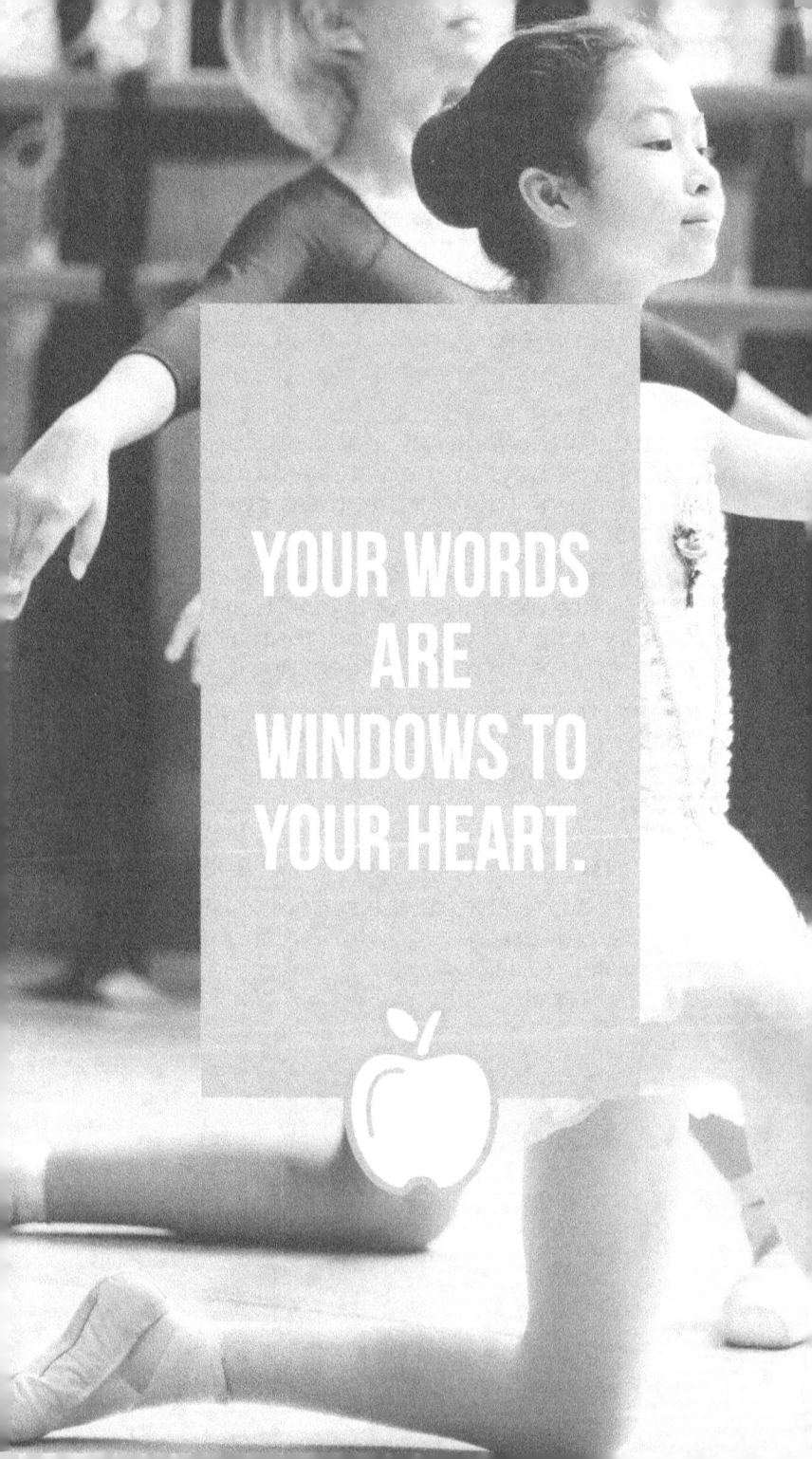

YOUR WORDS
ARE
WINDOWS TO
YOUR HEART.

E arly one morning in the locker room, Ruth overheard a cheerful voice say, "I really appreciate the book you picked up for me last week. I'm glad you suggested it." Then the voice went on to greet another person, "Good morning! Have you ever seen such a gorgeous day? I spied a pair of meadowlarks this morning."

Ruth imagined that only a wealthy woman with little to do but read and watch birds could be that cheerful. As she rounded the corner, she came face to face with a woman in a yellow housekeeping uniform— the cleaning lady—who put in long hard days with mops, brooms, and buckets. Yet she radiated sunshine!

After her laps in the pool, Ruth sank down into the warm, foamy whirlpool. Her two companions were deep in conversation—one intent on describing his woes with arthritic knees, a heart problem, sleepless nights, and pain-filled days. The water was too hot for him, he complained, and the whirlpool jets weren't strong enough. His heavy diamond ring flashed in the light as he wiped his face with a monogrammed towel. Ruth made a comparison to the cleaning woman and wondered what had made this man such a complainer when he had so much for which to be thankful.

Today, remember your blessings and light up your classroom with a smile![69]

For out of the abundance of the heart the mouth speaketh.

MATTHEW 12:34

THE HEART IS HAPPIEST WHEN IT BEATS FOR OTHERS.

D r. Richard Blaylock had a first-class reputation as a competent manager and skilled clinician. When his hospital merged with another facility, however, the new administrator promptly stripped Rick of all administrative duties.

Rick felt betrayed, his ideas ignored, and his talents underutilized. He remained in the system five more years, but the bounce had left his step, and his usual optimism was replaced by anger and hurt When he retired after twenty-two years of faithful service, he was not given as much as a thank you for his many contributions.

Rick has said, "I felt sorry for myself for about a month." Then he decided to let go of his bitterness. He heard about a rural hospital in need of a volunteer physician, and soon he was on staff—not only as a physician but also as an administrator. Two years later, the bounce in his step was back, hospital revenues were up, good nurses had joined the staff, and the hospital was on the road to recovery.

If you feel your talents as a teacher are unappreciated and underutilized, find a place to plant them. Those who aren't sowing, aren't growing.[70]

Greater love has no one than this, that he lay down his life for his friends.

JOHN 13:13 NIV

REAL FRIENDS
ARE THOSE WHO,
WHEN YOU'VE
MADE A FOOL OF
YOURSELF, DON'T
FEEL YOU'VE DONE
A PERMANENT
JOB.

After supper two little brothers were playing until bedtime. Bobby accidentally hit Joe with a stick, and Joe began to wail. Accusations were exchanged until their exasperated mother finally sent both boys to bed.

As she tucked them in, she said, "Now, Joe, before you go to sleep, you need to forgive your brother for the mistake he made."

Joe thought for a few moments and then replied, "Well, okay. I'll forgive him tonight, but if I don't die before I wake up, he'd better look out in the morning."

Holding a grudge or blowing a mistake out of proportion drives a wedge between two people, and if allowed to remain, that wedge can destroy a relationship. Be quick to recognize that some mistakes are not worth mentioning and some errors are not matters of eternal importance.

Those who are quick to forgive others tend to be those who are forgiven quickly. And we all must admit it's nice to be on the forgiven side of a mistake, whether we're a teacher or a student.[71]

Love does not delight in evil but rejoices with the truth. It always protects, always trusts, always hopes, always perseveres. Love never fails.

1 CORINTHIANS 13:6-8

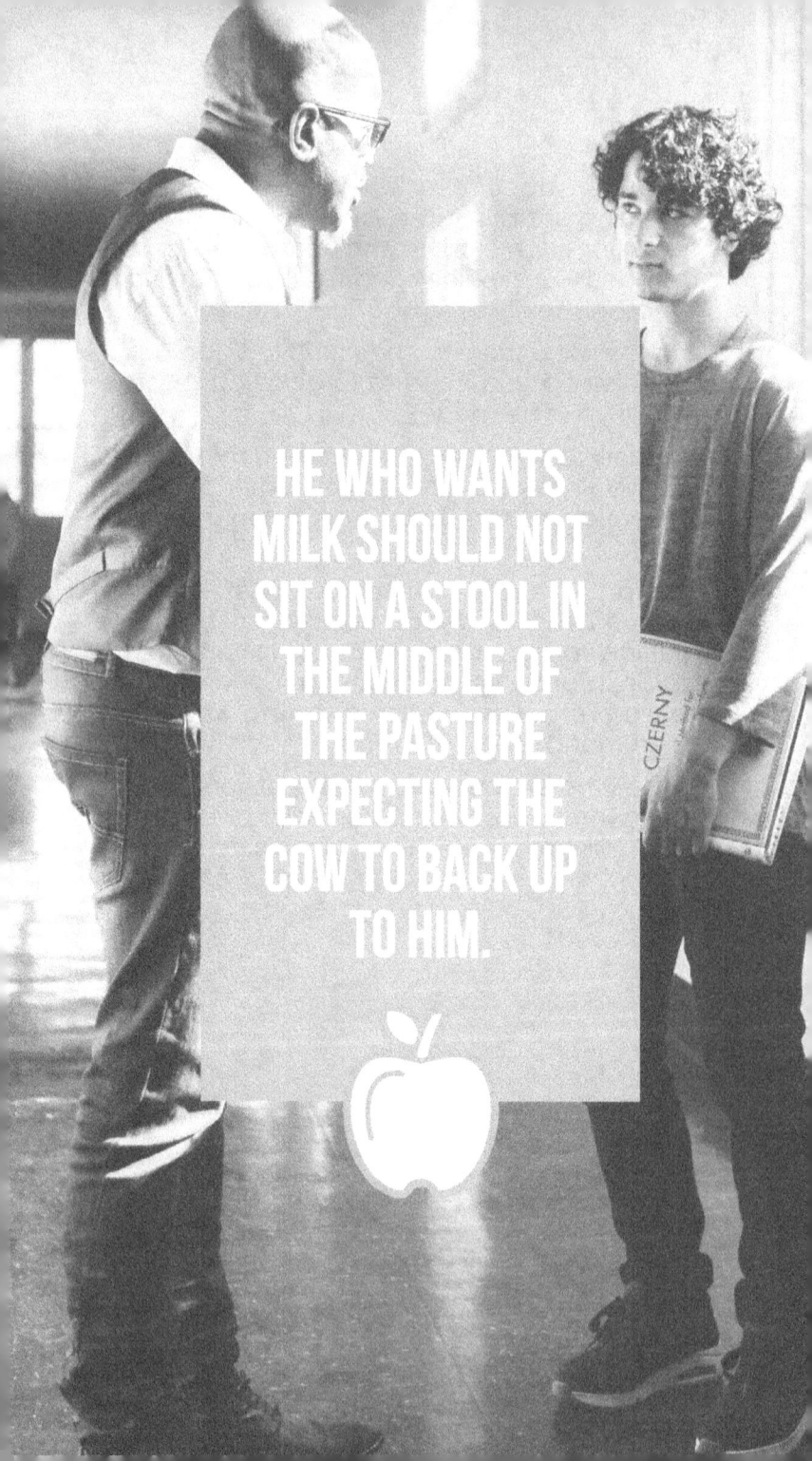

HE WHO WANTS MILK SHOULD NOT SIT ON A STOOL IN THE MIDDLE OF THE PASTURE EXPECTING THE COW TO BACK UP TO HIM.

Comedian Jay Leno may be regarded as a man who makes his living in "fun and games," but he is known by his friends for his work ethic, something he learned from his parents. He employed that work ethic in his first job at Wilmington Ford near his hometown of Andover, Massachusetts, the summer he was sixteen. There, he put in twelve-hour days as a *prepper*—the person who washed and polished new cars. Each night, the preppers removed all the hubcaps so they wouldn't be stolen, and put them back on each morning. This was no small chore since the dealership had seven acres of cars!

Later while in college, Leno wanted a job at a Rolls- Royce dealership, but the owner had no openings. He started washing cars there anyway. When the owner noticed him and asked what he was doing, Leno replied that he was working until he got hired. He was hired on the spot. Says Leno, "It takes persistence to succeed. Attitude also matters. I have never thought I was better than anyone else, but I have always believed I couldn't be outworked."

It is true for student and teacher alike: before we can produce our best work, we first must learn to work.[72]

Lazy hands makes a man poor, but diligent hands bring wealth.

PROVERBS 10:4 NIV

THE TRAIN OF
FAILURE
USUALLY
RUNS ON THE
TRACK OF
LAZINESS.

n the campaign of 1948, nobody in either political party—not a professional politician, not a reporter, not even his own mother-in-law—doubted that Tom Dewey would be the next president of the United States. A *Newsweek* poll of political commentators predicted the final vote Dewey, 50, Truman, 0.

No president in office had ever campaigned so hard or traveled as many miles as Truman, who was sixty-four years old. Younger men on the train with candidate Truman described it as the worst ordeal of their lives. The roadbed was rough, and Truman insisted the train fly at eighty miles an hour at night to reach as many destinations as possible. The food was bad, and the work was unrelenting. The only reason any of the staff stuck by Truman was . . . Truman. There was something about his heroic, memorable act of faith in the American public that compelled them to stick with him. As he crisscrossed the nation, Truman reminded his fellow countrymen, "Here I am, here's what I stand for. Here's what I'm going to do if you keep me in the job. You decide." Despite the odds against him, Truman won the election.

No success in life, including academic and career success, is ever maintained without an effort equal to that required to attain it.[73]

If a man is lazy, the rafters sag; if his hands are idle, the house leaks.

ECCLESIASTES 10:18 NIV

OUR CHILDREN
ARE LIKE
MIRRORS—
THEY REFLECT
OUR
ATTITUDES
IN LIFE.

I f you ever question whether children are listening and learning from our lives, consider these examples:

• A mother and her five-year-old son were driving down the street, when the little boy asked, "Mommy, why do the idiots only come out when Daddy drives?"

• After the church service, a little boy said to the pastor, "When I grow up, I'm going to give you money." "Thank you," the pastor replied, "but why?" "Because," the little boy explained, "my daddy says you're one of the poorest preachers we've ever had."

• A wife invited several family friends to dinner. At the table, she turned to their six-year-old daughter and said, "Would you like to say the blessing?" The girl answered, "I don't know what to say." The mother insisted, "Just say what you hear Mommy say." The daughter bowed her head and said, "Lord, why on earth did I invite all these people to dinner?"

Parents and teachers never know when little eyes are watching our actions and little ears are hearing what we say. If you want to avoid embarrassment, don't let your kids hear what you don't want repeated.[74]

The just man walketh in his integrity: his children are blessed after him.

PROVERBS 20:7

A LOT OF PEOPLE MISTAKE A SHORT MEMORY FOR A CLEAR CONSCIENCE.

In 1994 while competing in the Western Open, professional golfer Davis Love III moved his marker on a green to get it out of another player's putting line. A couple of holes later, he couldn't remember if he had moved his ball back to its original spot. Unsure, Love gave himself a one-stroke penalty.

That one stroke caused Love to miss the cut and be knocked out of the tournament. If he had made the cut and then finished last in the competition, he would have earned $2,000 that week. That amount came into play at the year's end. Love was $500 short in the annual winnings necessary to qualify for the following year's Master's Tournament. Love began 1994 needing to win a tournament to get into the event.

Someone asked Love how he would feel if he missed the Masters for calling a penalty on himself. Love said, "How would I feel if I won the Masters and wondered for the rest of my life if I cheated to get in?" As it turned out, the week before the 1995 Masters, Love won a tournament in New Orleans. Then in the Masters, he won $237,600 for finishing second.

Most teachers know the right thing to do. Be among the ones who actually have the courage to do it.[75]

Ill-gotten treasures have no lasting value, but righteousness delivers from death.

PROVERBS 10:2 NIV

THE PAST
SHOULD BE A
SPRINGBOARD,
NOT A
HAMMOCK.

As founders of Tom's of Maine, Tom Chappell and his wife, Kate, were a successful couple who had a vibrant and growing business. But in 1988, they decided to launch a new product, even though marketing research indicated no one would buy it. The Chappells, however, had learned to trust their instincts, and they also were willing to take a risk.

They knew if parents were buying natural toothpastes for themselves, they would want a similar product for their children. They pointed to an earlier successful venture. All of the so-called experts had predicted a natural fluoride toothpaste would never sell, but it had turned out to be more popular than the non-fluoride product.

The children's toothpaste was a big hit. Since its successful launch, this product has been cited at a number of business schools as a prime example of entrepreneurs not being content with the status quo or resting on their laurels. If a company isn't growing, it's stagnating.

What are you learning as a teacher? If you stop learning, you will stop growing, and eventually you will be less effective as a teacher. Keep learning—God always has more to teach![76]

Forgetting the past and looking forward to what lies ahead, I strain to reach the end of the race and receive the prize.

PHILIPPIANS 3:13-14 TLB

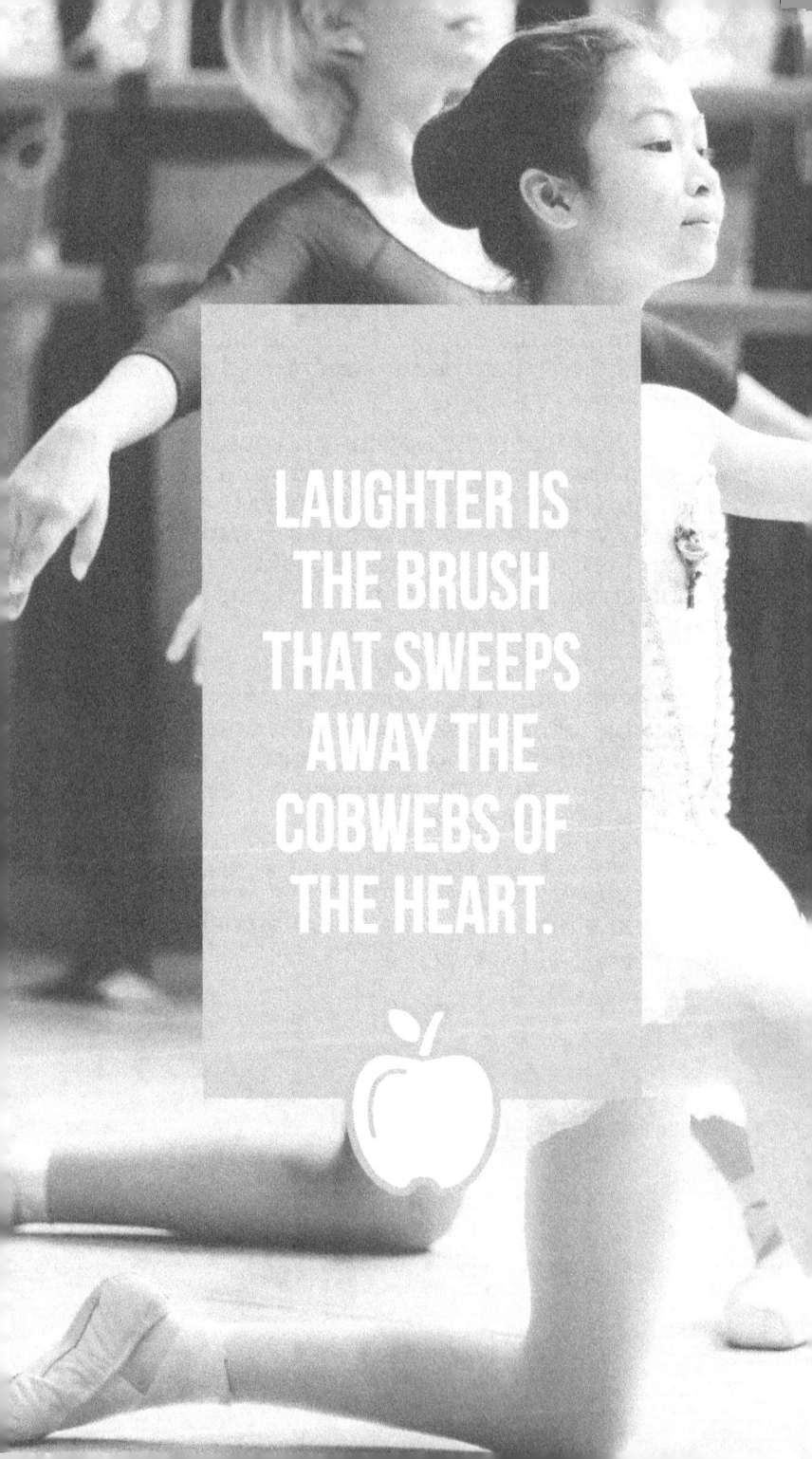

LAUGHTER IS
THE BRUSH
THAT SWEEPS
AWAY THE
COBWEBS OF
THE HEART.

George Mueller would not preach until his heart was "happy in the grace of God."

Jan Ruybroeck would not write while his feelings were low, he would retire to a quiet place and wait on God until he felt joy in his heart.

It was the happy laughter and joy of a group of Moravian Christians that convinced John Wesley of the reality of their faith and helped bring him to a point of genuine spiritual conversion.

Joy is both the responsibility and the privilege of every Christian. As Henry Evansen wrote:

"It costs nothing, but creates much.

It enriches those who receive it without impoverishing those who give it.

It happens in a flash, and the memory of it sometimes lasts forever.

None are so rich that they can get along without it, and none so poor but are richer for its benefits."

It fosters good will in a business, creates happiness in a home, and is the countersign of friends. It is rest to the weary, daylight to the discouraged, sunshine to the sad, and nature's best antidote for trouble What is it? A smile!

Teach with a smile and a happy heart today![77]

A happy heart is a good medicine and a cheerful mind works healing, but a broken spirit dries up the bones.

PROVERBS 17:22

SWALLOWING ANGRY WORDS BEFORE YOU SAY THEM IS BETTER THAN HAVING TO EAT THEM AFTERWARDS.

Jealous of the mayor's election victory, the wife of his opponent spread malicious lies about the mayor throughout the town. The rumors and gossip brought the life of the mayor under scrutiny, and although he had done nothing of which to be ashamed, he resigned, feeling it was impossible to continue in office without the respect of those he served.

Later, overcome with remorse, the woman went to the ex-mayor to beg his forgiveness. "Please tell me, how can I make amends?" she said. "I'll do anything you say."

The man replied, "Open a goose-down pillow and allow the feathers to spill to the ground."

She nodded, "And then what?"

He said, "Wait ten minutes and then pick up all the feathers."

The woman returned the next day with only a small portion of the feathers in the ripped-open pillow case. "How did you do?" he asked.

She answered, "The feathers blew everywhere, and I was unable to retrieve them all."

He said soberly, "Rumors and gossip are equally impossible to retrieve."

What you say about a student or a colleague has far-reaching, ripple effects. Make certain that what you say is not only true, but that it needs saying.[78]

From the fruit of his mouth a man's stomach is filled; with the harvest from his lips he is satisfied. The tongue has the power of life and death, and those who love it will east its fruit.

PROVERBS 18:20-21 NIV

n 1992, Hurricane Andrew completely destroyed the home of one Florida couple. Devastated at the loss of all their personal belongings, the couple retreated to their vacation home on the island of Kauai to recuperate and wait out the rebuilding of their Florida home. Shortly after their arrival, a hurricane struck the Hawaiian Islands, demolishing their vacation home!

The couple acknowledged their frustration and grief in the wake of this second tragedy, but it also forced them to take a hard look at their lives. They had survived two disasters! They still had their health and human abilities. They still had faith in God and their love for one another. These were their greatest assets! They also faced the fact that no matter where they might rebuild, their home would be vulnerable to some type of natural disaster. The point was to rebuild—not to remain in ruins—and to do it with optimism, and not fear.

Hard times, crises, and troubles come to all of us— even teachers. It's not the nature of the crisis but how we choose to respond to it that matters most. Those who live in faith and contentment will have the faith and inner peace required to weather any storm.[79]

For I have learned to be content whatever the circumstances.

PHILIPPIANS 4:11 NIV

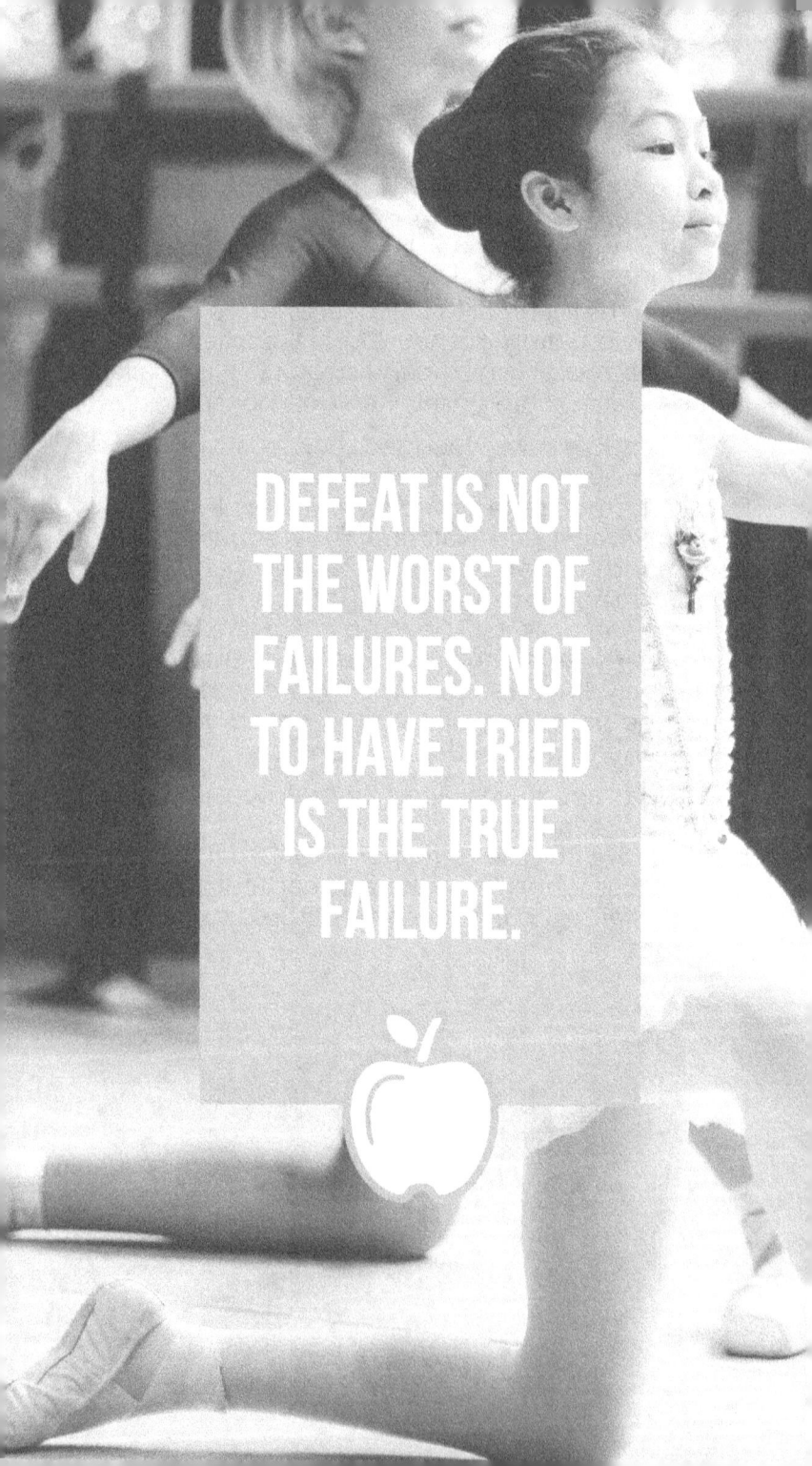

DEFEAT IS NOT
THE WORST OF
FAILURES. NOT
TO HAVE TRIED
IS THE TRUE
FAILURE.

Kicked out of her house as a teenager, Kim ended up living with friends who were negative about life. She was intelligent, but also angry and antagonistic. Her teachers discovered that although she had a hard time dealing with people, she had relevant suggestions to make and could often see problems others couldn't see. One of Kim's teachers said to her privately, "You have a great ability to see a problem and offer a workable solution."

Kim shrugged and said, "You're just saying that—you don't really believe it."

The teacher replied, "No, Kim, you don't really believe it. One day you will have to decide what you're going to believe about yourself. It's up to you."

About four months after Kim graduated from the program, she called to tell this teacher that she had a job at the phone company. She said, "The person who interviewed me asked why they should hire me. I couldn't think of anything so I said my teacher said I was good at solving problems. They hired me as a trouble-shooter. Now I believe you."

Two of the most valuable things a teacher can ever tell a student are those: here's what I believe you can do, and here's what you are doing that's right.[80]

Be strong and of a good courage; be not afraid, neither be thou dismayed: for the Lord thy God is with thee whithersoever thou goest.

JOSHUA 1:9

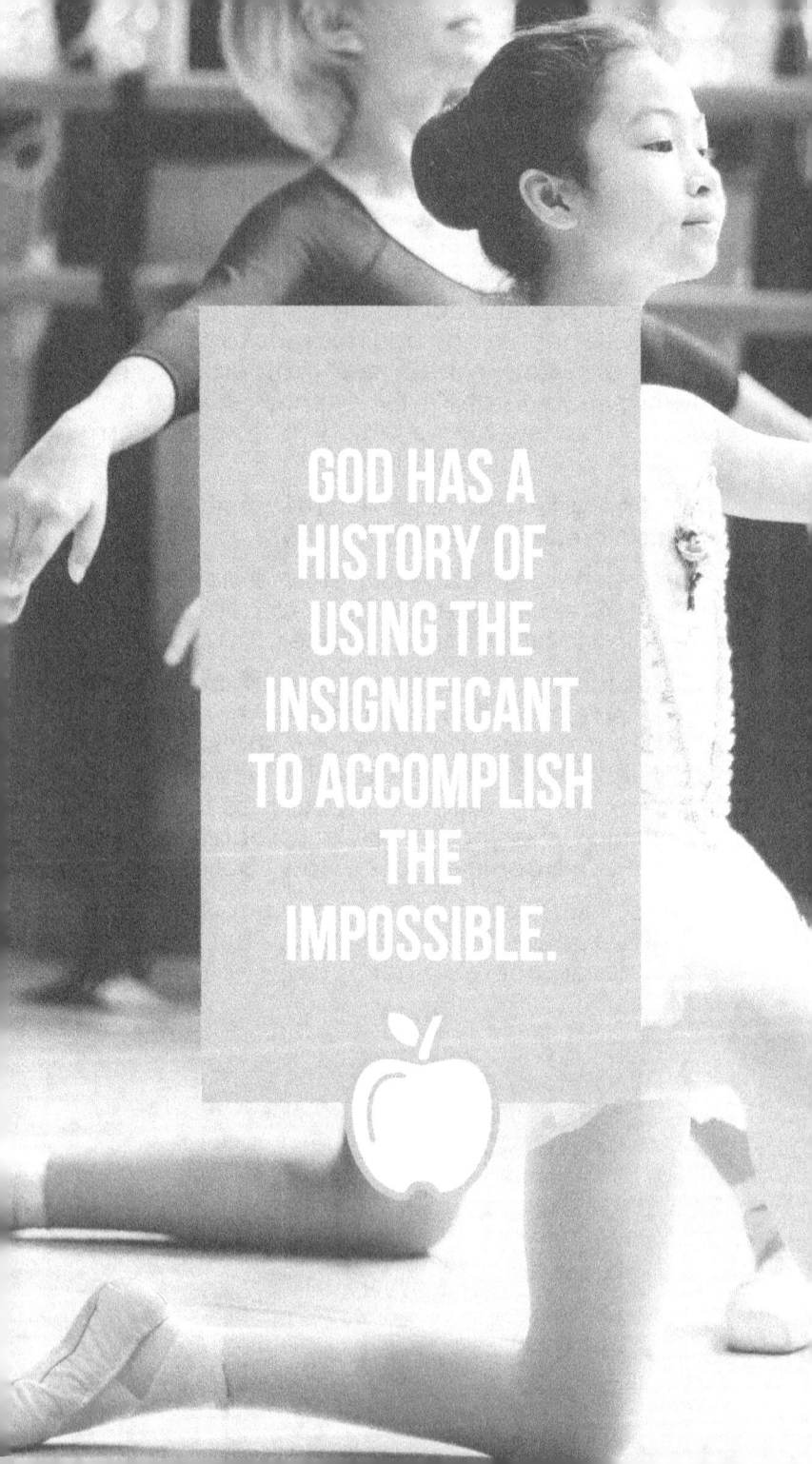

GOD HAS A HISTORY OF USING THE INSIGNIFICANT TO ACCOMPLISH THE IMPOSSIBLE.

The household was abuzz—the greatest religious leader in the nation was coming to supper! The finest meal was prepared, and the best dishes brought out. When he arrived, the leader said to the father, "God has sent me to meet with one of your sons about a leadership position."

The father asked, "Which son?"

The religious leader replied, "I don't know. God said I would know him when I see him."

At that, the father invited his eldest son to meet the leader. He was a tall, handsome young man, and the leader thought, Surely this is the one. But God spoke in his heart, "Don't look on appearances. He's not the one." The father called his next son . . . and the next. After the leader had met seven young men —none of them God's choice—he asked, "Have I met all of your sons?" The father admitted that one son was missing—the youngest, who was far from the strongest and possessed no known political or military skills. "Call him," the religious leader said.

When the young man came in, the Lord said, "This is the one!" And the religious leader—the great prophet, Samuel—anointed young David, the shepherd boy, to be the next king of Israel.

Never discount the potential of a child you teach. God has a purpose for each and every one.[81]

And Jesus looking upon them saith, "With men it is impossible, but not with God: for with God all things are possible."

MARK 10:27

On a cold December day in New York City a little barefoot boy about ten years old stood before a shoe store on Broadway. He peered longingly through the window, shivering with cold. A woman approached him and said, "Little fellow, why are you looking so earnestly in that window?"

The boy replied, "I was asking God to give me a pair of shoes."

The woman took him by the hand and entered the store, asking the clerk to get a half dozen pairs of socks for the boy. She then asked the clerk for a basin of water and towel. He quickly complied. She took the little boy to the back of the store, and removing her gloves she knelt down, washed his feet, and dried them. The clerk brought the socks to her, and she placed a pair on the child. After the boy tried on several pairs of shoes, she purchased a sturdy and handsome pair for him. The kind woman tied up the remaining pairs of socks and gave them to him. "I feel sure you feel more comfortable now," she said smiling.

The boy took her hand, looked up into her face, and with tears in his eyes asked, "Are you God's wife?"

God blesses us through the actions of His people . . . including your students. Be grateful today, both to Him and to them.[82]

I will remember the deeds of the Lord; yes,
I will remember your miracles of long ago.
I will meditate on all your works and
consider all your mighty deeds.

PSALM 77:11-12 NIV

As a child of English settlers in Africa, Peter often went on rounds with his mother, a doctor, to vaccinate children in rural areas. Even though she was authorized to vaccinate only Rhodesians, she was generous in vaccinating the Ndau people from Mozambique who were nomads in the region.

As an adult, Peter returned to the area as a reporter. He was kidnapped, labeled a spy, and taken to the rebel base camp. The longer he listened to the rebel leader speak, the more he understood. The leader was speaking Ndau! He recalled some of what he had learned as a child and spoke back in the language. The leader was shocked. "Where did you learn this?" he demanded. When Peter told him, he asked "What is your family name?"

Peter said, "Godwin."

The leader asked again, "Was your mother the doctor?"

Peter replied, "Yes."

The leader smiled broadly. "She vaccinated me when I was a child. Look now! I grew up strong!"

Peter immediately went from hostage status to honored guest. He considers a photo of his final day with the rebels to be a testament to the permanence of good deeds. Truly, the good we do as teachers always has an eternal seed in it![83]

In the same way, let your light shine before others, that they may see your good deeds and glorify your Father in heaven.

MATTHEW 5:16 NIV

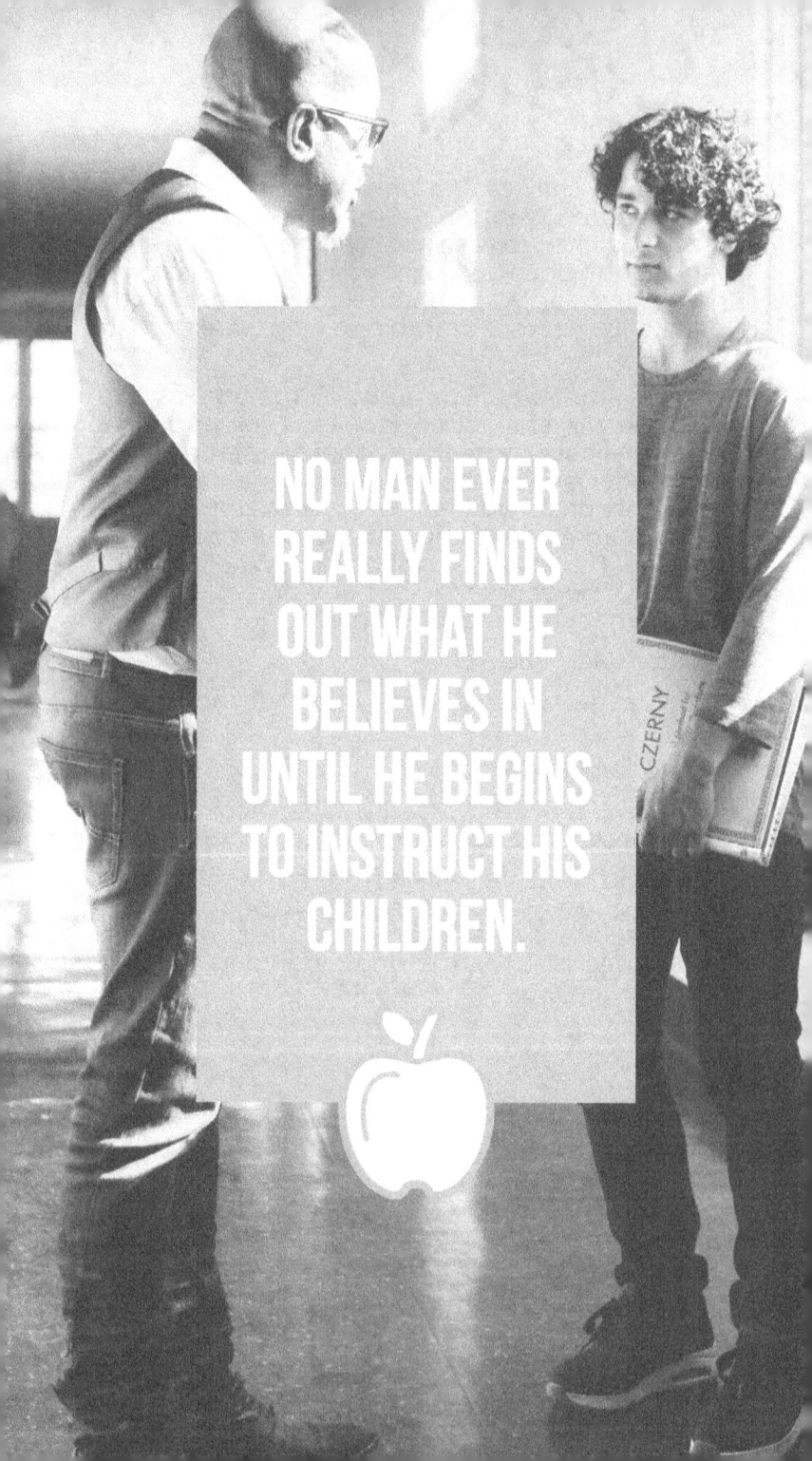

NO MAN EVER REALLY FINDS OUT WHAT HE BELIEVES IN UNTIL HE BEGINS TO INSTRUCT HIS CHILDREN.

A five-year-old boy was looking forward to visiting a planetarium while the family was on vacation. When the family arrived at the site, however, they learned that children under age six were not admitted. The mother said "Let's pretend you had a birthday. If the ticket man asks how old you are, I want you to say, 'I'm six.'"

The mother rehearsed this dialog with her son until he sounded convincing. As it turned out, she was able to buy tickets without her son ever being asked his age. When the planetarium show ended, the family moved on to the nearby museum. There, a large sign read, "Children under 5 admitted free." To avoid the admission fee, the mother had to convince her son to forget his pretend birthday.

As the family walked up to the last destination of the day, the aquarium, the mother came face to face with what she had been doing to her son. He looked up at her with a worried look on his face and asked, "Mommy, how old am I now?"

What we say to the children in our classroom today affects how they will act as adults tomorrow. If something is wrong for an adult to do, then it is wrong for a child to do.[84]

And, ye fathers, provoke not your children to wrath, but bring them up in the nurture and admonition of the Lord.

EPHESIANS 6:4

Most people are content in making "little mistakes." Stop to consider, however, that if 99.9% is "good enough" we would then live in a world in which:

· $791,900 would be spent each year on tapes and compact discs that won't play.

· 1,314 phone calls would be misrouted every minute

· 103,260 income tax returns would be processed incorrectly each year.

· 14,208 defective personal computers would be shipped this year.

· 18,322 pieces of mail would be mishandled each hour

· 20,000 incorrect drug prescriptions would be written a year.

· 880,000 credit cards would be produced with incorrect magnetic strips a year,

· 291 pacemaker operations would be performed incorrectly in a year.

· 22,000 checks would be deducted from the wrong bank accounts in an hour.

Little actions can produce huge results! Ask God to help you with the smallest of tasks and briefest of encounters with your students.[85]

Whatever you do, work at it with all your heart, as working for the Lord, not for human masters, since you know that you will receive an inheritance from the Lord as a reward. It is the Lord Christ you are serving.

COLOSSIANS 3:23-24

THE BEST WAY TO INSPIRE PEOPLE TO SUPERIOR PERFORMANCE IS TO CONVINCE THEM BY EVERYTHING YOU DO AND BY YOUR EVERYDAY ATTITUDE THAT YOU ARE WHOLEHEARTEDLY SUPPORTING THEM.

Many people admire and recite the love poetry of Elizabeth Barrett Browning, but few know the motivation for her writing.

Elizabeth grew up as one of eleven children under the absolute rule of an oppressive and dictatorial father. She was a sad and sickly teenager who became a sad and sickly adult. She did not meet Robert Browning until she was forty years old.

Robert saw Elizabeth as a beautiful, talented woman waiting to blossom. He loved her with all his heart and was willing to endure brutal confrontations with her father to win her hand in marriage.

After they married, Elizabeth explored her talents and emerged as a woman in love. She bore Browning a healthy child when she was forty-three, and it was then that she wrote "How Do I Love Thee?" as part of her *Sonnets from the Portuguese*.

When you see past physical shortcomings and take the time to value and encourage your students, they, too, will rise above physical attributes to meet their full potential.

But thou, O man of God, flee these things; and follow after righteousness, godliness, faith, love, patience, meekness.

1 TIMOTHY 6:11

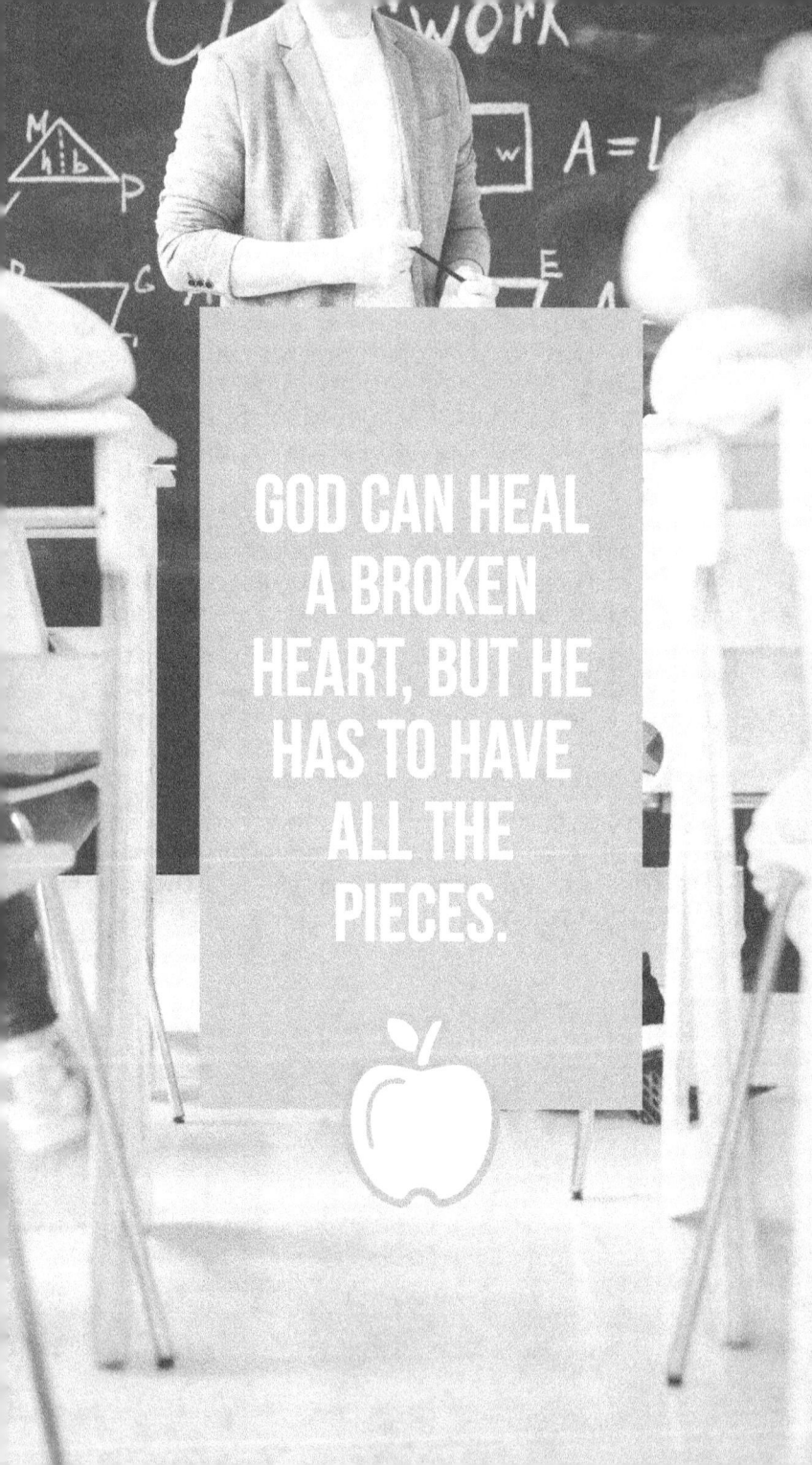

GOD CAN HEAL A BROKEN HEART, BUT HE HAS TO HAVE ALL THE PIECES.

When Christian singer Sheila Walsh gave birth to her son, Christian, she was on top of the world . . . until the physicians gave her a bad report. Her son had jaundice, which was the result of his early arrival, and a premature liver not yet able to function normally. A blood test showed something suspicious, and before Walsh knew what was happening, her son was in pediatric intensive care.

She found an empty room at the hospital and knelt down to pray. It was then that she had an inner understanding about who God really is—not a God who sends trouble to test or judge people, but a loving Father who carries our cares when times are tough. She writes in *Bring Back the Joy,* "I suddenly remembered that God had been there before me. He had watched his boy kneeling in a garden, blood flowing down his face. I knelt down broken and afraid; and when I left that room I was still afraid, but I was leaning on the Lord."

At times, keeping a "stiff upper lip" may be necessary to reassure our students, but with God, we never need to pretend to be brave. Bring your shattered hopes and stinging fears to Him so that He can heal you completely.[87]

My son, give me thine heart.

PROVERBS 23:26

THE SECRET OF CONTENTMENT IS THE REALIZATION THAT LIFE IS A GIFT, NOT A RIGHT.

A preacher once had a flat tire, and a young man with a yellow dog stopped to help him. As they worked on the tire, the preacher asked him about his relationship with the Lord. The young man seemed indifferent. Then the preacher asked about the dog. The young man lit up as he said, "That dog saved my life once." He told how he had been trapped in quicksand. There was not a human being within a couple of miles, but unexpectedly, out of nowhere, the dog appeared. The dog allowed him to put his arms around his haunches and pulled him to solid ground. The young man said, "That dog is always with me. He can have anything I have. I'd probably kill anybody who tried to hurt that dog."

The preacher then said, "Isn't it strange that you take such good care of a dog who saved your life at no cost to itself, yet you treat so indifferently the Savior who saved you at such great cost to Himself?"

A look of wonderment came over the man's face as he said, "You know, Mister, that's right. I reckon it's because I can't see Him and I can't feel hell like I sometimes feel that quicksand around my legs."

Keep God in your thoughts today. Your life as a teacher is one that you live because of His love, grace, and mercy toward you.[88]

But godliness with contentment is great gain.

1 TIMOTHY 6:6 NIV

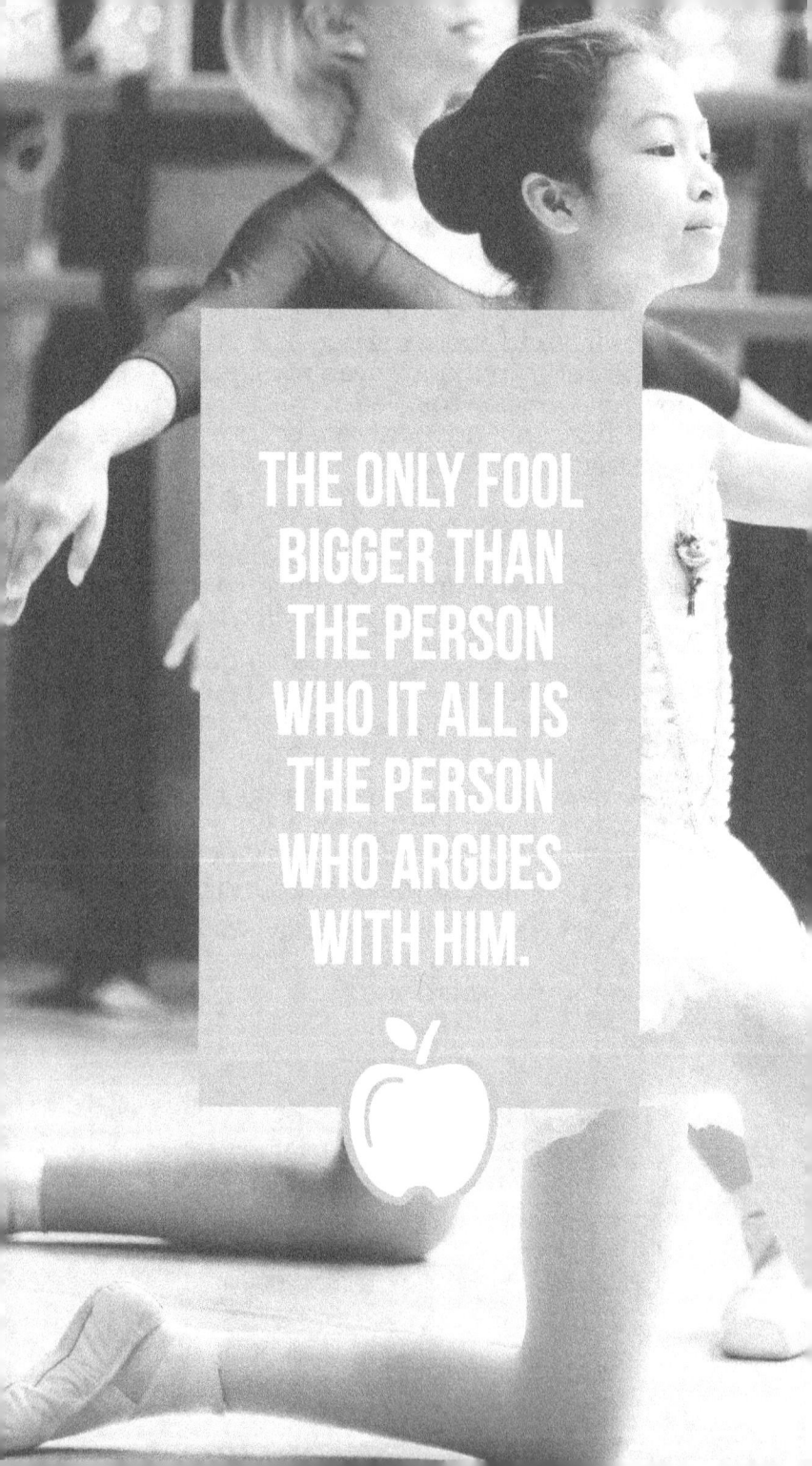

THE ONLY FOOL
BIGGER THAN
THE PERSON
WHO IT ALL IS
THE PERSON
WHO ARGUES
WITH HIM.

Recently, martial arts expert and actor Chuck Norris went into a Texas cafe and sat down to order something cool to drink. A large man came to the booth, towered over him, and said with an edge to his voice that Norris was sitting in his booth. Norris didn't like either the man's tone or his implied threat, but he didn't say anything. He just moved to another booth.

A few minutes later, the man moved in his direction. Norris thought, *Here it comes. A local tough out to make a name for himself by taking on Chuck Norris in a fight.* This time, however, the man said, "You're Chuck Norris." Norris nodded, and the man continued, "You could have whipped me back there a few minutes ago. Why didn't you?"

Norris replied, "What would it have proved?"

The man thought for a moment and then extended his hand. "No hard feelings?" he asked.

"None," Norris responded, and shook his hand. He had won a confrontation, not by a display of martial arts, but by losing his seat in a cafe. And he had made a new friend in the process.

What are you willing to lose in order to gain your students' respect and God's approval and reward?
89

Whoever corrects a mocker invites insult, whoever rebukes a wicked man incurs abuse.

PROVERBS 9:7 NIV

Few physicians make house calls these days, but one doctor decided to do so, believing that his patient would do better if she could be treated in the comfort of her own home. Cancer was causing fluid in her lung which needed to be drained periodically.

At each visit, the physician spent time talking with the woman about subjects that were of interest to her. One day after finishing his procedure, he commented on the beautiful flowers just outside her window. She said to him, "Those flowers are one of the reasons my home is so dear to me. It gives me great joy to look out the window and see them."

A short time later, the woman died. Her daughter came to the physician's office one day with a gift from his former patient—a jar filled with beautiful flowers from the woman's garden. The note with the flowers read: "It was my mother's desire to share with you some of the beauty you made possible for her to hang onto in her last days. Thank you for everything."

Who was the more loving? The sick woman no doubt thought the physician was—the physician had no doubt that his patient and her daughter were.

Love keeps on giving. Its message is an eternal one, that no student or colleague tires of hearing.[90]

Beloved, let us love one another: for love is of God: and every one that loveth is born of God . . . for God is love.

1 JOHN 4:7-8

The homed lizard uses a distinctive defense mechanism against aggressors. First, the lizard hisses and swells its body with air. If that doesn't work, the animal flattens its body into a dorsal shield and tips it up toward the attacker, projecting an image that would be difficult to swallow. When all else fails, however, the lizard's eyelids suddenly swell shut. A hair-like stream of blood comes shooting out from an opening near the animal's eyelids aimed directly at the enemy. The blood contains compounds that repel the attacker. Then the eyelids shrink to normal size.

People are not so different. Those who feel themselves under attack often rise to their full height, jut out their jaws, clench their fists, and "square off" for a fight. Angry words then spew out aimed at the greatest area of vulnerability in the other person's life.

Our words of criticism, ridicule, and name-calling may stop or stall an attack, but they never bring peace, reconciliation, or resolution. Only uplifting and positive words spoken with genuine love bring peace and harmony to a classroom or faculty lounge. Choose to speak healing words today.[91]

A person finds joy in giving an apt reply—
and how good is a timely word!

PROVERBS 15:23 NIV

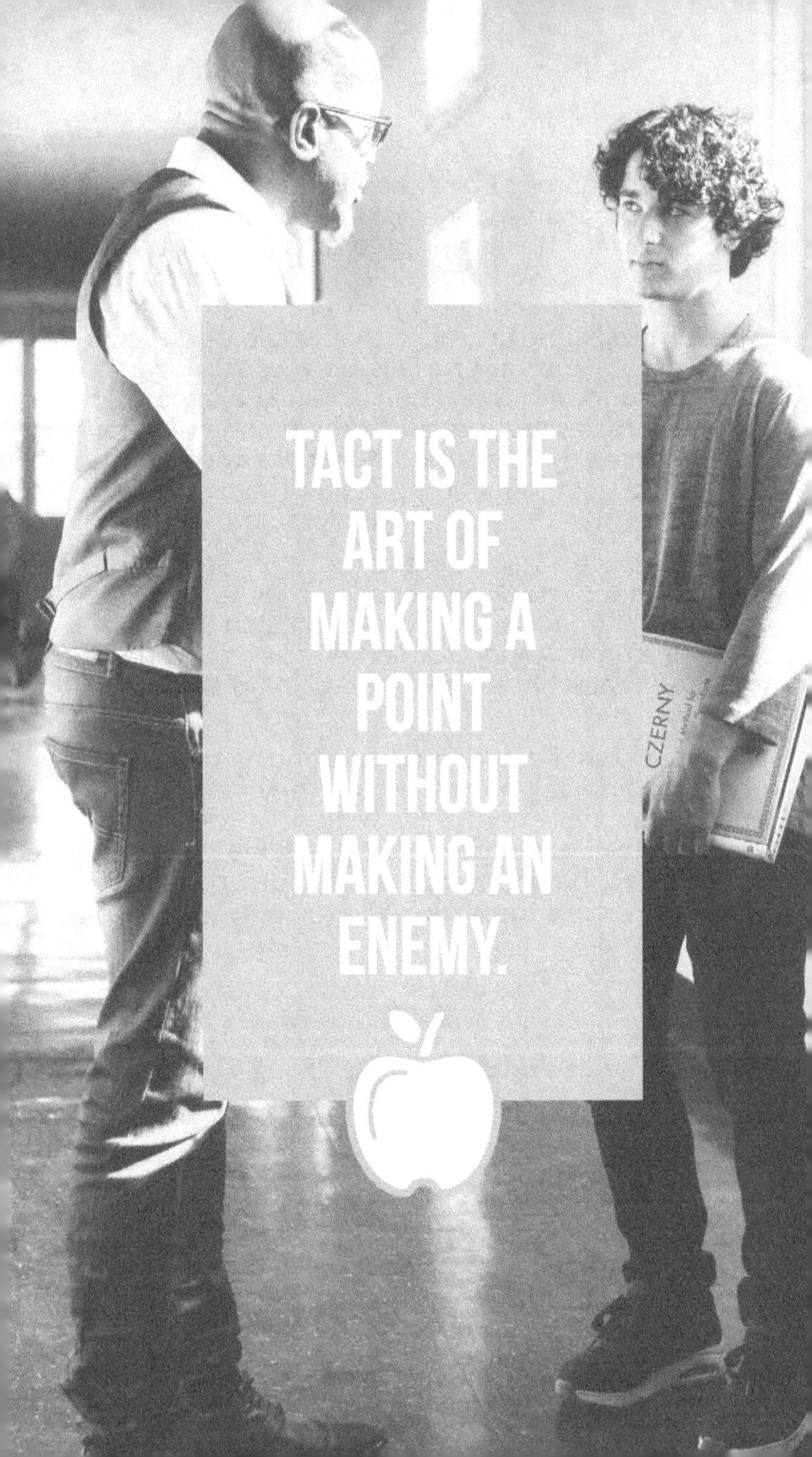

TACT IS THE ART OF MAKING A POINT WITHOUT MAKING AN ENEMY.

Soon after the grocery store closed, a woman knocked sharply at the glass door. The clerk responsible for locking up that evening tried to ignore her, but she kept knocking. "We're closed," the clerk shouted.

"Let me in," the woman shouted even louder. Reluctantly, the clerk opened the door, and before he knew it, the woman had pushed her way into the store. "I need a head of lettuce," she announced.

The clerk followed her to the produce section and watched as she examined every head of lettuce there. After five minutes of deliberation, she said, "I really only need half a head of lettuce." The tired clerk was eager to go home, but he didn't want to explode at the I woman, so he told her he had to get his manager's permission for such a sale.

He went to the back of the store and said to his manager, "You won't believe this. A stupid, idiotic, cranky, mean, difficult woman wants to buy only half a head of lettuce." At that point, he glanced over his shoulder and I saw that the old woman had followed him. He slowly I turned back to the manager and said, "But fortunately, we have another woman here who will take the other half."

Always remember that the slowest thing to heal in a person—student or principal—is a wounded spirit.[92]

Reckless words pierce like a sword, but the tongue of the wise brings healing.

PROVERBS 12:18 NIV

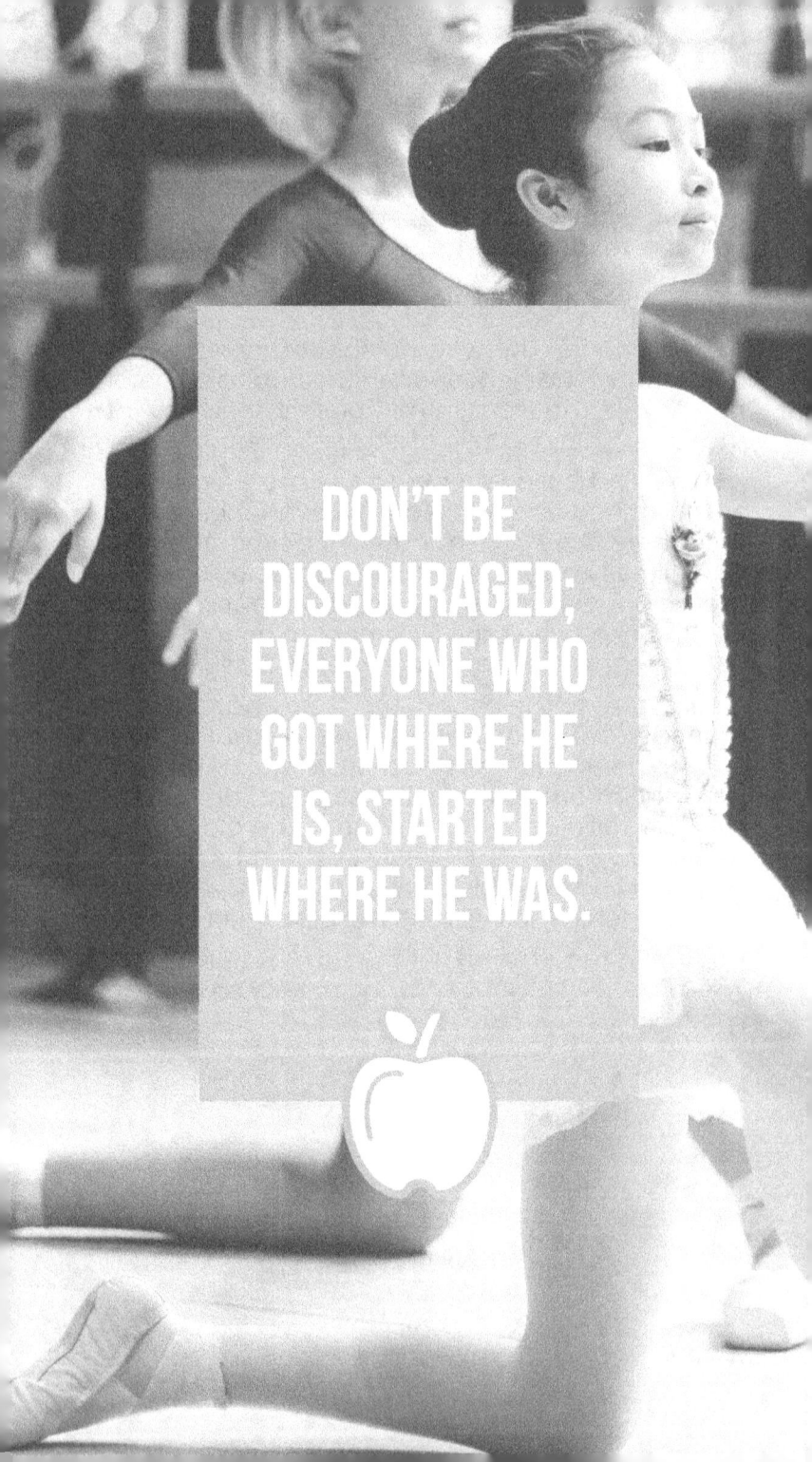

DON'T BE DISCOURAGED; EVERYONE WHO GOT WHERE HE IS, STARTED WHERE HE WAS.

He didn't just drop out of college, he was expelled. His major, like that of many students, was undeclared. He enjoyed taking a couple of acting classes in college, so it seemed like a good idea to head for Hollywood. Except for a few bit parts, he couldn't really call himself an actor. So after a few years, with bills to pay and children to raise, he learned carpentry skills and made his living as a Hollywood handyman, building everything from bookcases to sundecks.

When George Lucas was casting Star Wars, he ran into the unemployed actor, who was nailing boards at Goldwyn Studios in Hollywood. He remembered him from an earlier movie they had done together and asked him to act as a stand-in while other actors ran through their lines. The stand-in, however, turned out to be a lot more impressive than the other guys trying out for the part. He was given the role of Hans Solo, and Harrison Ford went on to become a major film star. Does Ford give credit to every setback along the way to that first big role as a step toward finally reaching his dream? Absolutely.

A student may earn a failing grade, but no student should ever be considered a failure.[93]

Though your beginning was insignificant, yet your end will increase greatly.

JOB 8:7 NASB

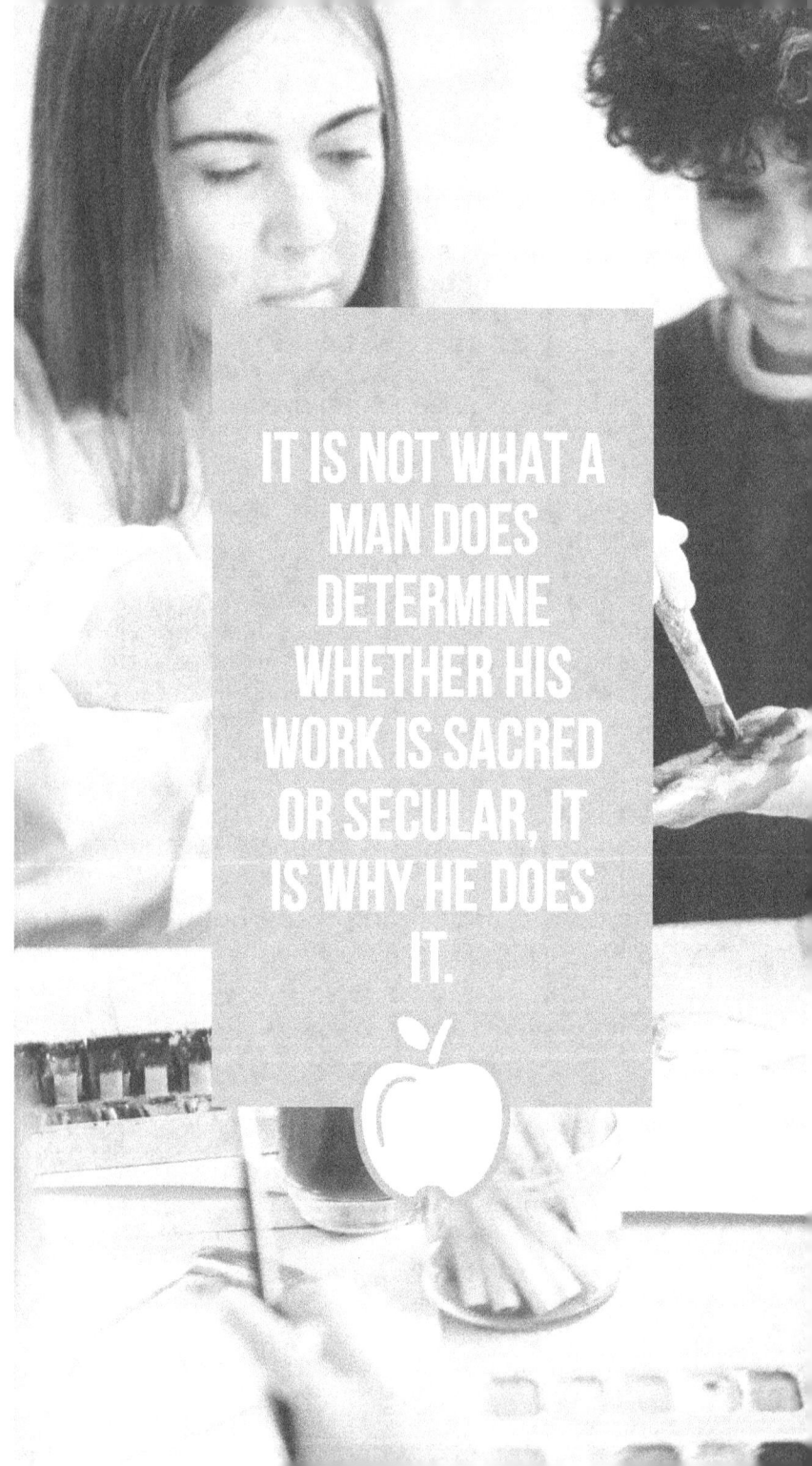

IT IS NOT WHAT A MAN DOES DETERMINE WHETHER HIS WORK IS SACRED OR SECULAR, IT IS WHY HE DOES IT.

On its fortieth anniversary, Fuller Seminary celebrated by inaugurating the President's Lectureship. The series featured Carl F. H. Henry, theologian; Samuel Hugh Moffett, professor emeritus of ecumenism and mission at Princeton; Mary Steward Van Leeuwen, professor of interdisciplinary studies at Calvin College; and Gary Wisiger III, retired pastor.

In his address, Wisiger displayed characteristic humility at having been chosen to be in the company of such noted academic giants. He said, "I have been a pastor by the grace of God. If I could do it all over again, I would be a pastor. I have never, frankly, regarded myself as a scholar. I have tried to be studious, and I want to thank Dr. David Hubbard for including me in this program today. A farmer once put his mule in a horse race and his friends said to him, 'Silly, that mule can't run with those thoroughbreds.' The farmer said, 'I know it, but you have no idea how good it makes him feel to be with all those horses.'"

No matter what you do today—from the most menial to the most noble task associated with teaching—do what you do as if you are doing it for the Lord. He is with you, which means you are on the best team and in the finest company possible!

94

Whatever you do, work at it with all your heart, as working for the Lord, not for men . . . It is the Lord Christ you are serving.

COLOSSIANS 3:23-24 NIV

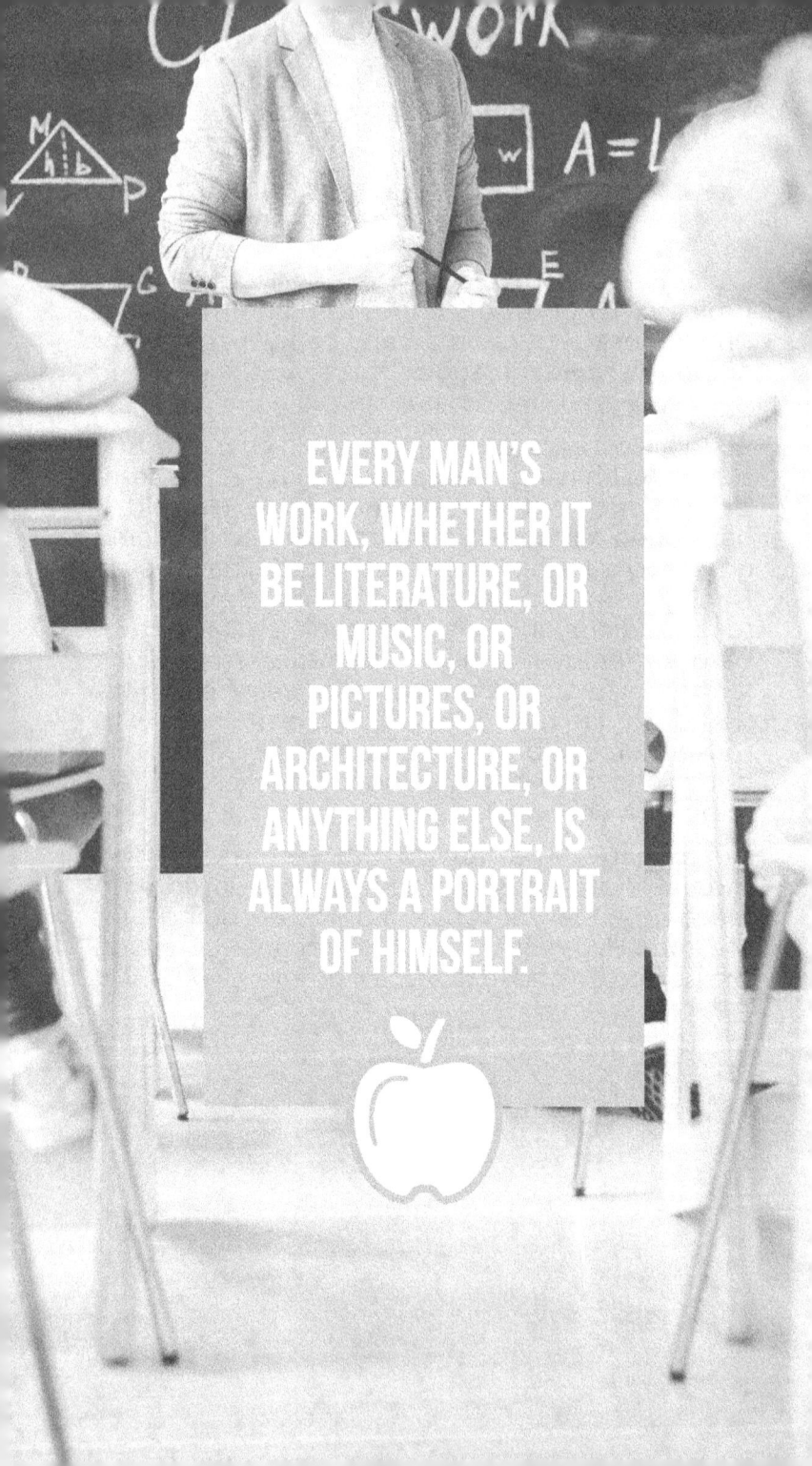

EVERY MAN'S
WORK, WHETHER IT
BE LITERATURE, OR
MUSIC, OR
PICTURES, OR
ARCHITECTURE, OR
ANYTHING ELSE, IS
ALWAYS A PORTRAIT
OF HIMSELF.

I n a book about the village of Akenfield in England, the author tells of old farmers who could look at a field where ten people had plowed and tell you the name of the man who had done each furrow.

There are those who frequent the Indian markets in South America who can tell by looking at a piece of rope who made it.

The difference in furrows was not a factor in whether a field produced more or fewer beans per acre. The difference in rope was not a factor in the usefulness of the rope. But in each case, the work was a reflection of the character of the worker. It was a statement about the diligence with which the person approached his work and the amount of pride he took in producing quality.

It was in this same spirit of endowing work with character that the great artisans of the Middle Ages often carved the backs of their art, knowing that God alone would see it—but caring greatly that He did!

No person may see your lesson plans today, monitor your classroom, or review your students' exams or homework, but God will. Give your best to your students as if God were sitting in your classroom.[95]

> As in water face reflects face, so the heart of man reflects man.
>
> PROVERBS 27:19 NASB

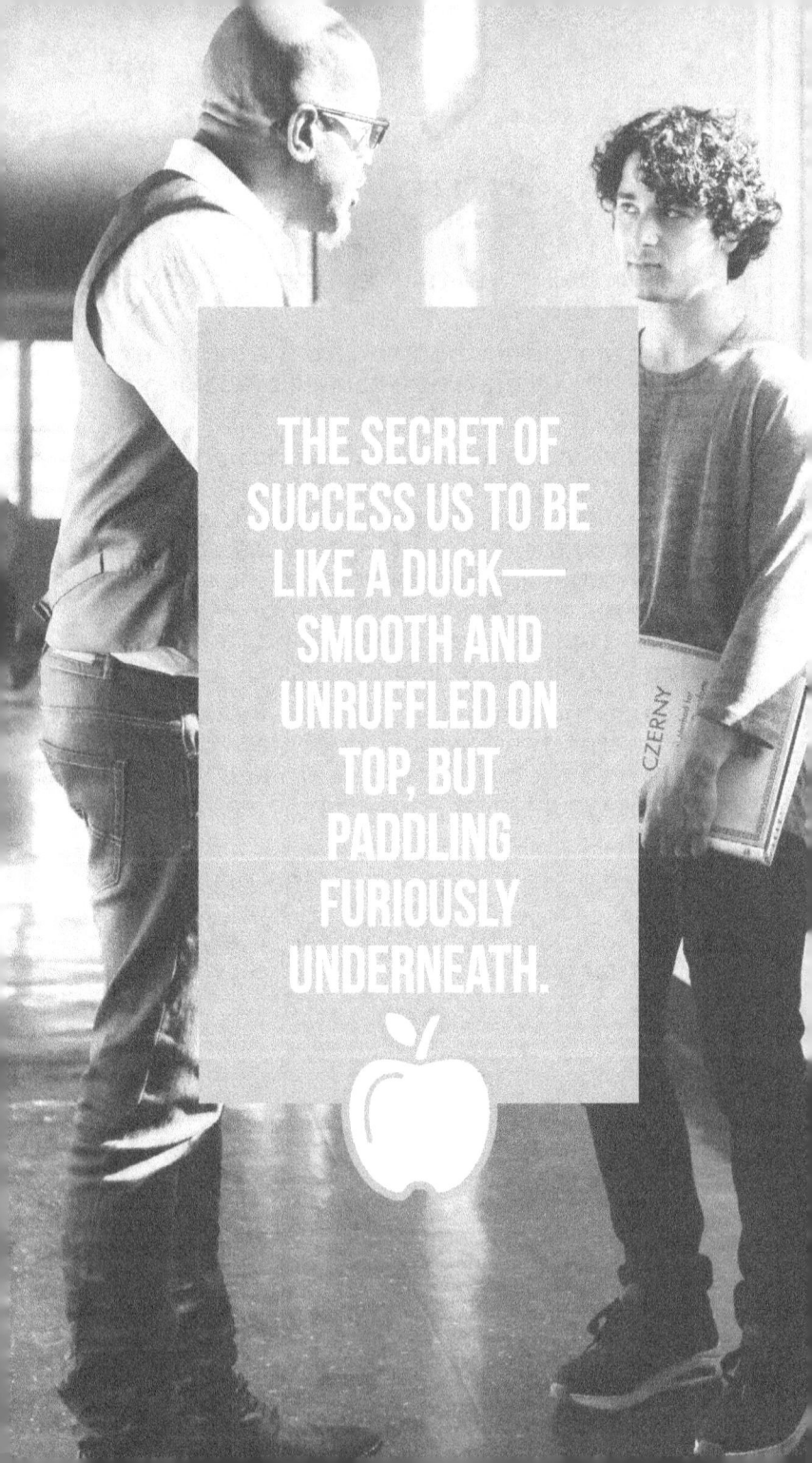

THE SECRET OF SUCCESS US TO BE LIKE A DUCK—SMOOTH AND UNRUFFLED ON TOP, BUT PADDLING FURIOUSLY UNDERNEATH.

I f ever a man presented an unflappable approach to life, it was Franklin D. Roosevelt. Stricken with polio and paralyzed at age 39, he was determined to carry on in strength. Even though he couldn't fight on a battlefield, he became the image of American strength and vitality during World War II. White House counsel Sam Rosenman watched Roosevelt's top military advisers—General George Marshall, Admiral Ernest King, and General Henry Arnold—leave the Oval Office after their daily consultations with the President. He has said, "I always remember their calm, determined, fighting faces . . . I always felt certain that a great deal of that calm confidence and firm determination were reflections of the spirit of the man whom they had just left."

Actor Gregory Peck recalls his first glimpse of the President when Peck was just a boy. He was stunned to see Roosevelt carried off a boat and placed in a wheelchair. "But then," Peck said, "he put his hat on his head, waved to the crowd, and suddenly I started clapping and everything was fine."

The wise teacher knows there is no substitute for hard work, and there is rarely a genuine cause for panic.[96]

But I laboured more abundantly than they all: yet not I, but the grace of God which was with me.

1 CORINTHIANS 15:10

MOST OF THE THINGS WORTH DOING IN THE WORLD HAD BEEN DECLARED IMPOSSIBLE BEFORE THEY WERE DONE.

W e can be grateful to God that somebody refused to believe these expert opinions:

• "Computers in the future may weigh no more than 1.5 tons."—*Popular Mechanics*, 1949.

• "I think there is a world market for maybe five computers"—Thomas Watson, IBM chairman, 1943.

• "This 'telephone' has too many shortcomings to be seriously considered as a means of communication. The device is inherently of no value to us"—Western Union internal memo, 1876.

• "Heavier-than-air flying machines are impossible."—Lord Kelvin, Royal Society president, 1895.

• "Drill for oil? You mean drill into the ground to try and find oil? You're crazy!"—drillers whom Edwin L. Drake tried to hire to drill for oil in 1859.

• "Man will never reach the moon regardless of all future scientific advances."—Dr. Lee DeForest, inventor of the vacuum tube and father of television.

• "Everything that can be invented has been invented."—Charles H. Duell, Commissioner, U.S. Office of Patents, 1899.

Don't be too quick to dismiss a student's idea or suggestion. It just may have life-changing merit![97]

But with God all things are possible.

MATTHEW 19:26

Years ago, a man riding on horseback came across a squad of soldiers who were trying to move a large piece of timber. The rider noticed a well-dressed corporal standing nearby, giving lordly commands to "heave." The piece of timber, however, was just a little too heavy for the squad to move.

"Why don't you help them?" the quiet man on the horse asked the corporal.

"Me?" the man said with a proud air. "Why, I'm a corporal, sir!"

At that, the stranger dismounted and carefully took his place with the soldiers. He smiled at them and said, "Now, all together boys—heave!" The piece of lumber slid into place. The stranger silently mounted his horse and then turned the horse around so that he could address the corporal.

'The next time you have a piece of timber for your men to handle, corporal, send for the commander-in-chief."

It was only as the man rode away that the corporal and his men realized that the helpful stranger was none other than George Washington.

Students may not remember much about their teachers' lectures, but they never seem to forget teachers who have helped them conquer personal problems.[98]

For the tree is known and recognized and judged by its fruit.

MATTHEW 12:33 AMP

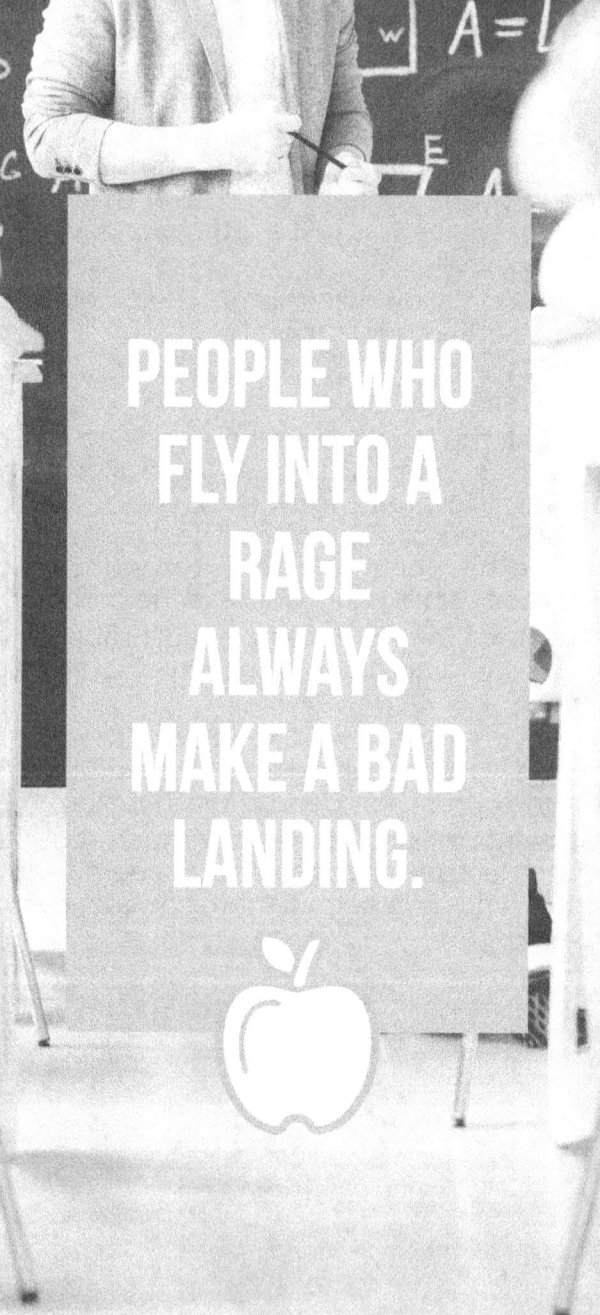

PEOPLE WHO
FLY INTO A
RAGE
ALWAYS
MAKE A BAD
LANDING.

Chuck Givens admits that he was once a pro at getting angry with both traffic and the drivers who caused traffic delays. He had a habit of venting his anger by pounding on the steering wheel of his car, usually while saying, "Those silly sons-of-guns . . . what do they think they're doing? What is this, a parade?"

On many days, he admits that he worked himself from fervor to frenzy. The more frustrated he got, the harder he pounded on his steering wheel until his face turned bright red in anger. It didn't matter to him who else was in the car with him. He knew he was "in the right," and he felt free to shout loudly, "Get out of my way! Don't you know I've got important things to do? If I had my way, nobody would drive on the highway when I'm using it!"

One day in 1967, his attitude changed. While riding with a friend and "up to his hubcaps in traffic," he pounded soundly on the steering wheel and—*crack*—it broke! In an instant, he rendered his car undrivable, and his anger dissolved into embarrassment.

In life and in the classroom, anger rarely solves a problem. Usually, it just makes things worse.[99]

Fools give full vent to their rage, but the wise bring calm in the end.

PROVERBS 29:11 NIV

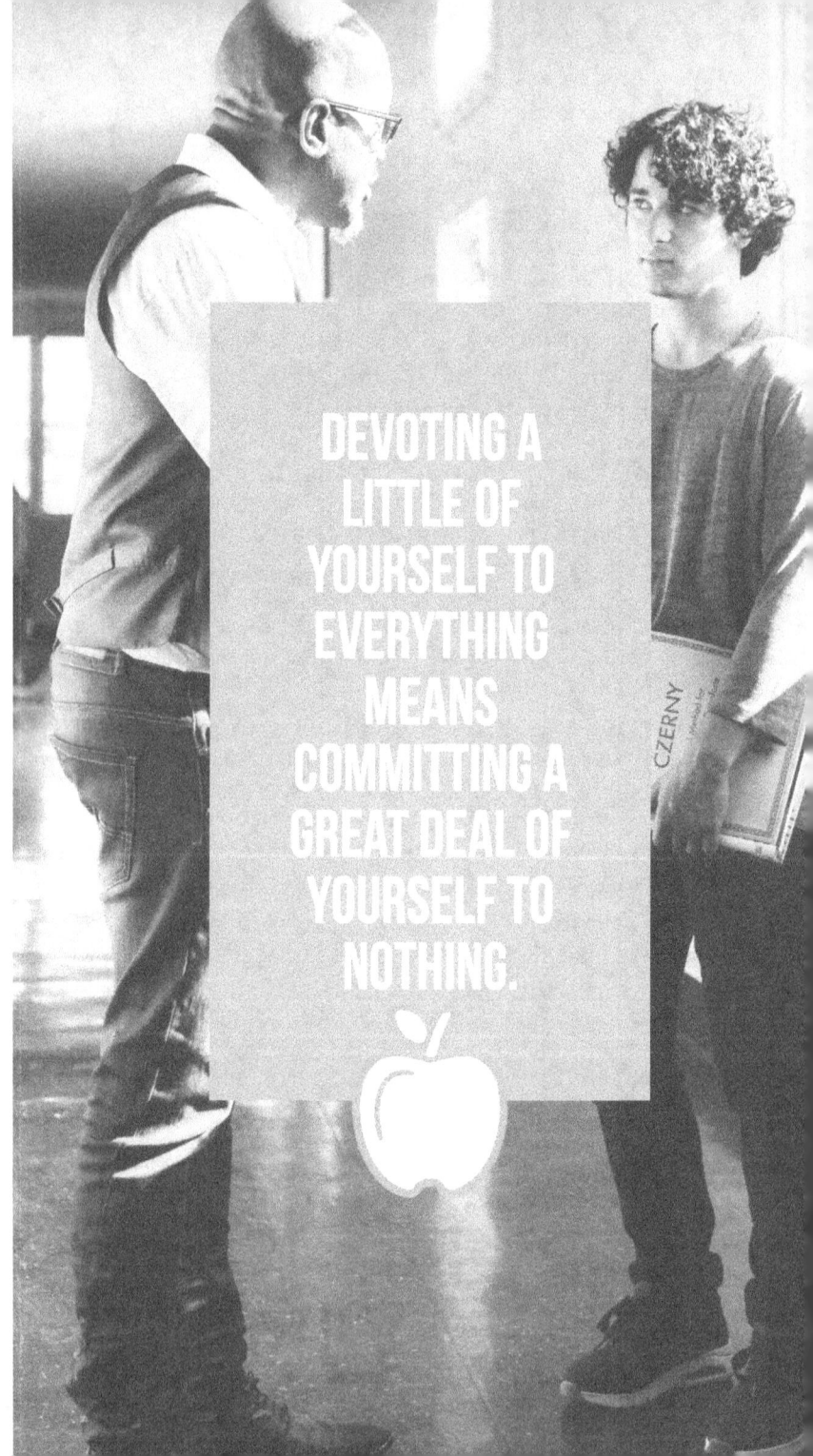

A young boy named Samuel was determined to build ships. He owned nothing but a penknife with which he whittled out little boats. Daily, he went to the harbor of Glasgow to examine the ships sailing into and out of the port. He loved everything about ships and the sea. As an unknown young man in the design and engineering field, someone asked Samuel Cunard to design what would become the first Cunard steamship.

Focus and a good aim are critically important to hitting any target. The student who gets bogged down by unimportant matters or who gives up in discouragement over what others say and think is a student who loses focus and eventually arrives at the poor and meaningless destination of "nowhere."

Help your students aim their lives toward specific goals, and then focus your efforts as a teacher toward helping them achieve their goals. A little graveyard beside a church in a small village in England gives tribute to a person who did just that. The epitaph on the gravestone reads: "She has done what she couldn't."[100]

Whatsoever thy hand findeth to do, do it with thy might.

ECCLESIASTES 9:10

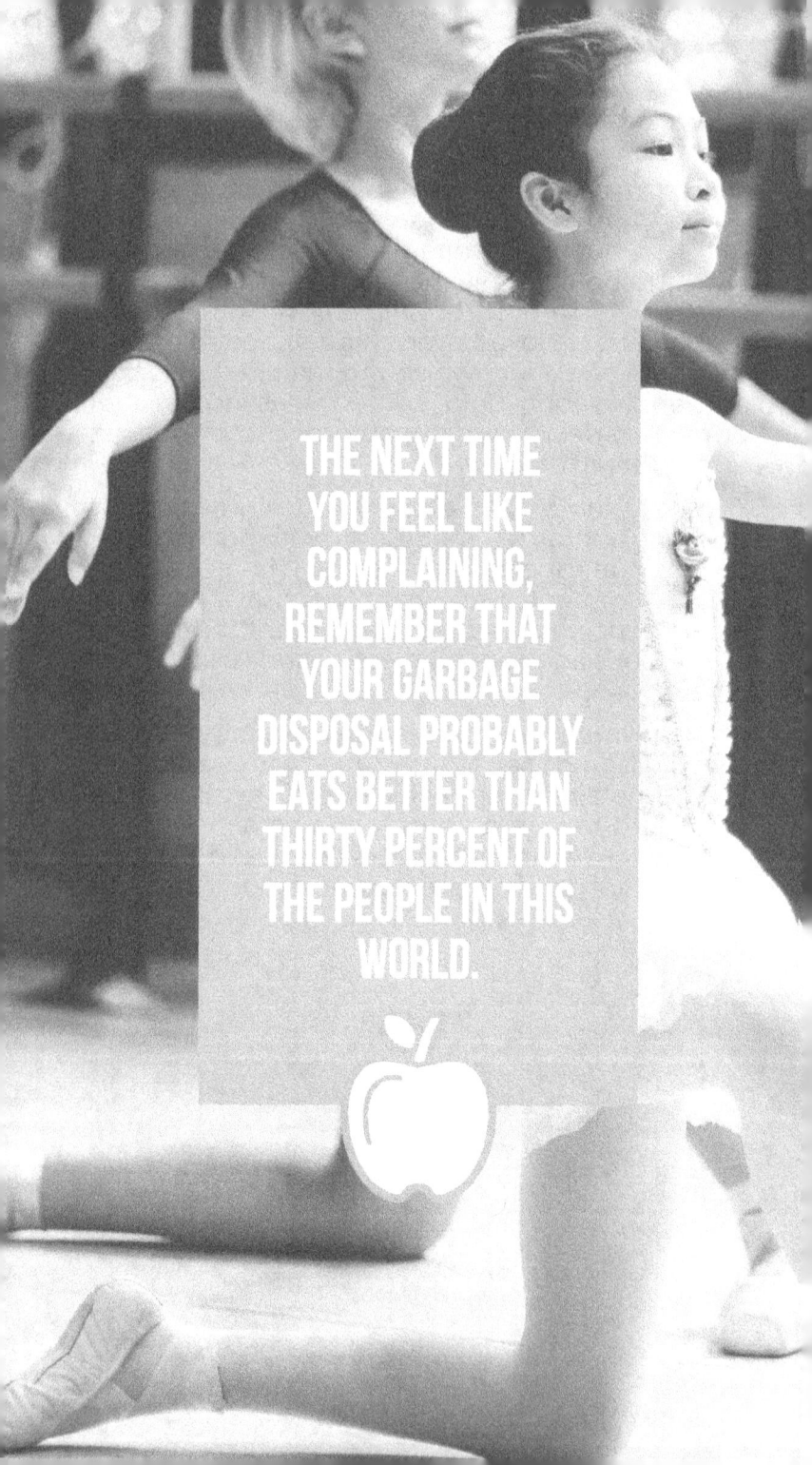

THE NEXT TIME
YOU FEEL LIKE
COMPLAINING,
REMEMBER THAT
YOUR GARBAGE
DISPOSAL PROBABLY
EATS BETTER THAN
THIRTY PERCENT OF
THE PEOPLE IN THIS
WORLD.

A woman whose only son had died went to a holy man and asked, "What powers do you have that will lift the ache from my heart?"

He said, "There is a wonderful thing you can do. But first you must bring me a mustard seed from a family that has no problems."

The woman went immediately to a beautiful mansion, thinking, *Nothing could possibly be wrong here!* She knocked at the door and said, "I have to find a mustard seed from a home where there are no problems. It's very important to me. May I have one of your mustard seeds?"

The people said to her, "Oh, you have come to the wrong house." They began listing all their problems. The woman thought, *I certainly know something about problems. Maybe I can help them.* She listened, consoled, and comforted.

At every home in the town, the same thing happened. Finally, she returned to the holy man and said, "I did not find the seed you wanted. Instead, I gave away all of the seeds of love I could give."

"And does your heart still ache?" the holy man asked. "No," she said, but then she added with a smile, "but I am thinking of growing some mustard and letting it go to seed."

Teach your students: Whatever you think you are on the outside, you likely are on the inside.[101]

So then, just as you received Christ Jesus as Lord, continue to live your lives in him, rooted and built up in him, strengthened in the faith as you were taught, and overflowing with thankfulness.

COLOSSIANS 2:6-7 NIV

BEING AT PEACE
WITH YOURSELF
IS A DIRECT
RESULT OF
FINDING PEACE
WITH GOD.

Gigi expected a routine visit to the doctor. Instead, her whole world changed. The doctor found a lump that required a biopsy, and the biopsy showed malignancy. Gigi went into surgery expecting the best.

"When I regained consciousness after the operation," she said, "my doctor was there to tell me more news. I just wanted to hear that they got it all. He said just the opposite. He told me cancer was running rampant all over my body. I was sick—physically, mentally, and emotionally. It was utter devastation. But it was an amazing time for me. I knew I had to grieve the loss of my body and ultimately my life."

Gigi found that she was more and more thankful for each day she awoke. She accepted the fact that it would do her no good to be angry, bitter, or vengeful. "I made peace with my situation on a sunny summer afternoon in August," she said. "I said, 'Lord, I want to live each day to the fullest. Help me to put aside anything that will keep me from doing that.' God answered my prayer. These last few months have been the most wonderful gift any woman or man could ever receive. I am a fortunate person."

Ask God today to give you His peace in your work as a teacher. There is no substitute for His grace.[102]

And the peace of God, which passeth all understanding, shall keep your hearts and minds through Christ Jesus.

PHILIPPIANS 4:7

Mary Ann Bird writes in *The Whisper Test*: "I grew up knowing I was different, and I hated it. I was born with a deft palate, and when I started school my classmates made it dear to me how I looked to others: a little girl with a misshapen lip, crooked nose, lopsided teeth, and garbled speech. When schoolmates asked, 'What happened to your lip?' I'd tell them I'd fallen and cut it on a piece of glass . . .

"There was, however, a teacher in the second grade that we all adored—Mrs. Leonard by name. She was short, round, happy—a sparkling lady. Annually we had a hearing test . . . Mrs. Leonard gave the test to everyone in the class, and finally it was my turn. I knew from past years that as we stood against the door and covered one ear, the teacher sitting at her desk would whisper something, and we would have to repeat it back—things like 'The sky is blue' or 'Do you have new shoes?' I waited there for those words that God must have put into her mouth, those seven words that changed my life. Mrs. Leonard said, in her whisper, 'I wish you were my little girl.'"

There is no known benefit from angry words fired to destroy, wound, or reject. In contrast, the benefit from words spoken to heal and restore can be eternal.[103]

A rebel shouts in anger; a wise man holds his temper in and cools it.

PROVERBS 29:11 TLB

THE WORLD
IS RUN BY C
STUDENTS.

There once was a nice young man who worked as a railroad express clerk in Minnesota. He went to work every day and enjoyed his job—an average man in an average role. One day, he received a large box of watches addressed to a local jeweler. The jeweler, however, did not want the watches. The clerk contacted the distributor who had sent the watches only to discover that he didn't want them back because the return postage was too expensive.

What was he to do with a box of watches? An idea dawned on the young clerk. He drew pictures of the watches, added descriptions about each one, and put together a little catalog which he then sent to other clerks on the rail line. In just a few weeks, they bought all the watches at what was nearly a hundred percent profit to him! His effort was so successful that he used the money to order more watches and enlarged his catalog.

The clerk's name? Sears. His catalog? Sears, Roebuck, and Company.

One of the greatest challenges any teacher will ever face is not in getting an F student to make a passing grade, but to get a C student to work hard enough and to think creatively enough to earn an A.[104]

The plans of the diligent lead to profit.

PROVERBS 21:5 NIV

A PINT OF EXAMPLE IS WORTH A BARRELFUL OF ADVICE.

A girl once went with her mother to a jewelry store after Christmas to exchange an expensive gift she had received for an item of the same type that was cheaper and more appropriate to her daily needs. She found an ideal replacement, and the clerk prepared a statement for the amount of cash refund to which she was entitled.

When the mother locked over the receipt, she found the owner had miscalculated. She called attention to the error. He denied the mistake, but she continued to quietly but assertively say, 'I wish you would check your figures again I believe you'll find the amount is different than what you calculated." She was polite but firm, and in the end he saw his error, made the correction, and apologized.

As the girl and her mother stepped outside the shop, she said to her mother, "I'm so glad you stood up for me. I also saw the error but I didn't know what to do. I probably would have gone my way, frustrated and angry at being ripped off. You showed me that I could be firm without being insulting and without anybody feeling bad in the end."

When errors are corrected and everybody walks away feeling good about it—that's good teaching!
105

Brethren, join in following my example,
and observe those who walk according to
the pattern you have in us.

PHILIPPIANS 3:17 NASB

BE CAREFUL
OF YOUR
THOUGHTS.
THEY MAY
BECOME WORDS
AT ANY
MOMENT.

On a rainy night, a salesman was driving on a lonely country road when he had a flat tire. He opened the trunk to discover he had no lug wrench, so he walked in the driving rain toward a dimly lit farmhouse. *Surely the farmer will have a lug wrench I can borrow,* he thought. *But it's late. The farmer will be asleep in his warm, dry bed. Maybe he won't answer the door.* The salesman began to panic as he stumbled toward the house, thinking, *If he DOES answer the door, he will be angry. He'll probably shout, "What's the big idea of waking me up at this hour?"* Soaked and uncomfortable, this thought made the man angry. What right did that farmer have to be rude or to refuse him the loan of a lug wrench? *That farmer is a selfish clod, no doubt about it!*

The salesman finally reached the house and banged loudly on the door. A light went on, and a window opened on the second floor. A voice called, "Who is it?"

His face white with anger, the salesman called back, "You know very well who it is. It's me! And you can keep your blasted lug wrench. I wouldn't borrow it now if you had the last one on earth!"

To govern the words you speak to your students, first govern your attitude.[106]

A wise man's heart guides his mouth

PROVERBS 16:23 NIV

IF THE ROOTS
ARE DEEP AND
STRONG, THE
TREE NEEDN'T
WORRY ABOUT
THE WIND.

A writer and a farmer were talking one day in a local cafe about the farmer's soybean and corn crops. Rain had been abundant in recent weeks, and the results were evident. The soybeans and corn were shooting up dramatically. "All of this rain must be a great relief to you," the writer said.

The farmer replied, "My crops are especially vulnerable now."

"What do you mean?" the writer asked.

The farmer replied, "Even a short drought could j have a devastating effect."

"Why is that?" the writer asked.

The farmer explained, "When it rains so much, the plants are not required to push their roots deeper into the earth in search of water. All of the roots remain near the surface. If a drought hits and begins to dry out the earth, it also dries out those shallow roots. The plants then die quickly." He concluded, "A good plant needs deep roots that can withstand what happens above the ground."

Choose to send down roots into what is truly eternal—reading the Bible, praising God, and worshipping regularly with other Christians. Then when times of stress hit your life, a deeply rooted love of God will give you the power to endure.[107]

"But blessed is the one who trusts in the Lord, whose confidence is in him. They will be like a tree planted by the water that sends out its roots by the stream. It does not fear when heat comes; its leaves are always green. It has no worries in a year of drought and never fails to bear fruit."

JEREMIAH 17:7-8 NIV

THE WORLD
WANTS YOUR
BEST, BUT
GOD WANTS
YOUR ALL.

There once was a wealthy man who was devastated when his only son was killed in a war. A friend of the son came to the house one day and gave the father a special gift a painting he had done of his friend. It became the man's most prized possession, even though he possessed a dazzling collection of priceless artwork.

When the man died, his art was auctioned off. Collectors flocked to the event. The first piece on the block was the portrait of the man's son. "Bring on the good stuff!" one collector shouted when he saw the painting. "Who wants a picture like that?"

The auctioneer replied, "The gentleman left orders that this piece must be auctioned first."

A friend of the deceased man finally made a bid of $10. In fact, his was the only bid, and he got the painting. The auctioneer immediately announced, "The auction is over."

A cry went up from the crowd. "What do you mean?" the collectors shouted. The auctioneer explained, "The will states that he who is willing to take the son will receive everything else."

God has said the same thing about His Son. For true success, God's will must be our first priority in the classroom.[108]

Thou shalt love the Lord thy God with all thy heart, and with all thy soul, and with all thy mind.

MATTHEW 22:37

There may be many reasons why a person might question why God would choose to use him or her. But don't be too concerned about your "faults." You're in good company:

- Moses stuttered.
- Timothy had stomach problems.
- Jacob was a liar.
- David had an affair.
- Abraham was too old.
- John was self-righteous.
- Naomi was a poor widow.
- Paul was a murderer.
- Jonah ran from God.
- Miriam was a gossip.
- Gideon doubted—and so did Thomas.
- Jeremiah was depressed and suicidal.
- Elijah was burned out.
- Martha was a worrywart.
- Amos' training was in fig-tree pruning.

God doesn't lock at our faults, finances, or failings. He only looks at our willingness. If you are willing today to bc used by God in the lives of your students and colleagues . . . get ready. You're just the right candidate for a job God has in mind!

A man's pride brings him low, but a man of lowly spirit gains honor.

PROVERBS 29:23 NIV

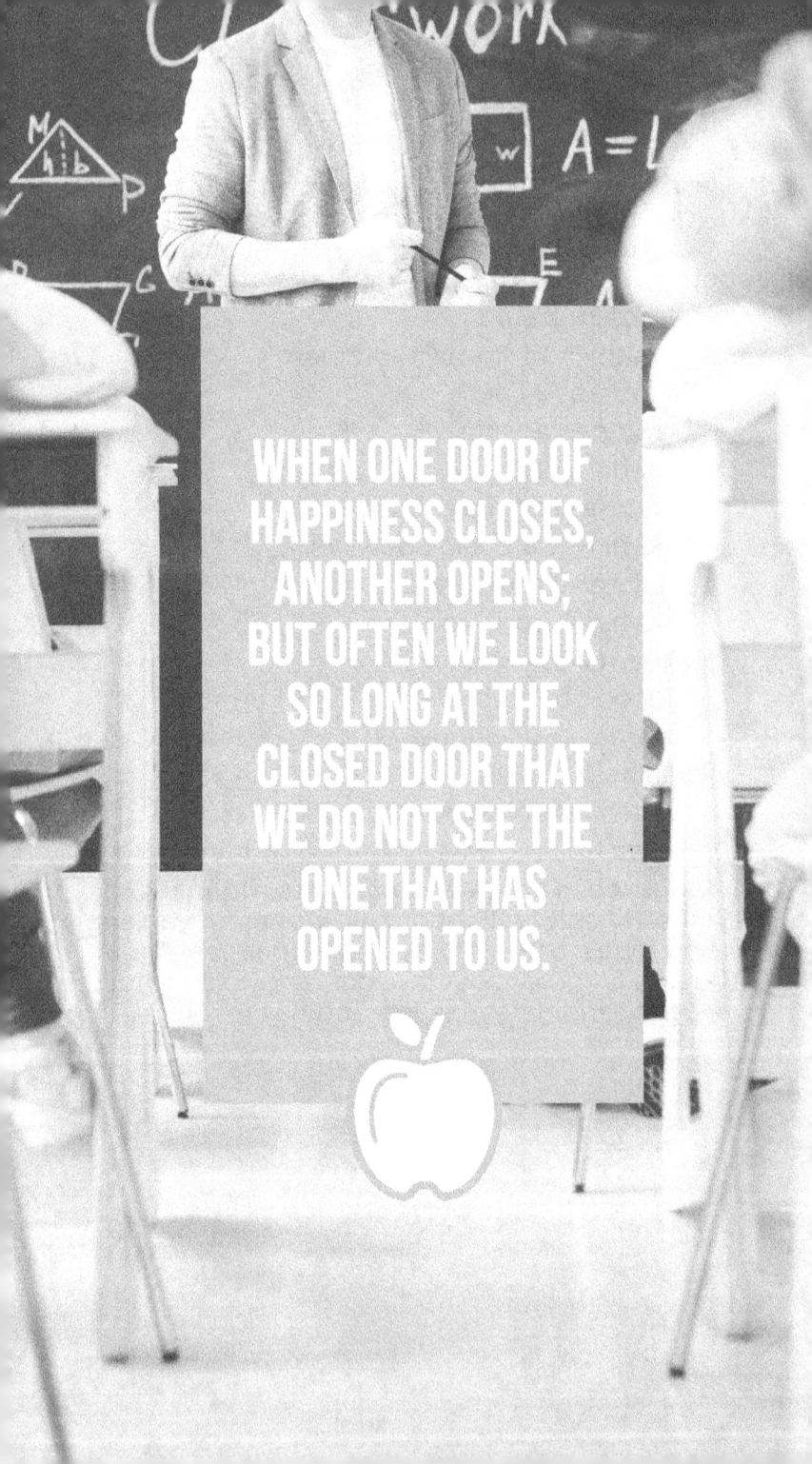

WHEN ONE DOOR OF
HAPPINESS CLOSES,
ANOTHER OPENS;
BUT OFTEN WE LOOK
SO LONG AT THE
CLOSED DOOR THAT
WE DO NOT SEE THE
ONE THAT HAS
OPENED TO US.

Fanny Crosby didn't start writing hymns until she was forty, but she certainly made up for lost time. She wrote more than eight thousand hymns, using more than two hundred pen names. Under contract for one music publisher, she wrote three hymns a week! Although she was blinded in infancy because of a physician's error, Crosby never reflects bitterness in her songs, but rather joy and longing for the Lord.

A Scottish minister once said to her that it was too bad God had allowed her to become blind. She quickly responded, "If I had been given a choice at birth, I would have asked to be blind . . . for when I get to heaven, the first face I will see will be the one who died for me." She also said about her blindness, "If I could meet that doctor now, I would thank him over and over for making me blind." The desire to see Jesus and to be close to Him always was foremost in her mind. She didn't see her blindness as a tragedy, but rather as a catalyst for keeping her focus on the fact that she was "Redeemed" with a "Blessed Assurance" that she would always be in a special relationship with her Savior "Close to Thee."

Give your weakness to God today. He will give back you strength and success as a teacher.[109]

And Jesus said unto him, "No man, having put his hand to the plough, and looking back, is fit for the kingdom of God."

LUKE 9:62

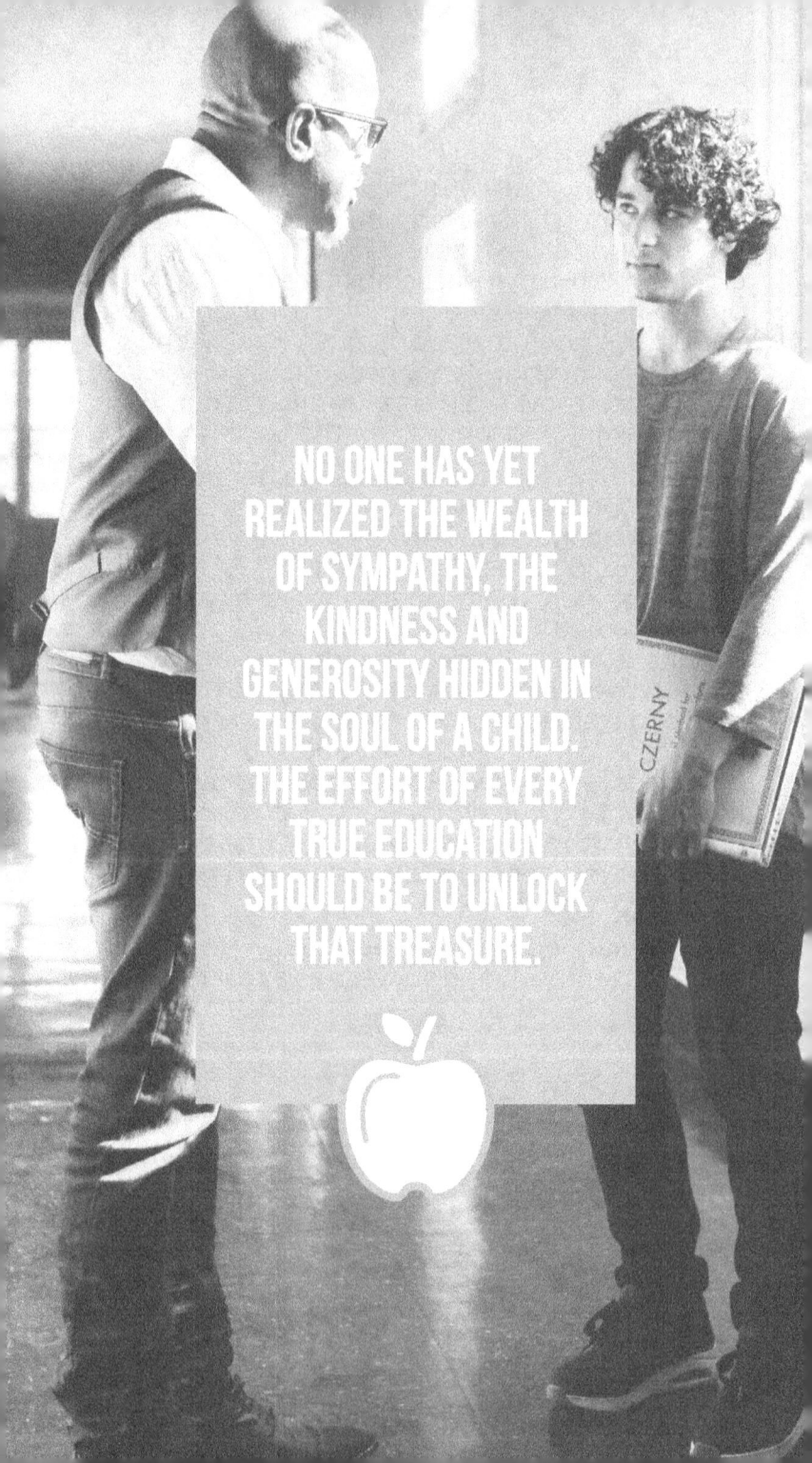

NO ONE HAS YET REALIZED THE WEALTH OF SYMPATHY, THE KINDNESS AND GENEROSITY HIDDEN IN THE SOUL OF A CHILD. THE EFFORT OF EVERY TRUE EDUCATION SHOULD BE TO UNLOCK THAT TREASURE.

One day, a man was throwing a Frisbee with his ten-year-old son. They were standing a little farther apart than usual, and the father's first throw was a bit off. He grimaced, but concluded, No big deal. His second toss veered quickly to the left. He shook his head—two bad ones in a row. His third throw was no improvement over the first two.

"Sorry," he called to his son, "another bad throw." After the next toss, he found himself saying, "Oh, no. Bad throw again!" And after yet another toss, "Sorry, son, it looks like nothing but bad throws today."

His son held the Frisbee and stood perfectly still for a moment. He looked thoughtfully at his dad and then said, "Dad, don't say 'bad throw.' It's a good chance for me to make a great catch!"

No matter how much a student may act out or misbehave, try on a new perspective. The behavior you see may be bad, but it also is an opportunity for you to become an even better teacher, perhaps even a great teacher! Your patient and consistent efforts to help a child develop character and unlock potential are never in vain, even though you may not see immediate fruit. God is able to work all things together for good.[110]

But encourage one another day after day, as long as it is still called "Today."

HEBREWS 3:13 NASB

HE WHO OPENS A SCHOOL DOOR CLOSES A PRISON.

A father once was asked to tell his son a bedtime story. He made up a fairly elaborate tale about a lost lamb that had found a hole in the fence and crawled through. The father went into great detail about how glad the lamb had been to leave the flock, and how a frightened the lamb was when it realized it couldn't a find its way back. The son's eyes grew wide when the father told about a wolf that chased the lamb, and then he relaxed as the father told how a shepherd had gone in search of the lamb, found it, and carried it back home on his shoulders. The little boy had only one question at the end of the tale: "Did they fix the hole in the fence?"

The best hope for curing juvenile delinquency and teenage gang violence lies in prevention. If we are able to influence children to believe in God's love and forgiveness and to share with them the bright future and hope that God has for them, we can do a great deal as teachers to turn the tide against crime.

Ask God today to reveal how to reach your students. Ask, "What will give them hope? What will cause them to dream big dreams and to work hard to reach them? What will cause them to trust You for Your help?"[111]

Each of you should look not only to your own interests, but also to the interests of others.

PHILIPPIANS 2:4 NIV

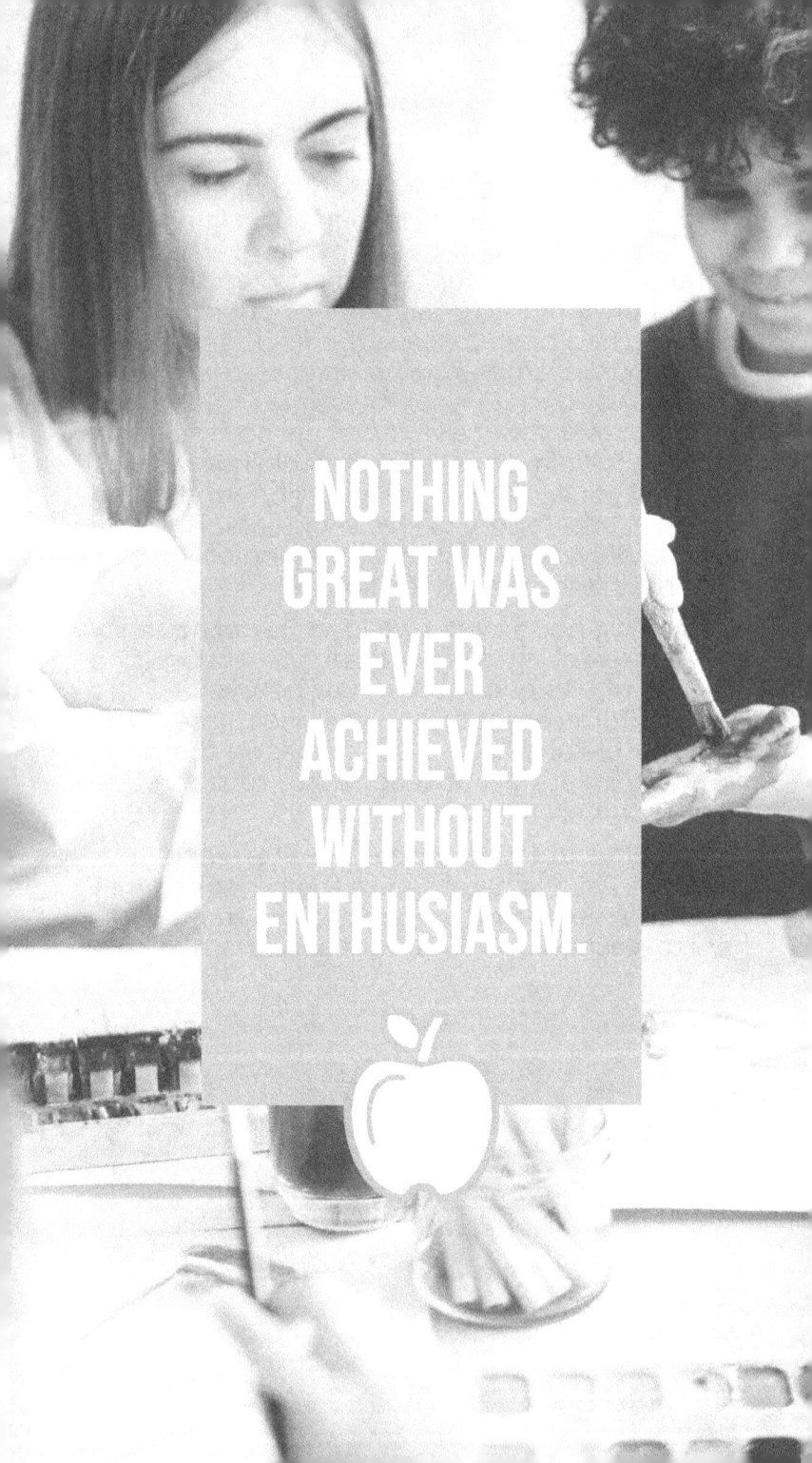

On the first day of class, a college teacher found that he had twenty-nine football players in his introductory philosophy course. On the first exam, twenty-six of them bombed badly. What was he going to do? He wanted them to learn, and he didn't fed he could give them passing grades solely because they were on the football team. His solution was to form a dub for any student, athlete or non-athlete, who had made a grade of C or lower on any previous assignment. He called it "The Below C Level Club." The club's slogan: "Keep your head above water."

More than fifty students came to the first meeting, many of them from the football team. They were used to being winners on the field, and now they were confronted with a failure. Dropping the class would have been the easy way out, but they opted instead to give the same effort to their class as to their football practices. The teacher soon found that his own enthusiasm and commitment were contagious. He began to think of himself as their "philosophy coach." The result? Every student who made a D or F on the first test got a C+ or B on the second!

Try incorporating a "pep talk" into every lesson.[112]

For the joy of the Lord is your strength.

NEHEMIAH 8:10 TLB

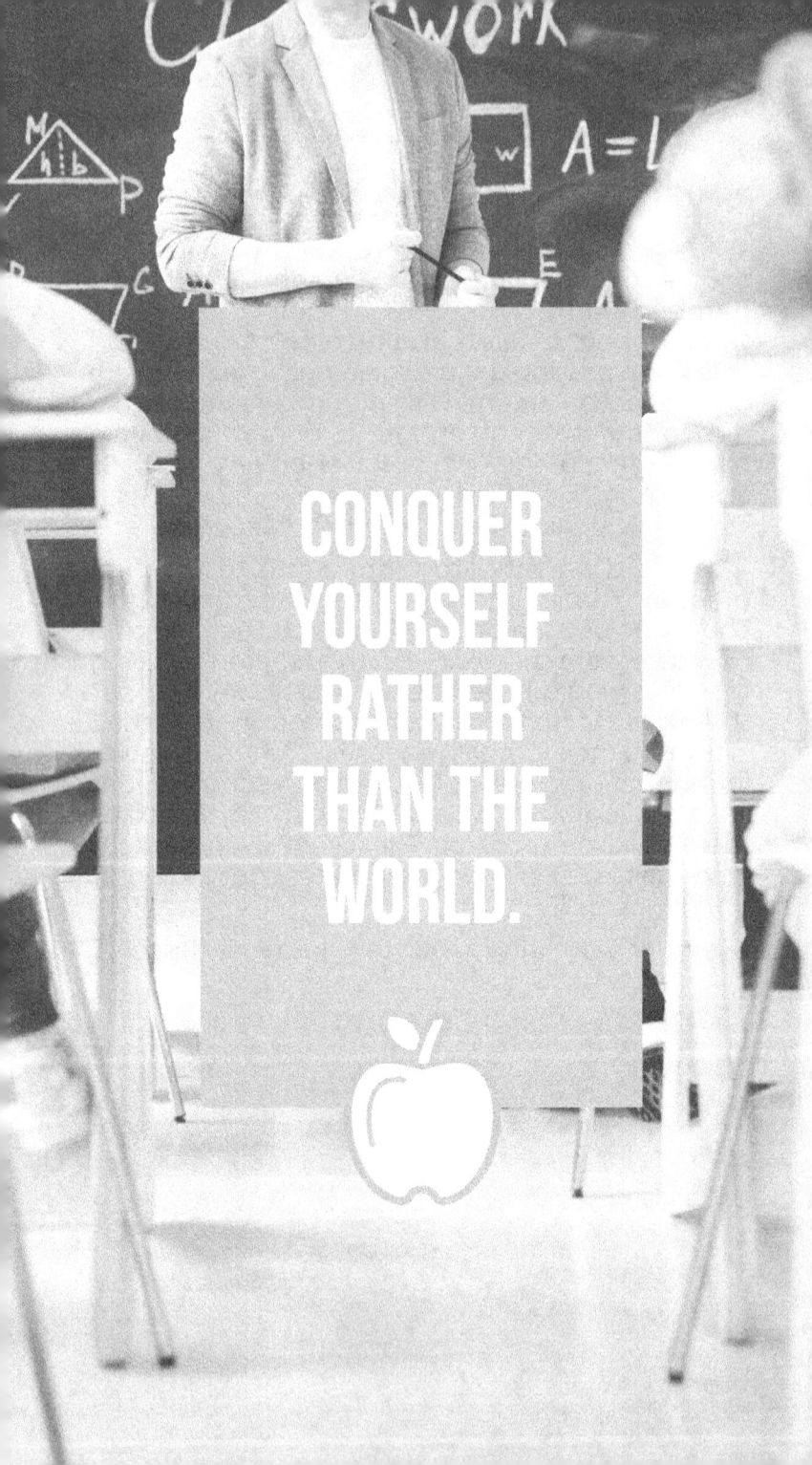

CONQUER
YOURSELF
RATHER
THAN THE
WORLD.

n 1975, an American doctor was invited to attend a conference in Finland. The conference was aimed at seeking a better understanding as to why heart disease was at epidemic proportions in Finland At a banquet held during the conference, Finland's president asked the doctor if he could explain the reason for this disturbing trend.

"Finland" the doctor said "has gone to war thirty- nine times in two hundred years. And Finland has never won!" The doctor went on to cite the fact that the Finns bordered the Soviet Union at that time. In fact, the closer a Finn lived to the border, more likely he was to die prematurely. In 1944, the Soviets had annexed a fifty-mile-wide strip of Finland property that was a beloved home to many Finns, and the people who forcibly were relocated never adjusted to this loss in their hearts and minds. Stress was a constant in their lives, and the stress, in turn, was linked to heart problems.

Don't allow students to dictate your mood—or your stress level. Instead pray, "God grant me the serenity to accept the things I cannot change, the courage to change the things I can, and the wisdom to know the difference."[113]

Similarly, encourage the young men to be self-controlled.

TITUS 2:6 NIV

A GOOD
REPUTATION
IS MORE
VALUABLE
THAN MONEY.

Amazing and heartwarming stories are told about a kind, Australian nurse whose gift was helping children to walk, especially those crippled with infantile paralysis. Sister Elizabeth Kenny is known all around the world.

On a trip to the United States, she was asked to demonstrate her treatments in several large hospitals. One day, one of her admirers asked what had motivated her to such success in her field. She replied quietly, "I'm no genius. I'm just a very ordinary person who still remembers and puts into action the stories my mother told me from the Bible."

Those who desire to know Jesus, to love as He loved, and to help others as He helped them are going to gain a reputation as friends of Jesus. They can be identified by their great interest in the happiness, health, and spiritual well-being of all. In that, they are like Jesus in spirit and purpose.

What motivates you as a teacher? What kind of reputation do you desire—not only as a teacher, but as a person?[114]

A good name is rather to be chosen than great riches.

PROVERBS 22:1

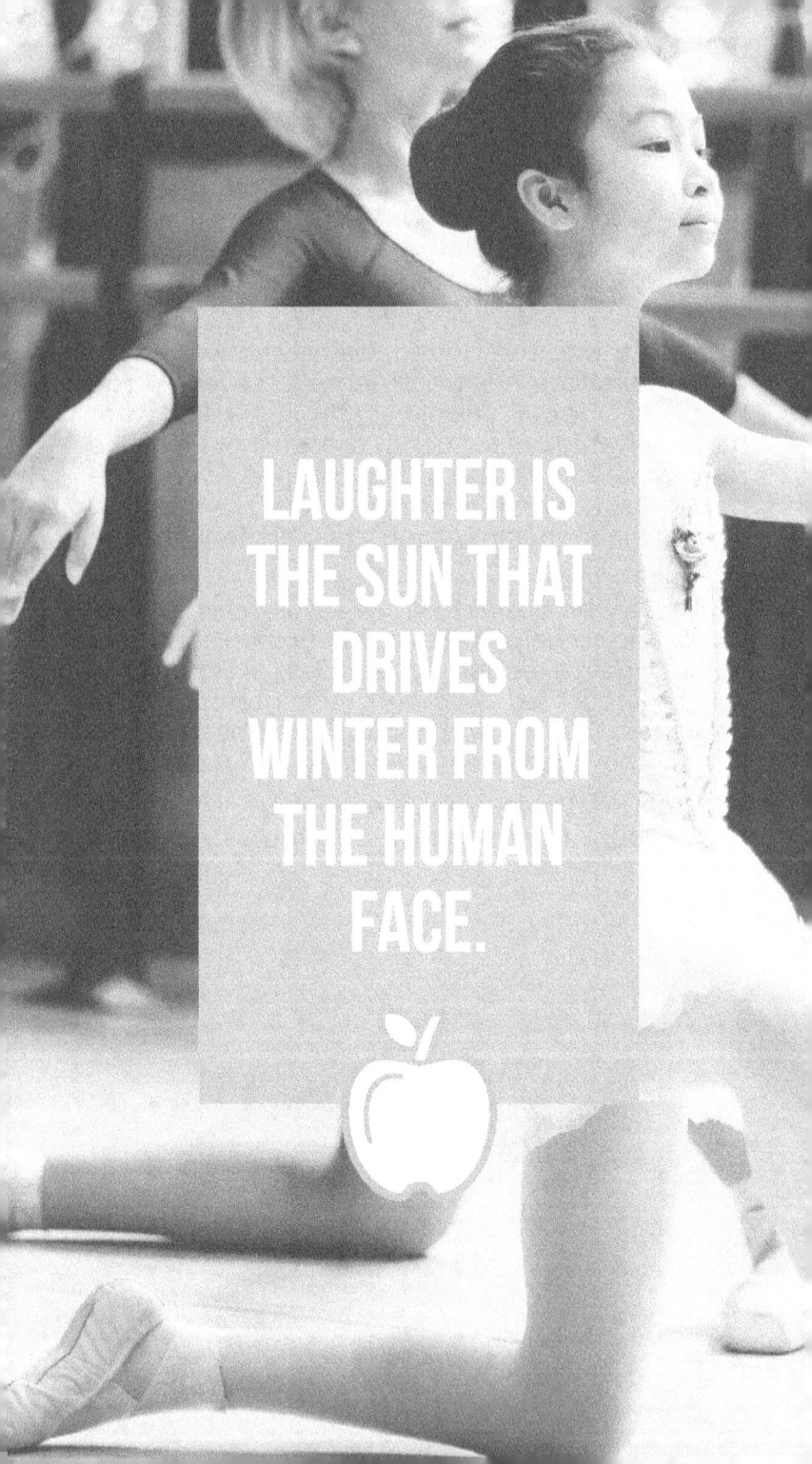

LAUGHTER IS
THE SUN THAT
DRIVES
WINTER FROM
THE HUMAN
FACE.

Jessica, a cute five-year-old, simply could not pronounce the word spaghetti. The harder she tried, the funnier the word seemed to come out. "Pasghetti," she would stammer. "No, I mean . . . saphetti." She usually ended up in tears because she was so humiliated that she couldn't conquer this one word.

Finally, her father advised her, "Jessica, don't take it so seriously. If you make a mistake, so what! Just laugh about it. You won't be embarrassed about it if you are the first one to laugh."

Jessica gave his advice a try. The next time she mispronounced spaghetti, she laughed at herself. She was amazed others laughed with her. They were having a genuinely good time with her, but as long as Jessica laughed first, neither she nor they felt they were laughing at her. In fact, as Jessica grew older and finally was able to pronounce spaghetti correctly, she almost was disappointed. She missed the good times she and her friends had shared over her "goof."

Every teacher has foibles and human weaknesses. Choose to laugh at yourself, and watch your students laugh with you—not at you.[115]

A merry heart maketh a cheerful countenance, but by sorrow of the heart the spirit is broken.

PROVERBS 15:13

THE DIFFERENCE
BETWEEN THE
RIGHT WORD AND
THE ALMOST RIGHT
WORD IS THE
DIFFERENCE
BETWEEN
LIGHTNING AND THE
LIGHTNING BUG.

John R. Bonee, a corporate communications expert, notes that word choice can make a difference in many areas, especially between a good speech and a great speech. He cites Franklin D. Roosevelt's declaration of war against Japan as an example.

Roosevelt's speech began with the words "December 7, 1941: A day that will live in infamy." The original manuscript, Bonee has observed, began differently. FDR's speech writer had typed, "December 7, 1941: A day that will live in world history." Roosevelt replaced world history with infamy. By changing only one word, he created a statement that can still send a chill through millions who lived through World War II.

The noted novelist Ernest Hemingway once was asked why he rewrote *For Whom the Bell Tolls* five times. The questioner wanted to know what was so difficult. Hemingway reportedly replied, "Getting the words right."

The childhood rhyme, "Sticks and stones may break my bones, but words can never hurt me," simply isn't true. Words matter! They convey emotional and spiritual life or death. As a teacher, it is especially important to choose your words wisely.[116]

A word aptly spoken is like apples of gold in settings of silver.

PROVERBS 25:11

EVERY CALLING IS GREAT WHEN GREATLY PURSUED.

One of the highest honors for any French chef is to be listed as chef of a three-star restaurant in the *Michelin Guide* to fine dining. In 1995, the Guide added to its three-star listing the Auberge de l'Eridan in Annecy, France. The owner and self-taught chef, Marc Veyrat, is considered by his peers and culinary critics to be something of a maverick. His unorthodox use of ingredients got him expelled from three hotel culinary schools, and local hotels in his home city would not even take him on as a kitchen apprentice.

Veyrat is from the French Alps. Key ingredients in his recipes are fresh alpine herbs, such as caraway, cumin, wild thyme, and chenopodium. Once a week at dawn, Veyrat ventures into the mountains to pick the herbs he will use throughout the week. Veyrat has said, "I know I'm not a traditional chef. I'm a student of nature because before you love cuisine, you have to love the ingredients."

To become a great teacher, a good teacher must first love learning. The teacher who never tires of learning is a teacher who will learn from students, as well as from books, experiences, events, and other sources. Such a teacher will always be open to new ideas and applications.[117]

I press toward the mark for the prize of the high calling of God in Christ Jesus.

PHILIPPIANS 3:14

PATIENCE IS BITTER, BUT ITS FRUIT IS SWEET.

A traditional Hebrew legend tells the story of Abraham and an encounter he had one evening with an old man who came to his tent. Abraham rushed out to greet the weary traveler and invite him into his tent for rest and refreshment. He washed the old man's feet and then served him food and drink. To Abraham's surprise, the old man immediately began to eat without saying a prayer or blessing. Abraham asked, "Don't you worship God?"

The old man replied, "I only worship fire. I have no other god."

Incensed, Abraham grabbed the old man by the shoulders and threw him out of his tent into the cdd night air After the old man shuffled away, God called to His friend, Abraham, and asked the whereabouts of the stranger. Abraham answered, "I sent him away because he did not worship You."

God answered, "I have suffered patiently with him for these eighty years, even though he dishonors Me and refuses even to recognize Me. And you could not put up with him for just one night?"

Any time you find yourself getting impatient with a student or school administrator, think about how long God has been dealing with you on some issues.[118]

You need to keep on patiently doing God's will if you want him to do for you all that he has promised.

HEBREWS 10:36 TLB

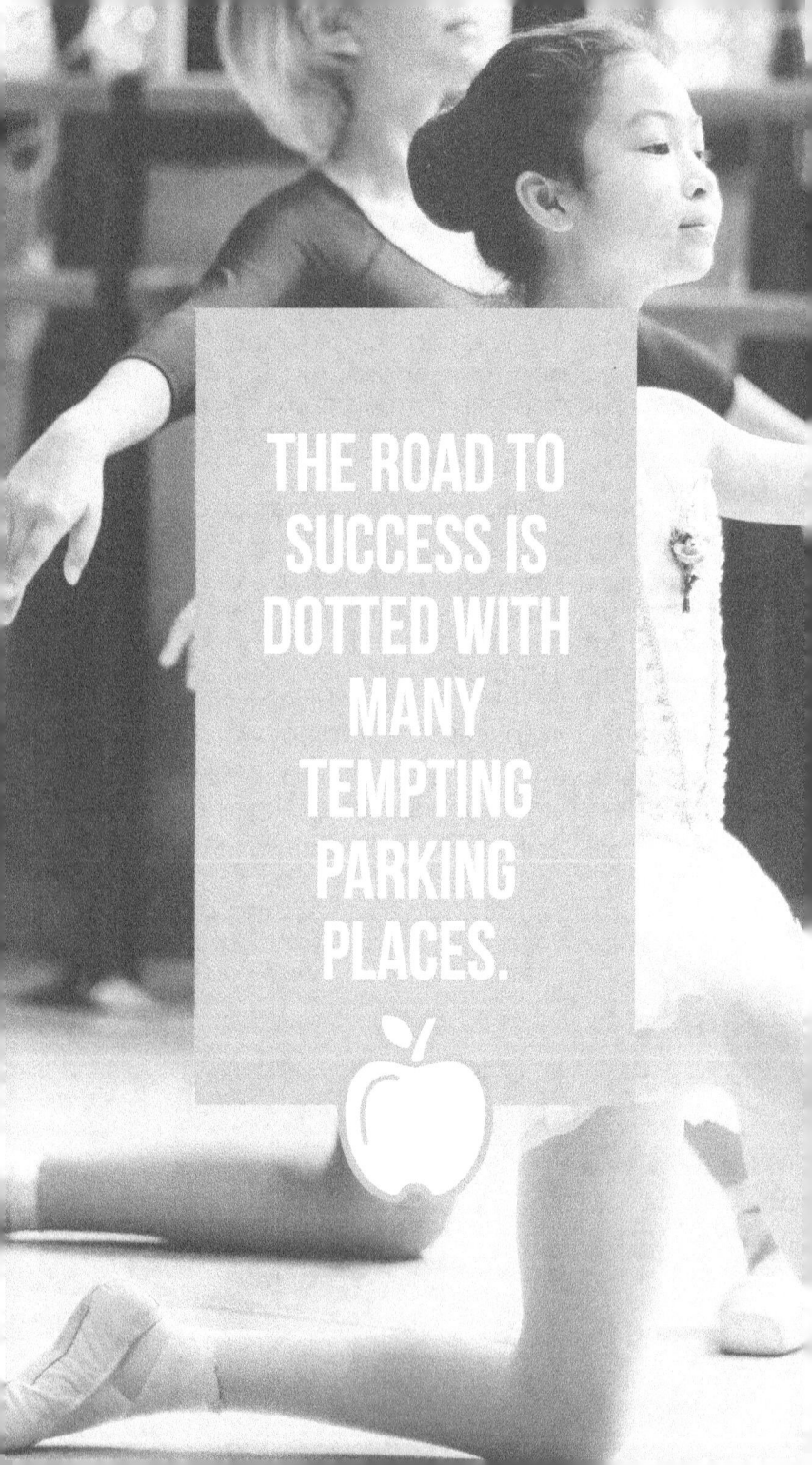

THE ROAD TO
SUCCESS IS
DOTTED WITH
MANY
TEMPTING
PARKING
PLACES.

A recently divorced man went to visit a friend who lived in the mountains. One night, the friend said, "Let's go hiking in the morning. You won't believe the view at sunrise from the top of the mountain." Morning seemed especially early that day, but before they had been on the trail ten minutes, the man realized the early hour was the least of his problems. He was out of breath and in pain. "Are you okay?" his friend asked.

"Oh, yes," he gasped. "Fine." The climb that would have taken an experienced hiker less than an hour took twice that long because of frequent stops to rest and drink water. At each stop, the man saw new and beautiful sights. *Why keep climbing?* he thought. *Things look fine here!*

Once at the top, however, the man realized what he g would have missed if he had stayed down below. The view was breathtaking! As he rested atop the peak, he saw parallels in his own life. The emotional trauma of his divorce had made him want to hide, or at least, stand still. He realized that if he was ever going to feel joy again, he needed to keep moving. The best direction, he concluded is the one God has for each of us.

As teachers, let's move forward and higher![119]

Let us lay aside every weight, and the sin which doth so easily beset us, and let us run with patience the race that is set before us.

HEBREWS 12:1

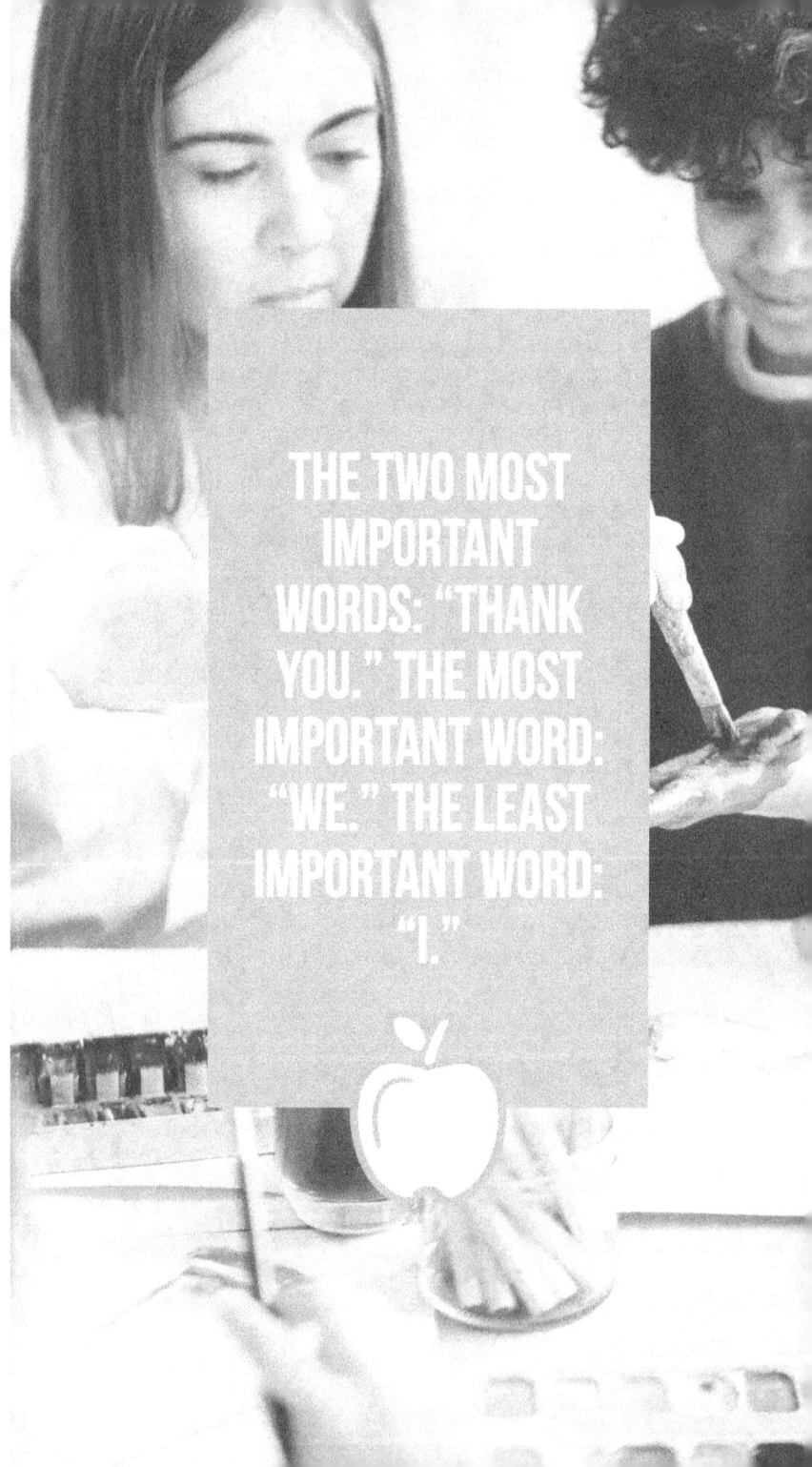

There once was a missionary woman, whom the Boxers in China had decided to execute for teaching about her western God. Forced to kneel so she might be beheaded, she looked up into her executioner's face and smiled. Without thinking, he smiled back. Then he stepped back a little . . . and stepped back a little more. Finally he turned around and walked away. As he and the other Boxers retreated, he turned and said to her, "You cannot die. You are immortal."

To this angry and hate-filled man, this woman's smile seemed supernatural. When she should have shown fear, she expressed love and concern.

Those who are self-centered rarely smile; those who are other-centered are quick to smile. A smile is always an expression of an inner heart, looking outward. It is a bridge to the soul of another person—the nonverbal expression of "we" and the unspoken expression of "thank you," "I care," and "I count you as valuable."

Give a personal smile to each of your students today?[120]

Don't be selfish . . . Be humble, thinking of others as better than yourself.

PHILIPPIANS 2:3 TLB

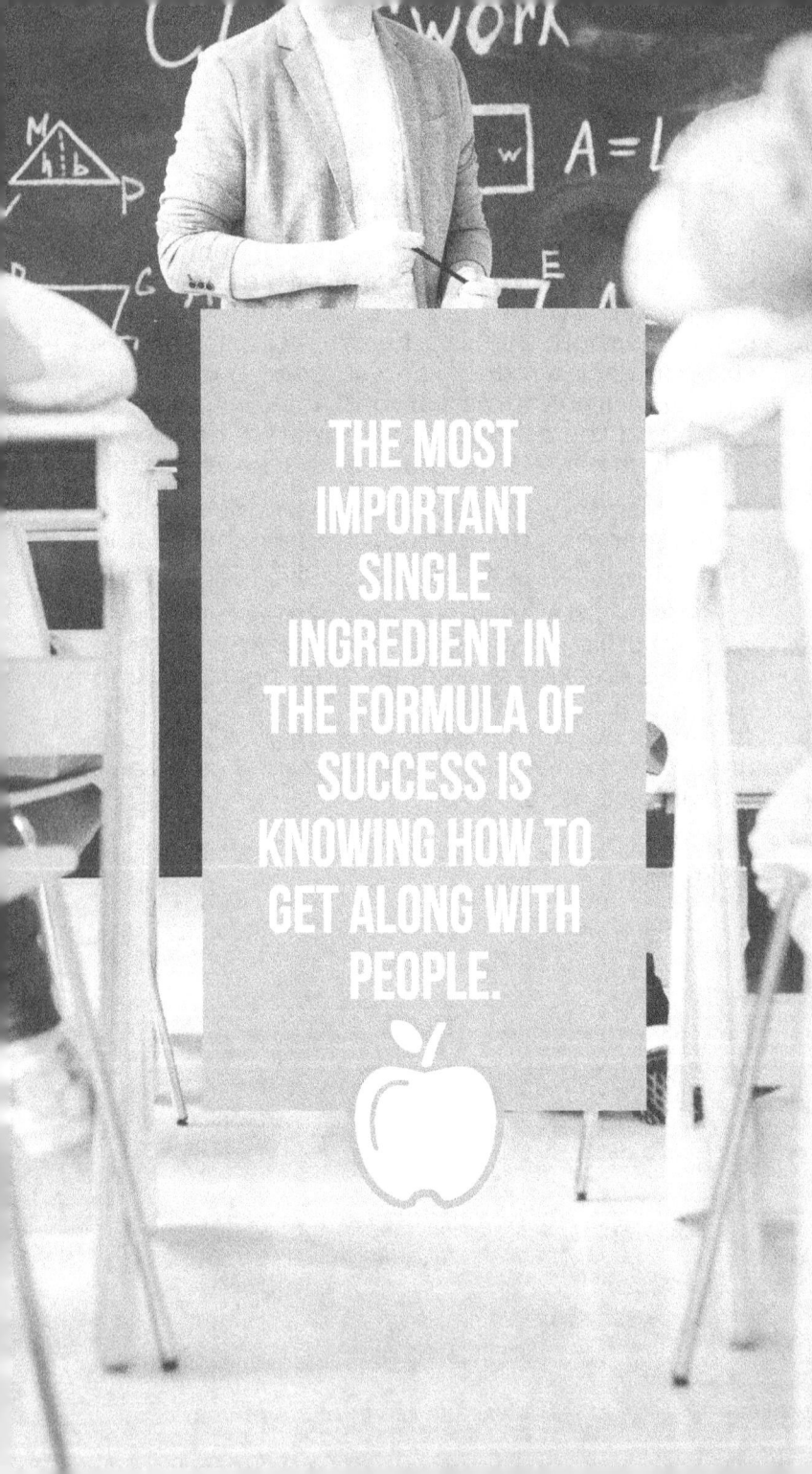

THE MOST IMPORTANT SINGLE INGREDIENT IN THE FORMULA OF SUCCESS IS KNOWING HOW TO GET ALONG WITH PEOPLE.

Jill Brand was only ten years old when she first began to sit with her grandmother behind the register at her Manhattan pharmacy. Before long, Jill was sitting at the register alone, having learned to treat customers politely and say "thank you" for each purchase. At first, she was paid in candy, but later she received fifty cents an hour. She worked every day after school, on weekends, and during the summer.

When Jill was twelve, her grandmother promoted her to selling cosmetics. She developed the ability to look each customer directly in the eye, taking a genuine interest in her customer's questions and translating them into make-up ideas. She sold a record amount of cosmetics. Says Jill, "That job taught me . . . to be a successful salesperson, you didn't need to be a rocket scientist—you needed to be a great listener. Today I still carry that lesson with me: I listen to customers."

Today those customers tend to be children who tell her which toys they want to see designed and developed. Jill is now chairman and CEO of Mattel, Inc., the world's largest toy maker.

Listening is more important than talking in virtually every profession, and especially so in teaching. It is in listening that we learn what to say.[21]

See that no one pays back evil for evil, but always try to do good to each other and to everyone else.

1 THESSALONIANS 5:15 TLB

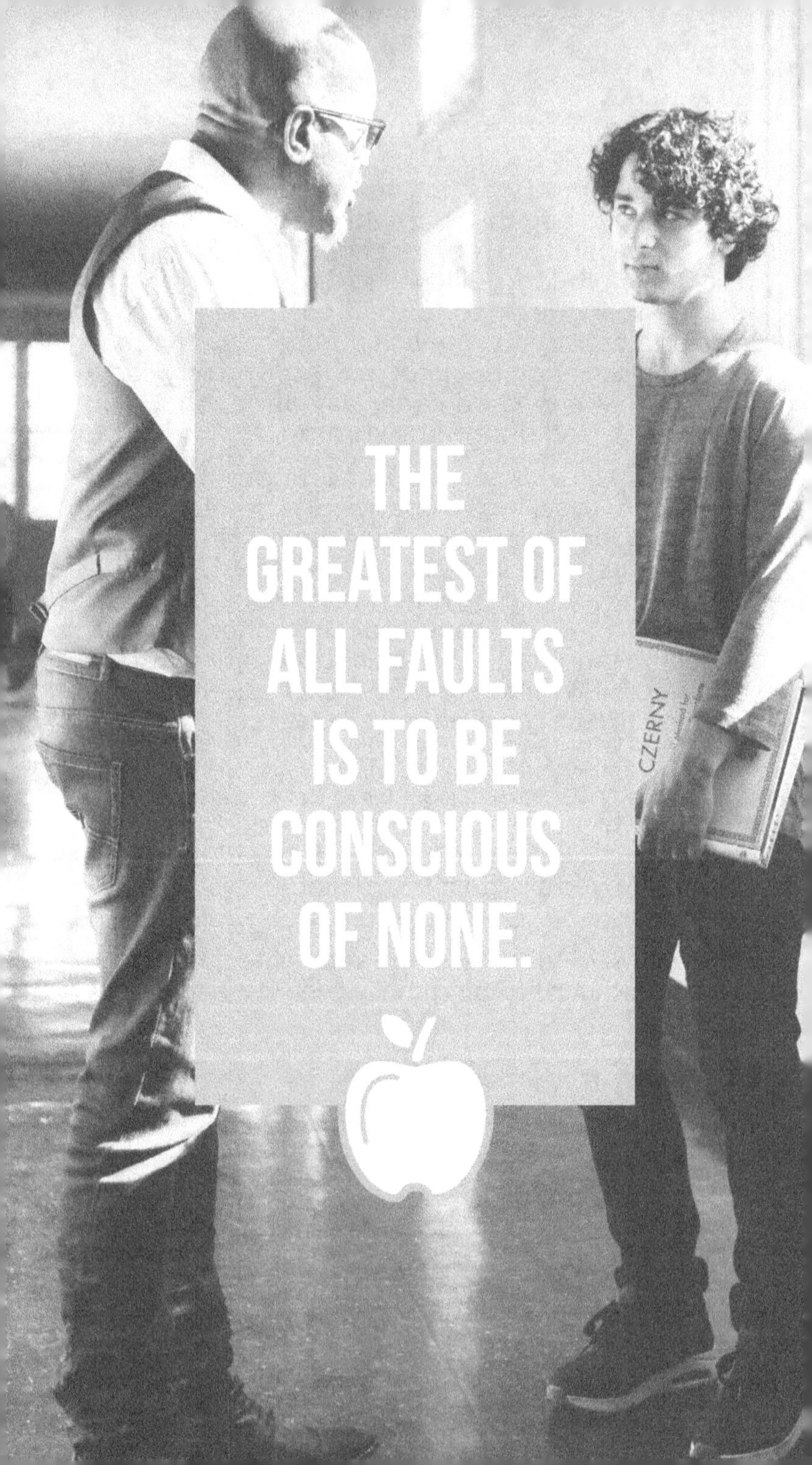

THE
GREATEST OF
ALL FAULTS
IS TO BE
CONSCIOUS
OF NONE.

A man once heard a top executive boast that he regularly gave positive feedback to his subordinates on their job performance. The man was encouraged that a top executive did this routinely and wanted to know more. He went to the man's place of business. The executive was not available, so he asked to speak to one of his subordinates. The receptionist asked which one. The man decided if what the executive had said was true, it wouldn't really matter. "Any one of them will do," he said.

Soon, one of the executive's assistants came to the lobby, and the man told him the reason for his visit "I heard that the top executive gives regular positive feedback to his subordinates on their job performance. I'd like to know if this is so, and if so, how frequently he does it."

The subordinate laughed loudly at the question and said, "Come with me back to my office, and I'll tell you exactly the last time he told me I was doing well. It was so unusual, I wrote it down on my calendar."

When you are grading your students' answers, grade your own as well. Ask God today to help you see yourself as others see you and correct the faults you find.[122]

A man's own folly ruins his life, yet his heart rages against the Lord.

PROVERBS 19:3 NIV

PEOPLE WITH
TACT HAVE
LESS TO
RETRACT.

A woman once took her son to a restaurant, and he asked if he could say grace. He prayed, "God is great. God is good. Thank you for the food, and I would thank you even more if Mom gets us ice cream for dessert. And liberty and justice for all! Amen!"

Several diners overheard the prayer and laughed. However, one woman remarked indignantly, "That's s what's wrong with our country. Kids don't know how to pray. Imagine asking God for ice cream!"

Upon hearing her, the boy burst into tears, asking, "Did I do it wrong? Is God mad?"

His mother comforted him, and then an elderly man came to the table, winked at the boy, and said, "I happen to know God thought that was a great prayer." He pointed to the critical woman and whispered, "Too bad she never asks God for ice cream. Ice cream is good for the soul sometimes."

When the mother ordered ice cream for dessert, her son stared at his sundae for a moment. Then he picked it up, walked over, and placed it in front of the critical woman. With a big smile he said, "This is for you. Ice cream is good for the soul sometimes, and my soul is already good."

What have you been saying to your students? Encouragement rarely requires an apology.[123]

The heart of the righteous weighs its answers, but the mouth of the wicked gushes evil.

PROVERBS 15:28 NIV

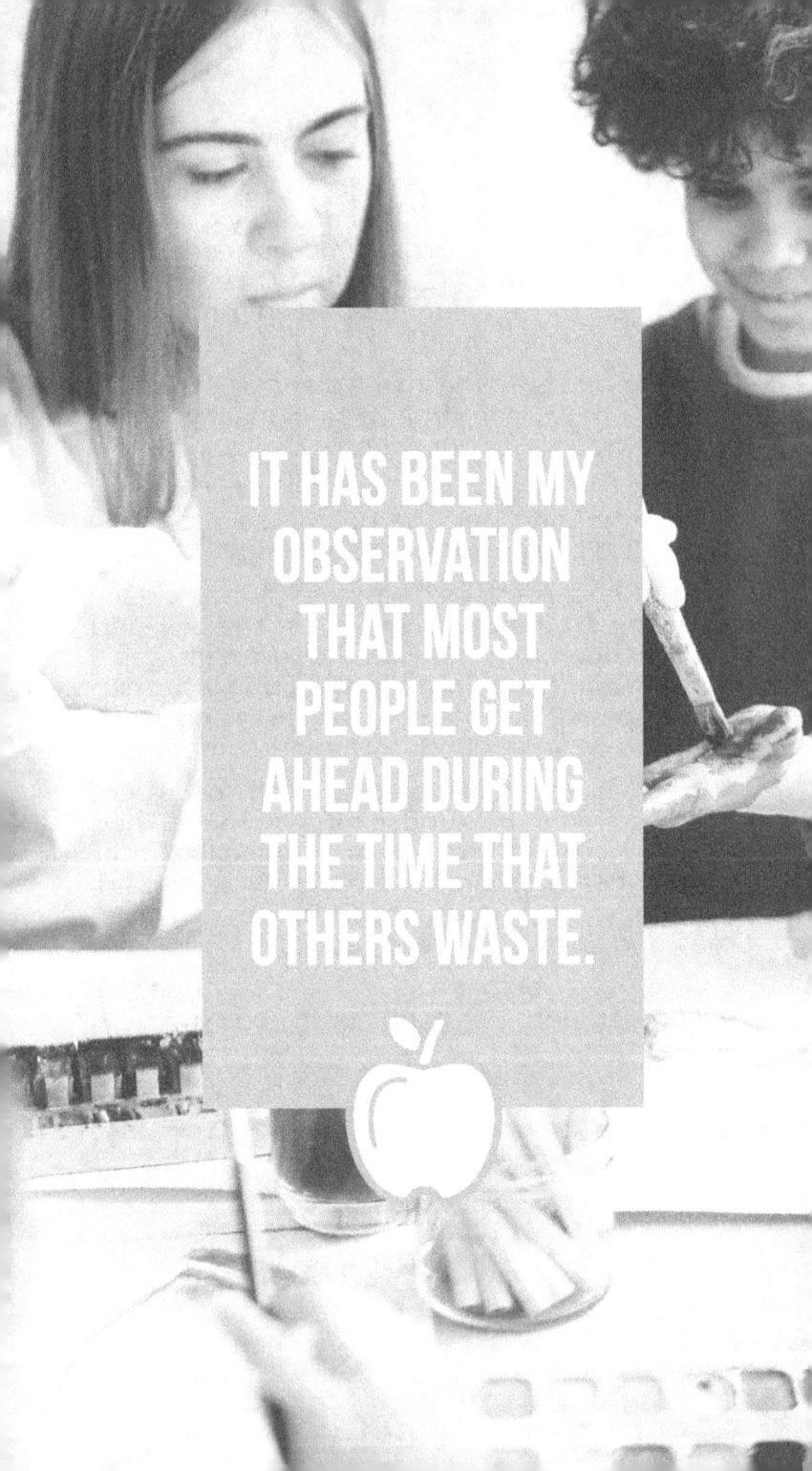

IT HAS BEEN MY OBSERVATION THAT MOST PEOPLE GET AHEAD DURING THE TIME THAT OTHERS WASTE.

Henry Ford considered the following tasks detrimental to a person's ability to be successful:

· They make too many telephone calls.

· They write letters that are three times as long as necessary.

· They work on little things and neglect big ones.

· They visit too often and stay too long on each visit.

· They read things that neither inform nor inspire them

· They spend hours with people who cannot stimulate them.

· They read every word of advertising circulars.

· They pause to explain why they did what they did when they should be working on the next thing.

· They hurry to the movies when they should be going to night school.

· They daydream at work when they should be planning ahead for their job.

· They spend time and energy on things that don't count.

Diligence includes the ability to focus and streamline your activities. Ask God to help you take full advantage of your time in the classroom.[124]

The plans of the diligent lead to profit as surely as haste leads to poverty.

PROVERBS 21:5 NIV

THE FIRST RULE OF HOLES: WHEN YOU'RE IN ONE, STOP DIGGING.

In *The Wonderful Spirit-Filled Life*, Charles Stanley writes: "In water-safety courses a cardinal rule is never I to swim out to a drowning man and try to help him as long as he is thrashing about. To do so is to commit suicide. As long as a drowning man thinks he can help himself, he is dangerous to anyone who tries to help him. His tendency is to grab the one trying to aid him and take them both down in the process.

"The correct procedure is to stay just far enough away so that he can't grab you. Then you wait. And when he finally gives up, you make your move. At that I point the one drowning is pliable. He won't work against I you. He will let you help."

It is wise to pray, "I can't do this job with my own strength and ability. I need You, God. Please help me to know what is right and best for the children that You have entrusted to my care." Such a prayer puts a teacher into the best possible position to receive help from the Master Teacher—the One who knows all the questions, all the solutions, and all the answers for all of eternity![125]

He lifted me out of the slimy pit . . . he set my feet on a rock and gave me a firm place to stand. He put a new song in my mouth, a hymn of praise to our God.

PSALM 40:2-3 NIV

Mary and Abe Ayala watched helplessly as their teenage daughter, Anissa, struggled with chronic myelogenous leukemia. Since CML had a fatality rate of 100 percent, physicians offered only one hope; replace her sick bone marrow with the marrow cells of a compatible donor. Neither Abe nor Mary, nor Anissa's brother, Airon, nor any other close relative was a donor match. In spite of a massive effort by Mary to increase the number of potential marrow donors nationwide, no donor was found. The Ayalas had only one option left—have a baby. They knew Mary only had a very slim chance to conceive since Abe had previously undergone a vasectomy and that if a healthy baby was born, there would be only a 25 percent chance he or she could become a donor. Even so, they pursued their only option.

Mary became pregnant. Marissa was born, and within hours, they knew from tests that she was a match. When she was fourteen months old, Marissa donated marrow to her sister—and it took! Anissa recently passed the five-year mark since her transplant with a clean bill of health.

See those you teach today as God sees them—potential life-givers to a sick and troubled world.[126]

Jesus said, "Let the little children come to me, and do not hinder them, for the kingdom of heaven belongs to such as these."

MATTHEW 19:14 NIV

ADVERSITY
MAKES A
MAN WISE,
NOT RICH.

Greg was a mover and shaker. As soon as he earned his MBA, he hit the ground running. Soon he was an executive. At age thirty, he started his own company, and success continued to follow him.

Unfortunately, Greg developed overconfidence. He spent too much time on the road, delegated too much responsibility, and lost touch with what his subordinates were doing. His business ended in failure.

At that point, Greg sought out his pastor for counsel. He suggested Greg count his blessings instead of his failures. He also suggested Greg "get out of himself" and volunteer at a local homeless shelter. At first Greg was insulted, but he finally agreed to go.

As Greg worked at the shelter, he wondered how it survived. He offered his services as a paid fund-raiser for the shelter, and in the process he found his true calling. The shelter grew and benefited from Greg's business skills, but Greg benefited more. The man who had always "looked out for number one" found it more rewarding to help others make it to the head of the line.

Teachers are helpers—not masters.[127]

Do not wear yourself out to get rich; have the wisdom to show restraint.

PROVERBS 23:4 NIV

BE SLOW IN CHOOSING A FRIEND, BUT SLOWER IN CHANGING HIM.

Late in the nineteenth century, one of the world's most distinguished astronomers was Sir Percival Lowell. In 1877, he heard an Italian astronomer had seen straight lines criss-crossing the surface of Mars. Lowell spent the rest of his life squinting into the eyepiece of a giant telescope in Arizona and mapping the channels and canals he saw. He was convinced the canals were proof of intelligent life on the red planet. Lowell was such a prominent scientist no one dared contradict him.

Today, the entire planet has been mapped; no canals were found. How could Lowell have seen so much that didn't exist? Lowell suffered from a rare eye disease that made him see the blood vessels in his own eyes. The canals were his own bulging veins. The malady is now called Lowell's Syndrome.

We must be cautious when we think we see fatal personality flaws in our students. The faults we see may well be our own. And even if the faults of others are valid, there is little benefit in drawing sweeping conclusions or voicing criticism about them. Faults are best left in the realm of prayer, faith, hope, and love.[128]

My dear brothers, take note of this: Everyone should be quick to listen, slow to speak and slow to become angry.

JAMES 1:19 NIV

THERE IS NOTHING HIDDEN BETWEEN HEAVEN AND EARTH.

Surgeon Viggo Olsen was eager to build a hospital for the Bangladeshi people, especially after watching hundreds die of typhoid and cholera in the wake of a devastating typhoon. When he laid the official forms on the desk of the chief surveyor, however, the man laughed. "It will be impossible for us to survey tomorrow," he said, reminding Olsen of the monsoon season. Olsen insisted, but the official only shrugged and said, "It has been raining for days, and it will rain for days to come."

Olsen had seen other obstacles moved. He replied, "We are God's men doing God's work. He will take care of the rain."

That night, Olsen and a companion prayed urgently for God to stop the rain. It rained all night and was raining in the morning when they went to the surveyor's office. Although they protested loudly, the crew agreed to go with Olsen on the thirty-two mile trip to the hospital site. As they drove, the rains only intensified, but soon the rain stopped and a patch of blue sky emerged. Half an hour after arriving at the site, the sloping land had drained enough for the surveyors to do their work!

You may not be able to move mountains in your school—but God can.[129]

The earth is the Lord's, and everything in it, the world, and all who live in it.

PSALM 24:1 NIV

RESTFUL SLEEP IS A DIRECT RESULT OF A CLEAR CONSCIENCE.

Coach Cleveland Stroud and the Bulldogs of Rockdale County High School in Conyers, Georgia, chalked up twenty-one wins and only five losses in a march to the Georgia boys' basketball tournament.

They then won a dramatic come-from-behind victory in the state finals. Conyers fans were ecstatic!

The new trophy case in the high school gymnasium is bare, however. It seems that the Georgia High School Association deprived Rockdale County of the championship after school officials reported that a player on the team who was scholastically ineligible had played forty-five seconds in the first of the school's five post-season games.

"We didn't know he was ineligible at the time," Coach Stroud said. "We didn't know it until a few weeks ago. Some people have said that we should have just kept quiet about it, that it was just forty-five seconds and the player wasn't an impact player. But you've got to do what's honest and right and what the rules say. I told my team that people forget the scores of basketball games. They don't forget what you're made of."

Obedience and forgiveness are the keys to a clear conscience. They also are excellent sleeping aids![130]

And herein do I exercise myself, to have always a conscience void to offence toward God, and toward men.

ACTS 24:16

A DAY HEMMED IN PRAYER IS LESS LIKELY TO UNRAVEL.

John Burrill has written, "I do a full day of work in the office, run a six-room house with two active sons, and consider it easy. My wife has been ill for years, but my house could stand a 'white-glove' inspection any Sunday afternoon. I also have found time to canvass neighbors in support of a school bond issue and to serve as treasurer of a Boy Scout troop and as a P.T.A. committeeman."

Burrill's secrets: "Two fine sons and organization, partly. But the real answer is that we three take time every day for prayer. God does the rest. If everybody would spend a few minutes daily in quiet self-inspection and rearrangement of real values, homes would be homes: places where each member of the family gathers strength for the next day."

Paul Yongi Cho, pastor of the world's largest church in Seoul, South Korea, once noted, "The more I have to do, the more appointments and the more decisions I have to make, and the greater the responsibility God gives to me for others, the more I have to pray. When the church was smaller, I only prayed an hour a day. Now I pray three hours."

Prayer paves the path God asks us to walk, including the path down the hall to a classroom.[131]

Pray about everything; tell God your needs and don't forget to thank him for is answers. If you do this you will experience God's peace . . . His peace will keep your thoughts and your hearts quiet and at rest.

PHILIPPIANS 4:6-7 TLB

WHEN
ANGER RISES,
THINK OF THE
CONSEQUENCES.

An old fable tells the story of a young lion and a cougar. Both were thirsty, and they both happened to arrive at the local watering hole at the same time. They immediately began to argue about who should satisfy his thirst first.

The argument became heated, and each decided he was due the privilege of being first to quench his thirst. Rulership of the territory was at stake! Pride was at issue! As they stubbornly confronted each other, their emotions turned to rage. Their roars and screeches could be heard for miles as they moved closer and closer to entangling in battle.

Then they both noticed strange shadows skirting across the ground. Both looked up at the same time. Circling overhead was a flock of vultures, waiting for the loser to fall. Quietly, the two beasts turned and walked away. The thought of being devoured was all they needed to end their quarrel.

Lashing out in anger always has consequences —not only to the one who receives the lashing, but to the one who lashes out, and to any observers who happen to be nearby. Before you wreak havoc in your relationship with a problematic student, pause and ask God to provide His alternative— peace.[132]

Those who guard their lips preserve their lives, but those who speak rashly will come to ruin.

PROVERBS 13:3 NIV

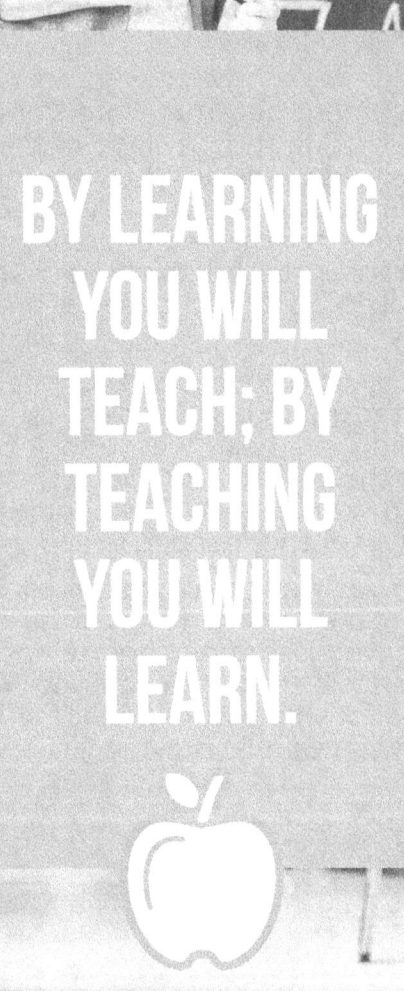

BY LEARNING
YOU WILL
TEACH; BY
TEACHING
YOU WILL
LEARN.

n *True Success*, Tom Morris writes, "A setback is not always bad." Morris learned this from personal experience. He lost several pages of his book after writing them out in longhand. For three days, he looked everywhere for them, both at home and at work. The search took up valuable writing time and produced little except unrelated items he had forgotten about.

A friend heard about Morris' problem and took it upon himself to search through a large, full dumpster outside his office building. He dug through mounds of refuse and paper, and within a couple of hours he knocked at Morris' office door and produced slightly wrinkled and "aromatic" sheets of paper. They were the lost pages!

Morris writes of the experience, "I learned some lessons and gained some insights I would have missed if things had gone smoothly and I never had lost those pages. Lessons that have helped me with my book. Insights that have helped me with my life." Ironically, the pages that Morris had lost were pages from a chapter in his book on "setbacks and detours!"

A wise teacher never stops learning from as many sources as possible.[133]

And the servant of the Lord must not be quarrelsome (fighting and contending). Instead, he must be kindly to everyone and mild-tempered [preserving the bond of peace]; he must be a skilled and suitable teacher, patient and forbearing and willing to suffer wrong.

2 TIMOTHY 2:24 AMP

Years ago, a minister spotted George T.B. Davis at one of his Sunday evening services. Mr. Davis was a well-known Christian leader who had led the distribution of several million copies of the New Testament to different nations and tribal groups. To the preacher's dismay, Mr. Davis left the meeting without his having a chance to talk to him. The minister went home and wrote a note, saying he was sorry to have missed speaking with him and outlining an idea that he hoped they might do together. He mailed the letter at midnight so Mr. Davis would receive it the next day.

In the morning's mail, the preacher found a note from Mr. Davis! In it he wrote that the Lord had laid it on his heart to write to him about a certain matter in which they might collaborate. He expressed precisely the same idea that the preacher had expressed! He, too, had mailed his letter at midnight.

A few moments after the mail arrived, the preacher's telephone rang. It was Mr. Davis. Within minutes the two had come into an agreement about the project—a project both believed had first been established by a spiritual agreement.

God arranges all things with precision in the lives of those teachers dedicated to doing His will.[134]

Who can put into words and tell the mighty deeds of the Lord? Or who can show forth all the praise [that is due Him]?

PSALM 106:2 AMP

All of her life, Sarah Flower Adams had dreamed of becoming a great actress. She had worked and studied toward that goal, and at last she had realized her ambition. She scored a dramatic triumph as Lady MacBeth and was hailed as a great actress. But then a devastating illness made her an invalid. For three years, she did little except lie in her bed and read her Bible and books about saints and martyrs. She also wrote poems, mostly on religious or Scriptural themes.

One day, her minister came to visit and found Sarah feeling sorry for herself. He quietly took her Bible from the shelf and opened it to the story of Jacob's vision of a ladder extending into heaven. Immediately, Sarah saw the parallel to her own life. She saw the darkness, the dream, the awakening, the sunshine, the triumph, the joy. She saw that each step of her suffering and affliction was a step that could bring her nearer to heaven, nearer to God. Almost without effort, she wrote all afternoon. The poem she produced became one of the world's most beloved hymns: "Nearer, My God, To Thee."

God can provide a calm center to the fiercest storm. Ask Him to create one in your heart and in your classroom today.[135]

And the peace of God, which transcends all understanding, will guard your hearts and your minds in Christ Jesus.

PHILIPPIANS 4:7 NIV

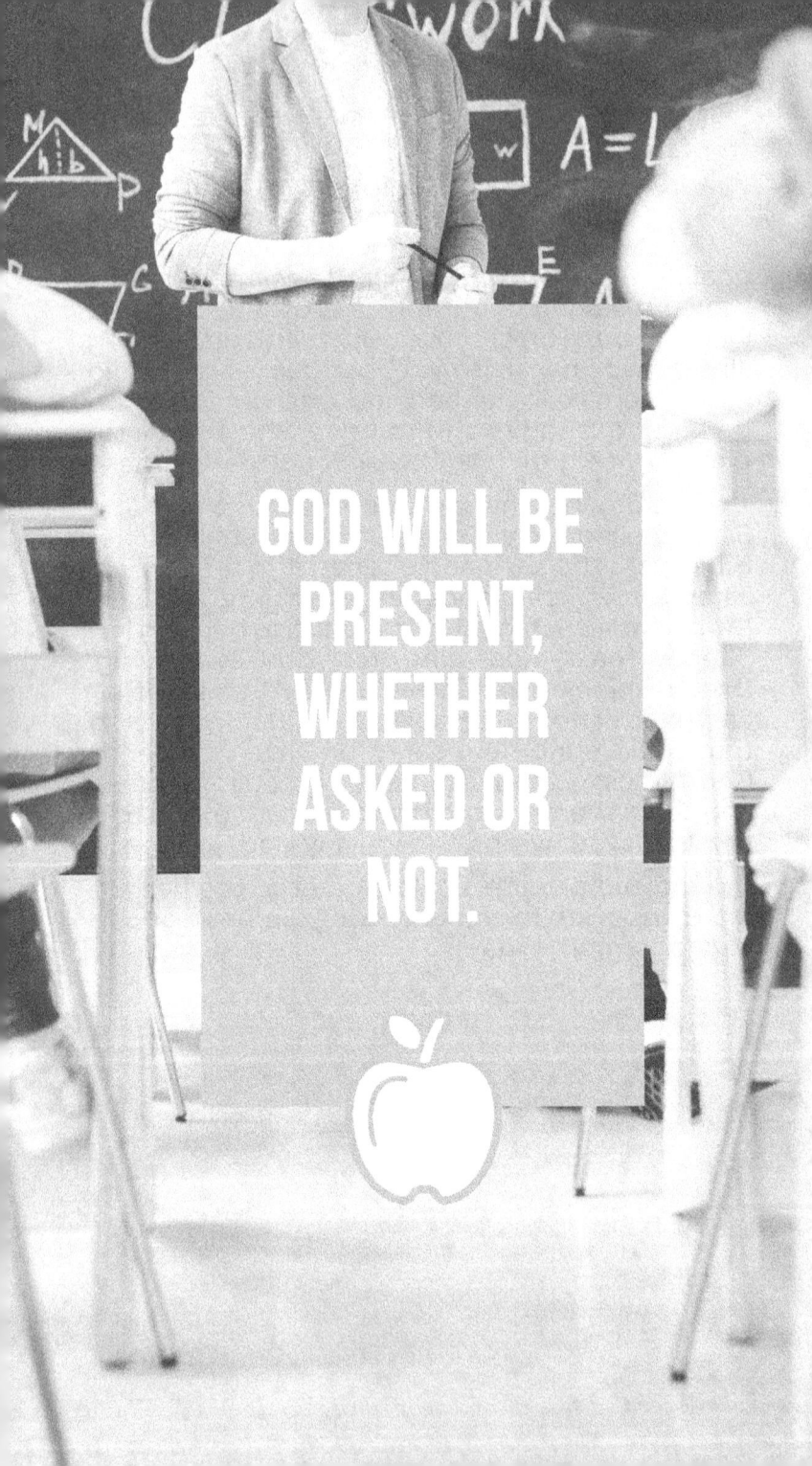

GOD WILL BE
PRESENT,
WHETHER
ASKED OR
NOT.

A Christian TV personality once partici-pated in a two-week crusade in Boston. While standing at the back of the hall after the evening's meeting, a couple walked up to her. They looked at each other and then the wife threw her arms around the woman and began to say, "Thank you, thank you, thank you."

The well-known woman was overwhelmed until the husband explained: "Two years ago, we were struggling financially. I had lost my job; it was a mess. I couldn't see a way out so I decided to make one. I decided to take my life. I checked into a cheap motel, and I had a gun. I was so desperate. I turned on the television and there you were. I hated Christian TV, but you said that God loved me. You told me that no matter how far away I felt, God loved me. I prayed with you, and I gave my life to God that night." Before she knew it, the woman was in tears herself. Sharing the Word of God in front of the cameras rarely gave her insight into just how God was using His own Word in the lives of those beyond the cameras.

We never fully know just how, when, and to what end God uses our words as teachers, but we can be assured that He uses them mightily, espe-cially when they are based on His Word, the Bible.[136]

The Lord reigns forever, he has
established his throne for judgment.

PSALM 9:7 NIV

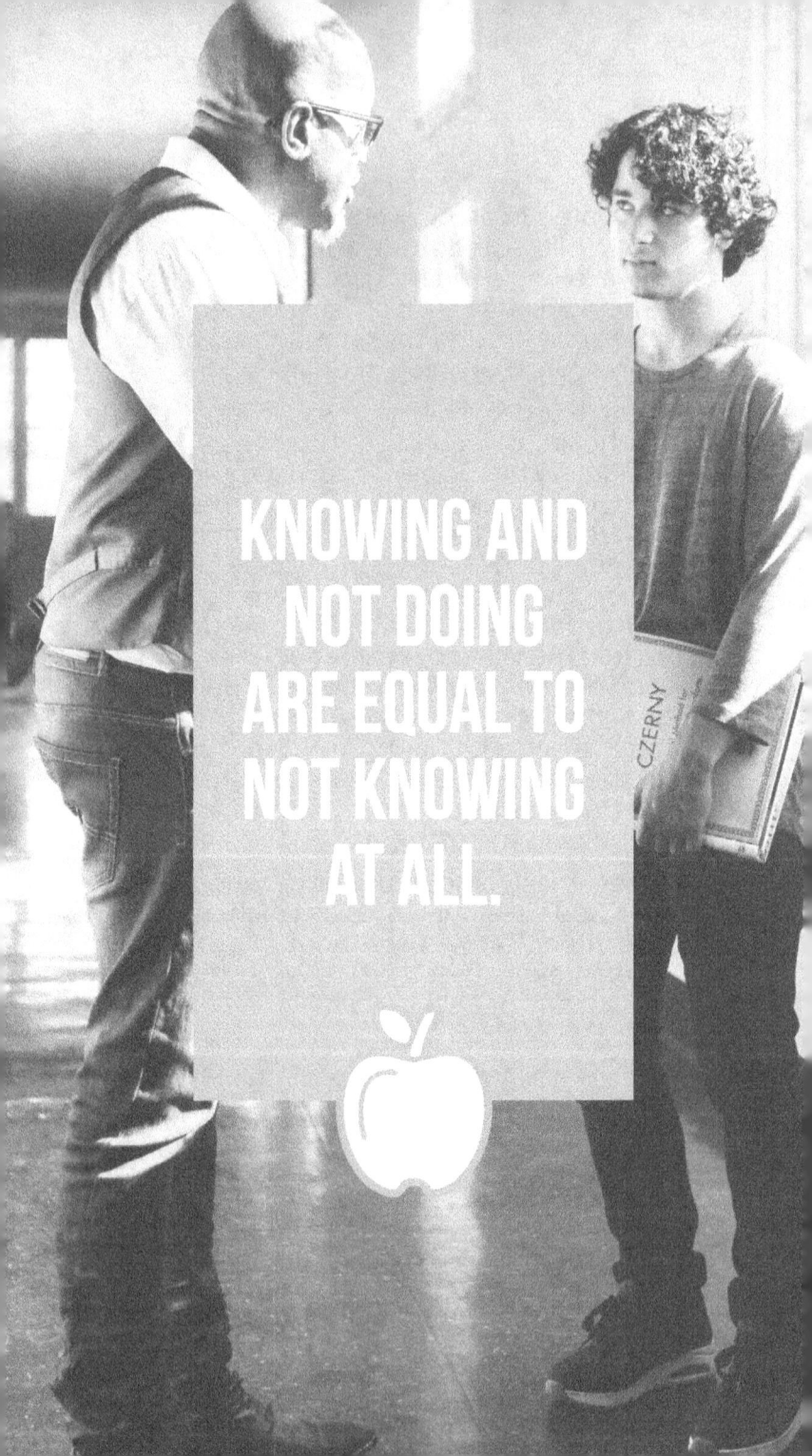

KNOWING AND
NOT DOING
ARE EQUAL TO
NOT KNOWING
AT ALL.

A missionary once faced the task of building a bed for his child who had grown to the point where his crib was no longer comfortable. After he had prepared the wood in an outside shed, his wife thought it too cold for him to work out there, so he brought the materials into the kitchen for assembly.

When the work was finished, the baby was brought to the kitchen and placed in the bed. Suddenly, the father had a disturbing thought What if the bed would not go through the door? Quickly, he measured the bed and door and discovered that the bed he had made was one inch too wide and one inch too high to pass through the doorway. Most of his work had been in vain.

Carpenters have a long-standing rule: measure twice and cut once. They know it takes less time to plan a project than to redo one.

The same is true in teaching and learning. To learn the wrong information is to learn nothing of value. To teach only part of the truth is to teach what can lead to error. Teach your students to plan wisely.[137]

Therefore, to one who knows the right thing to do and does not do it, to him it is sin.

JAMES 4:17 NASB

GOD PLUS ONE IS ALWAYS A MAJORITY!

When Dr. Ejnar Lundby visited Kristian Himler in prison, he found him lying on his bed, staring at the ceiling. Himler cursed him as he entered the cell Lundby knew Himler had been convicted of bombing a building in which an admired Norwegian leader died. He was facing execution in four days, but he seemed cold and unremorseful Lundby finally gave him a Bible and said, "You may not want to listen to me. But I've brought you the words of One who is divine and who can help you, because He cares for you in spite of all you've done."

The next day, Lundby returned to the prison. This time, Himler greeted Lundby warmly and thanked him for the Bible, which he had read all night. Himler prayed with Lundby to commit his life to Christ. He said, Tm ready to die now for the crime committed."

As Lundby prepared to leave, he suddenly turned and said to him, "Why did you lie to me?" Himler paled. His acceptance of Christ had been sincere, but he had lied about the bombing in an attempt to cover up for the real killer. Lundby embarked on a frantic effort to have Himler freed, and eventually he was released.

God knows more about how to help us as teachers than we know ourselves![138]

If God be for us, who can be against us?

ROMANS 8:31

A loving wife tried hard to please her ultra-critical husband. She rarely succeeded. He always seemed especially critical at breakfast. If she fried his eggs, he wanted them poached. If she poached them, he wanted them fried. One morning, she had an idea. She fried one egg and poached the other. She was certain he would approve, but instead he growled, "Can't you do anything right? You've scrambled the wrong one!"

A similar story involves a young man named Ted. Ted's boss asked him to pick up a newspaper on his way back from lunch. The boss then said to his secretary, "Ted has such a bad memory, I'm not sure he'll remember his way back to the office, much less bring a paper."

Just then Ted burst in the door. With great enthusiasm, he said, "Guess what? At lunch I ran into Smith. He hasn't given us an order in a year, but before lunch was over I talked him into a million-dollar contract!"

The boss sighed and said to his secretary, "I told you he'd forget the newspaper."

Most of us growl about things at school that really aren't important only uncomfortable or irritating. Let's focus on what really matters to making a difference in the lives of others.[140]

If it be possible, as much as lieth in you, live peaceably with all men.

ROMANS 12:18

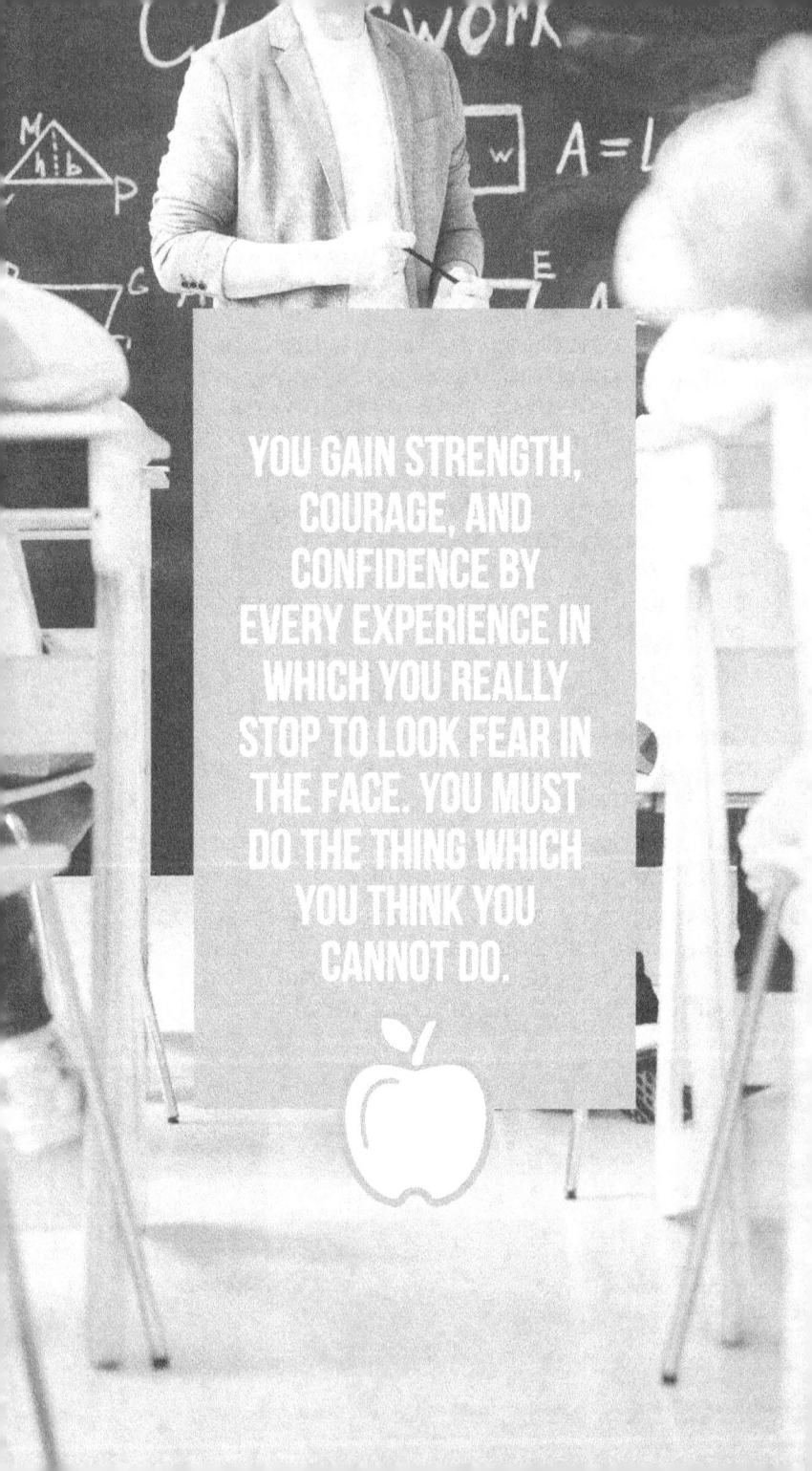

Montana rancher Lexy Lowler tried just about everything to stop the coyotes from killing her sheep. She used electric fences, odor sprays, and other devices. She tried placing battery-operated radios near them. She tried corralling them at night and herding them by day. She even tried sleeping with her lambs during the summer. Even with all of her efforts, she lost scores of lambs—fifty in one year alone!

Then Lexy tried llamas—the aggressive, funny-looking, fearless llamas generally associated with South America. She purchased several and began grazing them with her sheep. She said, "Llamas don't appear to be afraid of anything. When they see something, they put their heads up and walk straight toward it. That is aggressive behavior as far as the coyote is concerned, and they won't have anything to do with that. Coyotes are opportunists, and llamas take that opportunity I away." Not only did Lexy solve her problem, she gained the added benefit of llama wool spun into mohair!

Llamas intuitively seem to know the truth of the Bible; "Resist the devil, and he will flee from you" (James 4:7). When we are willing to resist evil in our schools, we take away an opportunity from the devil.[141]

Perseverance must finish its work so that you ma be mature and complete, not lacking anything.

JAMES 1:4 NIV

OUR CHILDREN
ARE LIKE
MIRRORS—
THEY REFLECT
OUR ATTITUDES
IN LIFE.

A reader recently sent this statement from an anonymous author to columnist Ann Landers:

"When you thought I wasn't looking . . .

". . . I saw you hang my first painting on the refrigerator, and I wanted to paint another one.

". . . I saw you feed a stray cat, and I thought it was good to be kind to animals.

". . . I saw you make my favorite cake just for me, and I knew that little things are special things.

". . . I heard you say a prayer, and I believed there is a God I could always talk to.

". . . I felt you kiss me goodnight, and I felt loved.

". . . I saw tears come from your eyes, and I learned that sometimes things hurt, but it's OK to cry.

". . . I saw that you cared, and I wanted to be everything that I could be.

"When you thought I wasn't looking, I looked —and wanted to say thanks for all the things I saw when you thought I wasn't looking."

Children are perhaps the ultimate "copycats." What you do today is what you will see your students do tomorrow.[142]

The just man walketh in his integrity; his children are blessed after him.

PROVERBS 20:7

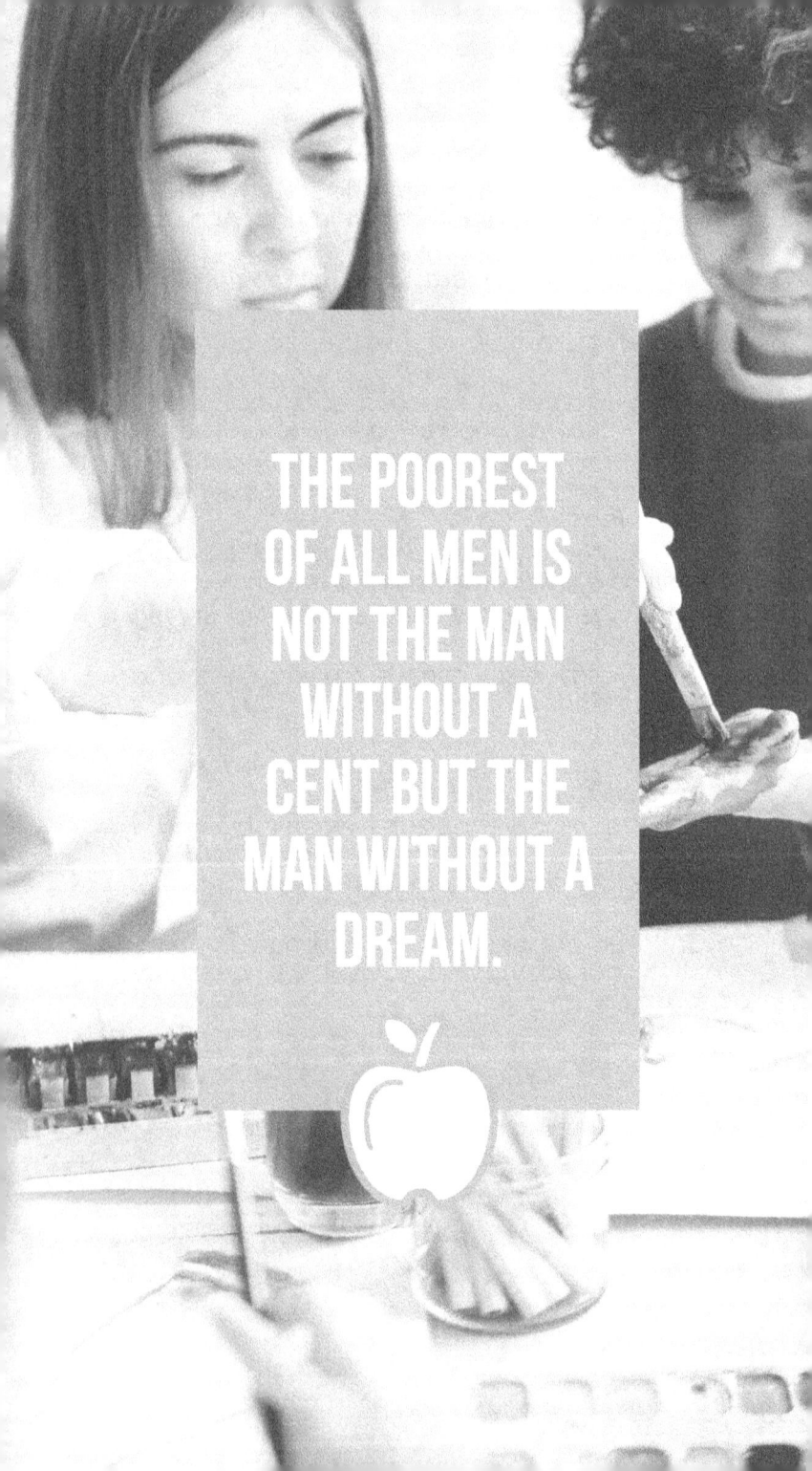

THE POOREST
OF ALL MEN IS
NOT THE MAN
WITHOUT A
CENT BUT THE
MAN WITHOUT A
DREAM.

Some three hundred and fifty years ago, a shipload of pioneers landed on the northeast coast of America. The first year, they established a town. The next year, they elected a town government. During the third year, the town government revealed plans to build a road five miles west into the wilderness.

In the fourth year, the people tried to impeach their government because they thought it a waste of public money to construct a road five miles westward into an unknown territory. Almost to the person, they voiced the opinion, "Why go there?"

These people had once had no trouble envisioning their own travel across three-thousand miles of ocean or setting their minds on overcoming the great hardships they knew such a voyage and new life would entail. But in four short years, they could not see five miles out of town! They had lost their pioneering spirit and their vision for what might be.

We lose heart any time we allow difficulty and stress to rob us of our God-given vision to see a better tomorrow, to see a failing student as succeeding, to see a task becoming easier, or to see talent emerging from a quiet and withdrawn child.

Ask God to renew your vision and your courage.[143]

Where there is no vision, the people perish.

PROVERBS 29:18

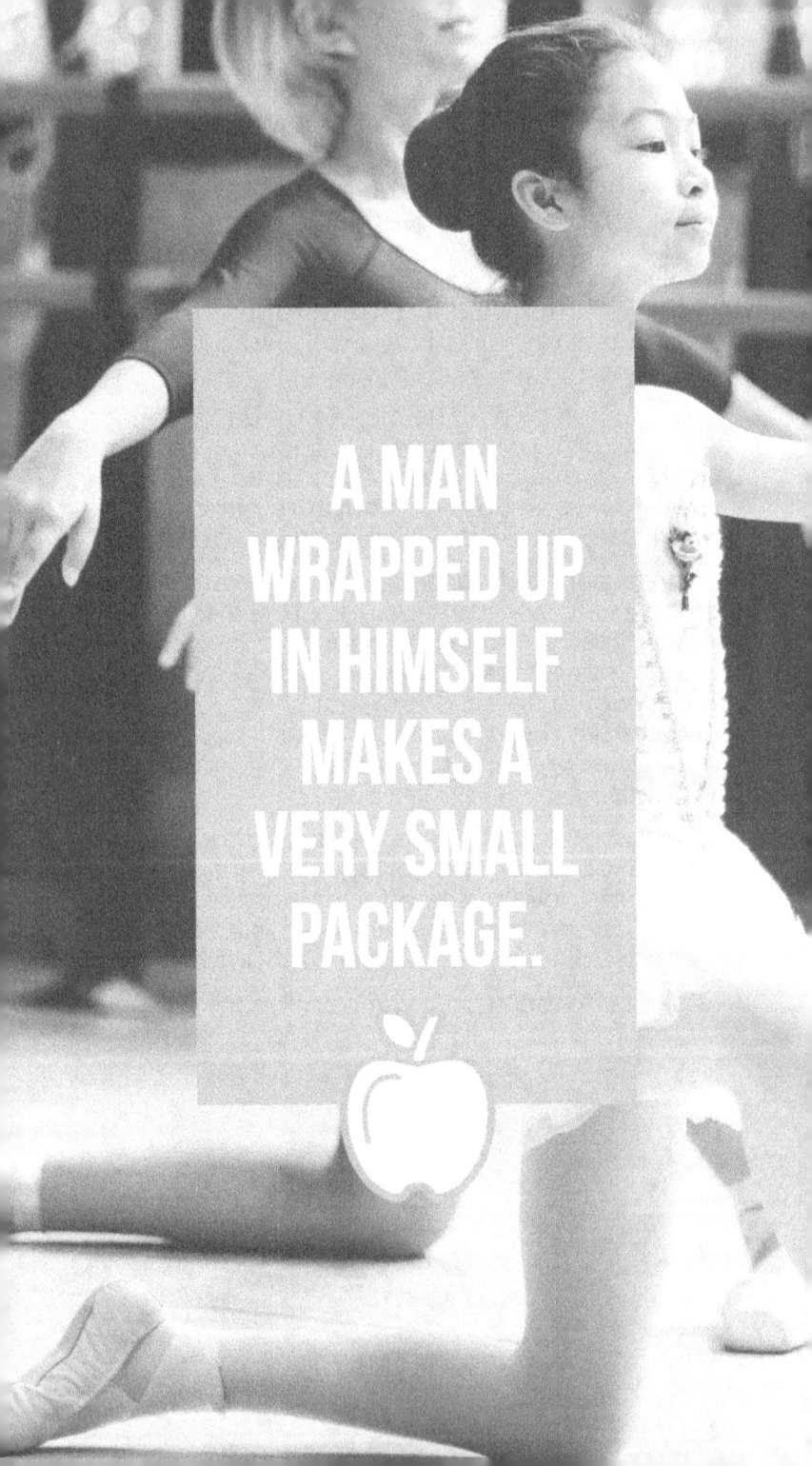

A MAN WRAPPED UP IN HIMSELF MAKES A VERY SMALL PACKAGE.

A speaker was once invited to address a community dinner in an effort to cheer up the people of the town as they faced difficult economic situations.

As part of her presentation, she took a large piece of white paper and made a black dot in the center of it. Then she held it up and asked the audience, "What do you see?"

One person quickly replied, "A black dot." Others nodded in agreement.

"Don't you see anything besides the dot?" she asked.

"No" came the resounding response from the audience.

The speaker continued, "The most important thing has been overlooked! No one noticed the sheet of paper!"

She then said, "In our business, family, personal, and social lives, we are often distracted by small, dot-like failures and disappointments. There is a tendency to focus on them and to forget the wonderful things around us. The blessings, successes, and joys are far more important than the little black dots that monopolize our attention and energies. Focus on the potential and the goodness all around your problems, and you will become strong and grow."

What might you write today in the "white space" surrounding the problems you face as a teacher?[144]

A fool finds no pleasure in understanding but delights in airing his own opinions.

PROVERBS 18:2 NIV

WHEN CONFRONTED WITH A GOLIATH-SIZED PROBLEM, WHICH WAY DO YOU RESPOND: "HE'S TOO BIG TO HIT," OR LIKE DAVID, "HE'S TOO BIG TO MISS?"

Marjorie, a nurse in the day-surgery unit, once said to a business consultant, "We can't wait for this time of cost-cutting to be over so we can go back to practicing the way we were trained." Marjorie had been a nurse for more than twenty years, and she had watched with dismay as hospital administrators and insurance executives seemed to place more and more emphasis on releasing people from the hospital "quicker and sicker." She and a number of other "good old days" complainers met at the hospital snack bar at break time each morning to moan together.

A nurse friend finally said to Marjorie, "The new policies are not going away, so why don't we go to the hospital fitness room together tomorrow and ride the stationary bikes instead." Marjorie tried her advice, and never went to the morning meetings at the snack bar again. While she and her friend rode their bikes, they brainstormed about ways to teach self-care to patients and patients' caregivers to make up for the shortened hospital stays. Marjorie not only became healthier physically, but emotionally happier . . . and her patients benefited, too!

Ask God today to help you focus your efforts on innovative solutions for your classroom and school.[145]

The Lord that delivered me out of the paw of the lion, and out of the paw of the bear, he will deliver me out of the hand of this Philistine.

1 SAMUEL 17:37

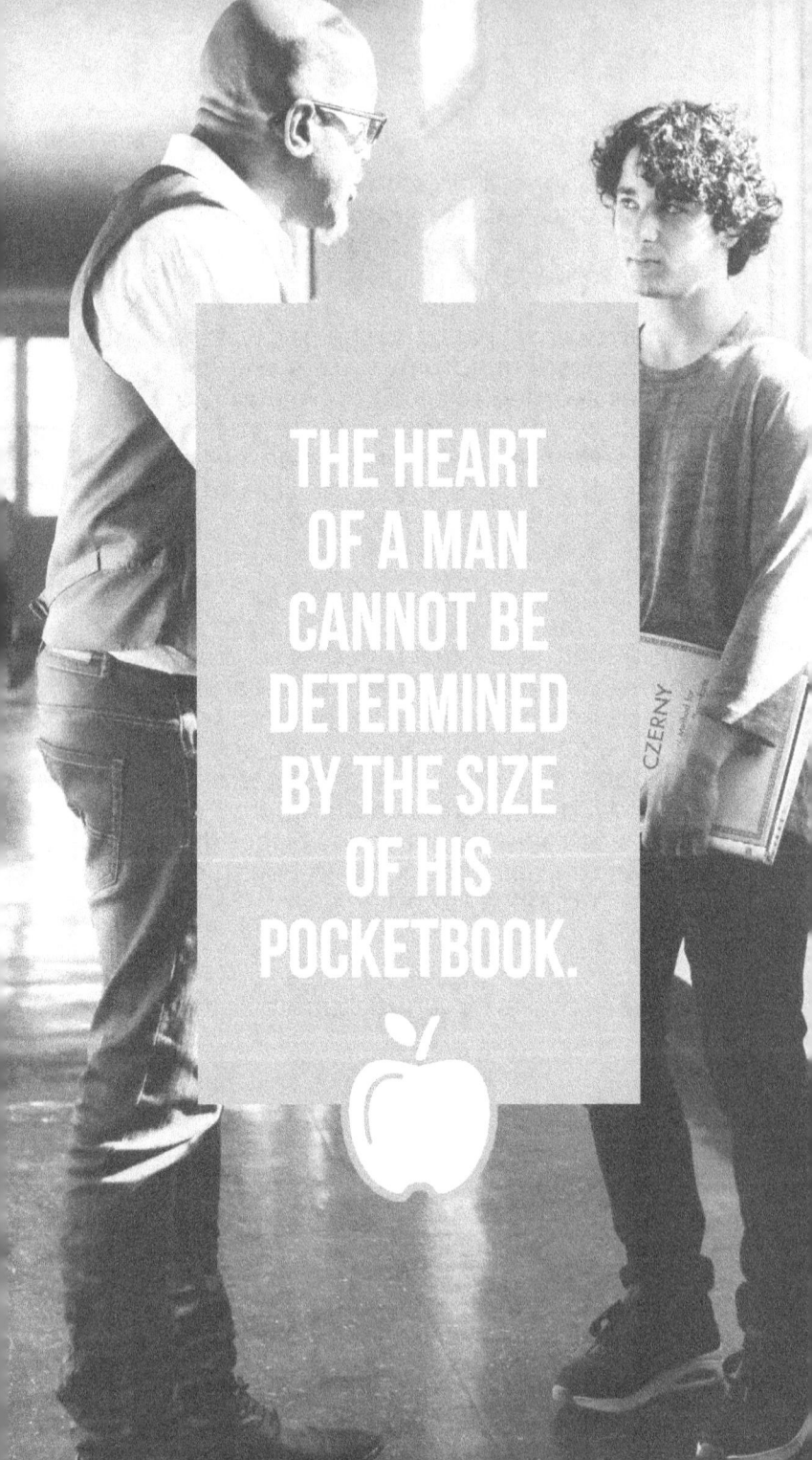

THE HEART
OF A MAN
CANNOT BE
DETERMINED
BY THE SIZE
OF HIS
POCKETBOOK.

A boy and his two sisters felt challenged when their pastor announced that a special Easter offering was going to be taken to help a poor family. They earned money by baby-sitting, housecleaning, and doing yard jobs. They also made pot holders to sell. By Easter they had seventy dollars, which they converted to three twenty-dollar bills and a ten-dollar bill. They could hardly wait to get to church!

That afternoon, the preacher showed up at their house with the envelope! After he left, they found eighty-seven dollars in it three twenty-dollar bills, a ten-dollar bill, and seventeen one-dollar bills. The children had never felt so poor in all their lives.

Next Sunday, the children were silent as they went to church The speaker was a missionary who told how one-hundred dollars could put a roof on a church in Africa. And the children decided to put that eighty-seven dollars they had been given back into the offering. The missionary exclaimed when he heard that just over one-hundred dollars was donated; "This church must have a rich family!" Yes, indeed!

Never underestimate the power and significance of your personal investments into your students.[146]

For what shall it profit a man, if he shall gain he whole world, and lose his own soul? Or what shall a man give in exchange for his soul?

MARK 8:36-37

EVERYONE HAS
PATIENCE—
SUCCESSFUL
PEOPLE LEARN
TO USE IT.

Tanya once watched a family build a log home next to her house in the mountains. The home was a "kit house"—all of the logs arrived pre-cut and pre-notched, along with roof beams and boxes of doors and windows. The family worked one weekend just sorting and stacking logs Then two weeks later, they returned to the mountain to begin construction, consulting the instructions frequently to make sure they were placing each log in its proper position. The building process took several months of weekend work.

Eventually, the weekend arrived when the support beams were positioned for the roof and the roof could be put on. Another weekend, windows were inserted and doors hung. After six months of weekend work, the family finally was ready to finish the interior and furnish their mountain home.

Tanya noticed two things about the family members at work. First, they didn't hurry. They had a goal and instructions, and they were content to let the home take shape over time. Second, they truly enjoyed the process of building their house. Many times, she heard laughter from the building site.

Patience also means giving students time to learn in a way that is joyous and satisfying.[147]

But let patience have her perfect work,
that ye may be perfect and entire,
wanting nothing.

JAMES 1:4

ACKNOWLEDGMENTS

Katherine Graham

C. Everett Koop

Willa Cather

C. C. Colton

Confucius

Benjamin Disraeli

Dale Carnegie

Ralph Waldo Emerson

Erik Erikson

Harvey Firestone

Oliver Wendell Holmes

Betty Smith

Benjamin Franklin

Lorene Workman

Buckminster Fuller

Les Brown

Ben Hogan

William H. Danforth

Jesse Jackson

Jean Kerr

John Lubbock

Austin O'Malley

Diane Sawyer

Charles H. Spurgeon

Bill Cosby

William James

Earl Nightingale

Say

Solon

Eleanor Roosevelt

George Edward Wood-berry

Harold Geneen

A.W. Tozer

Samuel Butler

Louis D. Brandeis

Frank Crane

Helen Keller

Emma Goldman

Victor Hugo

Descartes

Mark Twain

Theodore Roosevelt

Thomas Carlyle

Carl Sandburg

ENDNOTES

[1] Drawn from information in Tom Chappell, *The Soul of a Business—Managing for Profit and the Common Good*. NY: Bantam Books. 1993. p. x-xi.

[2] From Michael Hodgin. *1001 Humorous Illustrations for Public Speaking*, Grand Rapids, MI: Zondervan Publishing House. 1994, number 125 (attributed as a submission by Don Cheadle to "Pastor's Story File" in May 1986).

[3] Adapted from Della Reese. *Angels Along the Way: My Life with Help from Above*, New York: G.P Putnam's Sons. 1997.

[4] Drawn from Jake Steinfeld. *PowerLiving by Jake*. NY Random House, 1997. p. 116.

[5] Based upon information found on website: www. centralhigh57.org.

[6] Story adapted from "Heroes for Today." *Reader's Digest*. Pleasantville, NJ: Readers Digest Association, June 1997, p. 101.

[7] Based upon anecdote found in Martin Yate. *Beat the Odds*. NY: Random House. 1995. p. 47-48.

[8] From Craig Brian Larson. *Contemporary Illustration for Preachers. Teachers, and Writers*. Grand Rapids. MI: Baker Books. 1996. number 101. (Article first appeared in *Guideposts*. September 1980.)

[9] Found in Glenn Van Ekeren. *Words for All Occasions*. Paramus, NJ: Prentice Hall. 1988. p. 29-30.

[10] Based upon *Tulsa World* articles November 26,1998 (Section B-1 and following) about renewal ol contract for TU's coach, Dave Rader.

[11] Drawn from Craig Brian Larson. *Contemporary Illustrations for Preachers, Teachers, and Writers*. Grand Rapids. MI: Baker Books. 1996. number 156. (Information originally appeared in *Chicago Tribune*. December 1991.

Sec 5, Page 1. article titled "Epic in the Making.")

[12]Both anecdotes adapted from Glenn Van Ekeren, *Words for All Occasions*. Paramus. NJ: Prentice Hall. 1988. p. 35-36 and 198-199.

[13]Adapted from Anna B. Mow. *Your Child*. Grand Rapids, MI: Zondervan Publishing House. 1971. p. 34.

[14]From Donald Grey Barnhouse. *Let Me Illustrate*. Grand Rapids, MI: Baker Book House (reprint from Fleming H. Revell 1967 material), p. 25.

[15]Adapted from Anna B. Mow. *Your Child*. Grand Rapids, MI: Zondervan Publishing House. 1971. p. 88-89.

[16]Adapted from article released by Associated Press. Found in *Chicago Tribune*. October 29.1993, titled "In California City, Acts of Kindness Are Becoming Contagious." Also found in Craig Brian Larson. *Contemporary Illustrations for Preachers, Teachers, and Writers*. Grand Rapids, MI: Baker Books, 1996. number 114.

[17]Adapted from Glenn Van Ekeren, *Words for All Occasions*, Paramus, NJ: Prentice Hall. 1988, p. 10-11.

[18]Adapted from Lou Holtz, *Winning Every Day—The Game Plan for Success*. NY: HarperCollins Publishers. 1998. p. 48.

[19]Adapted from Craig Brian Larson. *Contemporary Illustrations for Preachers, Teachers, and Writers*. Grand Rapids, MI: Baker Books. 1996. number 138. Prisoner anecdote from Michael Hodgin, *101 Humorous Illustrations of Public Speaking*, Grand Rapids. Michigan. Zondervan Publishing House. 1994, number 650.

[20]Edited from Steven R. Mosley. *God: A Biography*. Phoenix, AZ: Questar Publishers, 1988, p. 201-202.

[21]Revised from Sheila Walsh with Evelyn Benee, *Bring Back the Joy*, Grand Rapids. MI Zondervan Publishing House, 1998. p. 150-151.

[22]Based upon story reported in *Chicago Tribune*. November 8,1994. "In Traffic Disputes, Turn Away and Live" by Eric Zorn, section 2. page 1.

[23]Adapted from an article titled. "My Dad, The Worrier" by Meg Cimino, in *Reader's Digest*. June 1997. p. 137-139. Originally from *The Atlantic Monthly*. March 1997.

[24]Revised from Charles J. Givens, *Super Self*. NY: Simon & Schuster, 1993. p. 165-166.

[25]Adapted from Craig Brian Larson. *Contemporary Illustrations for Preachers, Teachers, and Writers*, Grand Rapids, MI: Baker Books, 1996, number 119. Based upon a Phillip Yancey article that first appeared in *Christianity Today*.

[26]Lewis Carroll excerpt found in Glenn Van Ekeren, *Words for All Occasions*, Paramus, NJ: Prentice Hall. 1988. p. 187.

[27]Significantly revised from an anecdote in Barbara Bailey Reinhold, *Toxic Work*, NY: Penguin Books. 1996. p. 58-60.

[28]Adapted from Donald Grey Barnhouse, *Let Me Illustrate*, Grand Rapids. MI: Baker Book House (Fleming H. Revell). 1967. p. 108.

[29]Based upon anecdote found in Dr. Ray Guarendi. *Back to the Family*, NY: Villard Books. Random House. 1990. p. 115.

[30]Quote John H. Timmerman found in *Moody* September 1994. p. 14. article titled "Black Gold: Nurturing the Heart."

[31]Anecdote found in Glenn Van Ekeren, *Words for All Occasions*, Paramus, NJ: Prentice Hall. 1988. p. 290.

[32]Based upon anecdote found in Allan Cox, *Straight Talk for Monday Morning*. NY: John Wiley & Sons, 1990, p. 235-236.

[33]Fry and MacFadden information from Charles Davis, *Parables*, April 1987. Found in Michael Hodgin. *1001 Humorous Illustrations for Public Speaking*, Grand Rapids. MI: Zondervan Publishing House. 1994, number 520.

[34]Facts about Rudy's life found in Reader's Digest, March 1996, p. 46. Article titled "Make Your Own Breaks."

[35]Dialog for Corrie ten Boom anecdote found in Craig Brian Larson. *Contemporary Illustrations for Preachers, Teachers, and Writers*, Grand Rapids, MI: Baker Books, 1996, number 181.

[36]Hybels quote found in Craig Brian Larson. *Contemporary Illustrations for Preachers, Teachers, and Writers*, Grand Rapids, MI: Baker Books, 1996, number 221. Quote from *Honest to God*, p. 26-27.

[37]Anecdote found in Frederic and Mary Ann Brussat,

Spiritual Literacy: Reading the Sacred in Everyday Life. NY Scribner, 1996, p. 36-37.

[38] Adapted from anecdote found in Dr. Ray Guarendi, *Back to the Family*, NY: Villard Books, Random House, 1990, p. 162-163.

[39] Store adapted from Donald Grey Barnhouse, *Let Me Illustrate*. Grand Rapids. MI: Baker Book House, 1967, p. 171.

[40] Adapted from excerpt in Alice Gray, *Stories for the Heart*, Sisters, OR: Questar Pub. 1996, p. 75-76.

[41] Found in Malcolm Kushner, The Light Touch—How to Use Humor for Business Success, NY: Simon & Schuster, 1990, p. 235.

[42] Charlie Brown information found in Michael Hodgin. *1001 Humorous Illustrations for Public Speaking*, Grand Rapids. MI: Zondervan Publishing House. 1994, number 319.

[43] Summarized from Lou Holtz, *Winning Every Day—the Game Plan for Success*, NY: Harper Collins Publishers, 1998, p. 112-113.

[44] Information found in William A. Cohen, *The Art of the Leader*, Englewood Cliffs, NJ: Prentice Hall 1990, p. 4.

[45] Adapted from information found in Carrie Book and Kimberly Colen, *Hold Fast Your Dreams*, NY: Scholastic Inc. 1996, p. 48-50.

[46] Adapted from anecdote found in Mark Victor Hansen and Barbara Nichols with Patty Hansen, *Out of the Blue*, NY: Harper Collins. 1996, p. 100-102.

[47] Information found in *Renders Digest*, "Heroes for Today" column, June 1997, p. 99-100.

[48] Adapted from Paul Azinger with Ken Abraham, *Zinger*, Grand Rapids. MI: Zondervan Publishing House, 1995, p. 200-201.

[49] Information found in Craig Brian Larson, *Illustrations for Preaching and Teaching*, Grand Rapids. MI: Baker Books, 1993, p. 41.

[50] Adapted from Glenn Van Ekeren, *Words for All Occasions*, Paramus, NJ: Prentice Hall, 1988, p. 204.

[51]Information found in *USA WEEKEND*, December 11-13, 1998, p. 10-14.

[52]Information found in Craig Brian Larson. *Illustrations for Preaching and Teaching*, Grand Rapids, MI: Baker Books, 1993, number 250.

[53]Adapted from Charles R. Swindoll, *The Finishing Touch*, Dallas, TX: Word. 1994. p. 622-624

[54]Information found in Martin Yate, *Beat the Odds*, NY: Random House, 1995, p. 157.

[55]Based on information found in Paul Lee Tan, *Encyclopedia of 7700 illustrations*, Rockville, MD: Assurance Publishers. 1979, p. 1396-1397.

[56]Found in Glenn Van Ekeren. *Words for All Occasions*, Paramus. NJ: Prentice Hall. 1988. p. 325.

[57]Information and quotes found in Carrie Boyko and Kimberly Colen, *Hold Fast Your Dreams,* NY: Scholastic, Inc., 1996, p. 11-18.

[58]Information found in James S. Hewett, *Illustrations Unlimited*, Wheaton. IL: Tyndale House Publishers, 1988, p. 235.

[59]Adapted from Alice Gray, *Stories for the Heart*. Sisters, OR: Questar Pub. 1996, p. 109.

[60]MacArthur anecdote found in Michael Hodgin. *1001 Humorous Illustrations of Public Speaking,* Grand Rapids, MI: Zondervan Publishing House, 1994, p 145.

[61]Found in Glenn Van Ekeren. *Words for All Occasions*, Paramus, NJ: Prentice Hall. 1988. p. 65-66.

[62]Information from Robert S. Eliot, M.D., *From Stress to Strength—How to Lighten Your Load and Save Your Life*. NY: Bantam Books. 1994, p. 155-156.

[63]Some of information from Donald Grey Barnhouse, *Let Me Illustrate*, Grand Rapids, MI: Baker Bark House, 1967, p. 222.

[64]Found in Mark Victor Hansen and Barbara Nichols with Patty Hansen, *Out of the Blue*. NY: Harper Collins. 1996, p. 60-61.

[65]Information from Janet Bukovinsky. *Women of Words*. Philadelphia, Running Press, 1994. p. 97-99.

[66]From "Mikey's Funnies." by Mike Atkinson @ YOUTH SPECIALITIES; online ® aol. titled "Another Lesson in Life." 10/7/98 date of publication.

[67]Information from Porter B. Williamson. *General Patton's Principles for Life and Leadership*. Tucson, AZ: Management Systems and Consultants, Inc., 1988.

[68]From "Mikey's Funnies," by Mike Atkinson @ YOUTH SPECIALITIES; online @ aol, titled "Smarter Than You Think." 9/15/98 date of publication.

[69]Adapted from Alice Gray. *Stories for the Heart*. Sisters, OR: Questar Pub, 1996, p. 91-92.

[70]Information found in Robert L. Yeninga. *Your Renaissance Years*, Boston: Little, Brown & Co., 1991. p. 237-238.

[71]Adapted from Michael Hodgin. *1001 Humorous Illustrations of Public Speaking*. Grand Rapids. MI: Zondervan Publishing House, 1994, number 385.

[72]Adapted from *Reader's Digest*. January 1998, p. 157-158. Article compiled by Daniel Levine titled "My First Job."

[73]Information found in Robert A. Wilson, *Character Above All*. NY: Simon & Schuster. 1995. p. 58.

[74]Children anecdotes from Michael Hodgin. *1001 Humorous Illustrations of Public Speaking*. Grand Rapids. MI: Zondervan Publishing House, 1994, number 301; and from Mikey's Funnies" @ YOUTH SPECIALITIES, title "A Christian's Kids." online @ aol; 9/23/98.

[75]Information about Love found in *Reader's Digest*. March 1996, p. 38 in the "Personal Glimpses" column.

[76]Drawn from information in Tom Chappell. T*he Soul of a Business—Managing for Profit and the Common Good*. NY: Bantam Books, 1993, p. 107-108,113-114.

[77]Both poem and information found in Paul Lee Tan, *Encyclopedia of 7700 Illustrations*. Rockville, MD. Assurance Publishers, 1979, p. 678-679.

[78]Story adapted from Glenn Van Ekeren. *Words for All Occasions*, Paramus, NJ: Prentice Hall, 1988. p. 88-89

[79]Information found in Roger Connors, Tom Smith, Craig Hickman, *The Oz Principle*. Englewood Cliffs. NJ: Prentice Hall. 1994. p. 139.

[80] Adapted from entry in Mark Victor Hansen and Barbara Nichols with Patty Hansen. *Out of the Blue*. NY: Harper Collins. 1996. p. 79-80.

[81] Based upon information found in 1 Samuel 16.

[82] Found in "Mikey's Funnies," @ YOUTH SPECIALITIES, title "God's Wife." Forwarded by Pat Gray online @ aol. 9/29/98.

[83] Summarized from information in Peter Godwins, Mukiwa: a White Boy in Africa, NY Grove, Atlantic 1996.

[84] Found in Craig Brian Larson. *Contemporary Illustrations for Preachers, Teachers, and Writers*, Grand Rapids, MI: Baker Books, 1996, number 137.

[85] Facts from "Mikey's Funnies," by Mike Atkinson @ YOUTH SPECIALITIES; article titled "Strive for Perfection," forwarded by Dan Bonin, online @ aol, 9/23/98.

[86] Based upon information found in Glenn Van Ekeren. *Words for All Occasions*, Paramus, NJ: Prentice Hall, 1988. p. 253-254.

[87] From Sheila Walsh with Evelyn Benee, *Bring Back the Joy*, Grand Rapids MI: Zondervan Publishing House. 1998. p. 47-49, 71-72.

[88] Drawn from Donald Grey Barnhouse. *Let Me Illustrate*. Grand Rapids. MI: Baker Books House. 1967. p 149-151.

[89] Quotes and information adapted from *Reader's Digest,* March 1990. p. 37.

[90] Based on anecdote found in Richard A. Swenson. M.D. Colorado Springs. CO: NavPress Publishing Group. 1992. p. 241-242.

[91] Information about horned lizard from Susan Hazen-Hammond. "Horny toads enjoy a Special Place in Western Hearts." *Smithsonian,* December 1994. p. 90.

[92] Based upon story found in Lewis R. Timberlake. *It's Always Too Soon to Quit*. Grand Rapids, MI Fleming H. Revell. 1988, p. 109-110.

[93] Adapted from information found in Jake Steinfeld. *PowerLiving by Jake*. NY Random House. 1997, p. 43-44.

[94] Wisiger quote from Michael Hodgin. *1001 Humorous Illustrations of Public Speaking*. Grand Rapids. MI: Zondervan Publishing House, 1994, number 473.

[95]Furrow, rope, and artisan information found in Frederic and Mary Ann Brussat, *Spiritual Literacy: Reading the Sacred in Everyday Life*. NY: Scribner. 1990. p 306.

[96]Information and Rosenman quote from Robert A. Wilson, *Character Above All*. NY: Simon & Schuster 1995. p. 16-17, 24-25. Chapter on "Franklin D. Roosevelt" is by Doris Kearns Goodwin.

[97]From "Mikey's Funnies," by Mike Atkinson @ YOUTH SPECIALITIES; article titled "The Fad," forwarded by Mark Rayburn, online @ aol, 5/19/98.

[98]Washington anecdote found in Glenn Van Ekeren. *Words for All Occasions*. Paramus, NJ: Prentice Hall, 1988. p. 218.

[99]Edited from Charles J. Givens. *Super Self*. NY: Simon & Schuster. 1993. p 188-189.

[100]Both Cunard and epitaph information found in Paul Lee Tan, *Encyclopedia of 7700 Illustrations*. Rockville, MD: Assurance Publishers. 1979, entries 4104-4105.

[101]Revised from story found in Glenn Van Ekeren. *Words for All Occasions*, Paramus NJ: Prentice Hall. 1988. p. 344.

[102]Quote found in Bill Butterworth. *When Life Doesn't Turn Out Like You Planned*. Nashville, TN: Thomas Nelson. 1995. p. 71-72.

[103]From Craig Brian Larson, *Contemporary Illustrations for Preacher, Teachers, and Writers*. Grand Rapids, MI: Baker Books, 1996. entry 80.

[104]Information found in Glenn Van Ekeren. *Words for All Occasions*, Paramus, NJ: Prentice Hall 1988. p 289.

[105]From Patricia H. Berne and Louis M. Savary. *Building Self-Esteem in Children*, NY: The Continuum Publishing Co.. 1981. p. 71.

[106]Story found in *Parables Etc*. February 1986: quoted from *Economics Press* in Fairfield. NJ. column titled "Bits and Pieces".

[107]Adapted from an entry found in Craig Brian Larson, *Illustrations for Preaching and Teaching,* Grand Rapids, MI: Baker Books, 1993, p. 65.

[108]Found in "Something Good." the weekly newsletter circulated for staff and faculty at Oral Roberts University.

December 20, 1998 issue.

[109] Information from Robert K. Brown and Mark R. Norton, *The One Year Book of Hymns*. Wheaton, IL. Tyndale House. 1995. entries for April 25, May 1, June 16. Also quote about doctor from Glenn Van Ekeren. *Words for All Occasions*, Paramus, NJ: Prentice Hall, 1988, p. 49-50.

[110] Summarized from Tom Morris, *True Success*. NY: Grosset/Putnam, 1994. p. 95.

[111] Adapted from Donald Grey Barnhouse. *Let Me Illustrate*. Grand Rapids, MI: Baker Book House. 1967, p. 90.

[112] Found in *Reader's Digest*. March 1996, p. 46, 48, article titled "Make Your Own Breaks" condensed from *True Success* by Tom Morris.

[113] Information found in Robert S. Eliot. M.D.. *From Stress to Strength—How to Lighten Your Load and Save Your Life*. NY: Bantam Books, 1994, p. 49-51. (Eliot was doctor who went to Finland.)

[114] Based upon information found in E. Paul Hovey. *The Treasury of Inspirational Anecdotes. Quotations, and Illustrations*. Grand Rapids, MI: Baker Book House, 1959, p. 23.

[115] Adapted from Glenn Van Ekeren. *Words for All Occasions*. Paramus, NJ: Prentice Hall. 1988. p. 287-288

[116] Hemingway and Bonee information both found in Malcolm Kushner. *The Light Touch—How to Use Humor for Business Success*. NY: Simon & Schuster. 1990, 75.

[117] Based upon article that appeared in the *Chicago Tribune*, titled "Self-Taught Chef Has Star Quality." March 6, 1995, section 1, page 2.

[118] Found in Craig Brian Larson. *Illustrations for Preaching and Teaching*, Grand Rapids, MI: Baker Books, 1993, p. 172.

[119] From Bill Butterworth *When Life Doesn't Turn Out Like You Planned*. Nashville. TN: Thomas Nelson. 1995, p. 54-58.

[120] Based upon information in Walter B. Knight. *Knight's Master Book of 4,000 Illustrations*. Grand Rapids, MI: Wm. B. Eerdmans Publishing Company, 1956, p. 218.

[121] From *Readers Digest*. January 1998. p. 160, article titled "My First Job" compiled by Daniel Levine.

[122]Based upon information found in Allan Cox. *Straight Talk for Monday Morning*, NY: John Wiley & Sons, 1990. p. 24.

[123]Found in "Mikey's Funnies" @ YOUTH SPECIALTIES, article titled "Ice Cream Is Good for the Soul" from unknown contributor. Online @ aol, 9/17/98.

[124]Found in Glenn Van Ekeren. *Words for All Occasions*. Paramus, NJ: Prentice Hall. 1988, p. 21.

[125]Quote from Charles Stanley. *The Wonderful Spirit-Filled Life*, Nashville. TN: Thomas Nelson Publishers, 1992. p. 48-49.

[126]Summarized from *Reader's Digest*. June 1997, p 147-258. article titled "A Healing Birth" by Lawrence Elliott.

[127]Adapted from Bill Butterworth. *When Life Doesn't Turn Out Like You Planned*. Nashville, TN: Thomas Nelson, 1995. p. 155-157.

[128]Lowell information found in Craig Brian Larson. *Illustrations for Preaching and Teaching*, Grand Rapids, MI: Baker Books, 1993, entry 110.

[129]Found in Steven R Mosley. *God: A Biography*, Phoenix. AZ: Questar, 1988. p. 187-189.

[130]Found in Craig Brian Larson, *Illustrations for Preaching and Teaching*. Grand Rapids, MI: Baker Books. 1993, number 105.

[131]Burrill quote found in E. Paul Hovey, *The Treasury of Inspirational Anecdotes, Quotations, and Illustrations*. Grand Rapids, MI: Fleming H. Revell, 1959. p. 257-258.

[132]Found in Glenn Van Ekeren. *Words for All Occasions*. Paramus, NJ: Prentice Hall. 1988. p 54.

[133]Summarized from Tom Morris, *True Success*, NY: Grosset/Putnam, 1994, p. 131.

[134]Information found in Donald Grey Barnhouse. *Let Me Illustrate*, Grand Rapids, MI: Baker Book House. 1967, p. 250-251.

[135]Summarized from Lillian Eichler Watson. *Light From Many Lamps*. NY: First Fireside/Simon & Schuster. 1979, p. 45-46.

[136]Adapted from Sheila Walsh with Evelyn Bence, *Bring Back the Joy*, Grand Rapids, MI: Zondervan Publishing

House. 1998, p. 145.

[137]Information about missionary found in Donald Grey Barnhouse, *Let Me Illustrate*. Grand Rapids, MI, Baker Book House, 1967, p. 359-360.

[138]Summarized from Steven R Mosley. *God: A Biography*. Phoenix, AZ: Questar, 1988. p. 259-261.

[139]Found in Craig Brian Larson. *Contemporary Illustrations for Preachers, Teachers, and Writers*. Grand Rapids, MI: Baker Books. 1996, p. 236.

[140]Both anecdotes drawn from James S. Hewett. *Illustrations Unlimited*, Wheaton, IL: Tyndale House Publishers. 1988. p. 135.

[141]Llama information found in Craig Brian Larson, *Illustrations for Preaching and Teaching*, Grand Rapids, MI: Baker Basks, 1993. p. 259.

[142]Statement was attributed as a "poem on the Internet" submitted by Jennifer B. to Ann Landers, published as part of her Creators Syndicate. Inc. column and appearing in the *Tulsa World*. December 5, 1998.

[143]Information about pioneers found in Craig Brian Larson, *Illustrations for Preaching and Teaching*. Grand Rapids, MI: Baker Books. 1993, entry 260.

[144]Adapted from Glenn Van Ekeren. *Words for All Occasions*. Paramus, NJ: Prentice Hall. 1988. p. 60-61.

[145]Adapted from anecdote in Barbara Bailey Reinhold, *Toxic Work*, NY: Penguin Books. 1996. p. 105.

[146]From "Mikey's Funnies" @ YOUTH SPECIALTIES, article submitted by Eddie Ogan titled "The Rich Family in Church." found online @ aol, 4/9/98.

[147]Adapted from anecdote in James G. Kink. *Meditations for Advent and Christmas*. Louisville, KY: Westminster/John Knox Press, 1989, p. 35.

Additional copies of this book and other titles in
the *God's Little Devotional Book* series are available
online at www.honorbooks.com.

God's Little Devotional Book for the Workplace
God's Little Devotional Book for Moms
God's Little Devotional Book for Dads
God's Little Devotional Book for Couples
God's Little Devotional Book for Men
God's Little Devotional Book for Women
God's Little Devotional Book for Parents
God's Little Devotional Book for Leaders
God's Little Devotional Book for Students
God's Little Devotional Book on Success
God's Little Devotional Book on Prayer
God's Little Devotional Book on Graduates